IN PRAISE OF *THE TALENT DELUSION*

'Tomas Chamorro-Premuzic is a rare voice of reason in a field where most people talk gibberish.'
Lucy Kellaway, *Financial Times*

'This book shows how to find, attract, develop, motivate and retain stars. It's full of evidence and provocative ideas to help every talent leader.'
Dr Adam Grant, Wharton Professor,
NYT* bestselling author of *Originals* and *Give and Take

'A must-read for leaders and HR professionals who want to apply science to drive better business outcomes, and for individuals who want to better understand and leverage their own talents.'
Jonas Prising, Chairman and CEO, ManpowerGroup

'A clear-eyed, deeply researched account of what the science really tells us about finding, attracting and retaining talented people, while staying alert to talent's surprising dark sides.'
Oliver Burkeman, the *Guardian*, author of *The Antidote*

'In a world of clutter and hype, Tomas casts off HR folklore by providing a clear, data-driven direction on the topic that drives us all: finding and nurturing talent to pursue its potential. An enlightening book that will impact our world at work; a journey not for the faint-hearted!'
Adam Yearsley, Global Head of Talent Management, Red Bull

'This is the book I want to hand every manager I've ever worked with who mistakenly assumes "give me 5 minutes with a candidate and I'll tell ya if they are a good hire". Every chapter is filled with quotes, findings and ideas that I want to post on Twitter and share with the world.'
Dr Todd Carlisle, VP of HR, Twitter

'Provocative, funny and extremely useful, this incredible psychological tour de force will help you find and unleash the talent you've been looking for. A brilliant book!'
Nathalie Nahai, Web Psychologist, author of *Webs of Influence*

D1089453

ABOUT THE AUTHOR

Dr Tomas Chamorro-Premuzic is an international authority in psychological profiling, talent management and people analytics. He is the CEO of Hogan Assessment Systems, Professor of Business Psychology at University College London (UCL) and Visiting Professor at Columbia University. He has previously taught at New York University and the London School of Economics.

He has published 8 books and over 140 scientific papers, making him one of the most prolific social scientists of his generation. His work has received awards from the American Psychological Association and the International Society for the Study of Individual Differences. He is the director of UCL's Industrial-Organisational and Business Psychology programme, an Associate to Harvard's Entrepreneurial Finance Lab and has been named as one of the most influential thought teachers in talent management by *HR* magazine, *Workforce*, and *Thinkers50*.

Dr Chamorro-Premuzic has been a consultant to a range of clients in the financial services (such as JP Morgan, HSBC and Goldman Sachs), advertising (Google, Havas and BBH), media (Yahoo!, MTV and the BBC), fashion (LVMH and Net-a-Porter) and government (the British Army, Royal Mail and the NHS).

His media career comprises over 85 TV appearances, including for the BBC, CNN and Sky, and regular features in *Harvard Business Review*, the *Guardian*, Fast Company, Forbes and the Huffington Post. He is a keynote speaker for the Institute of Economic Affairs and the co-founder of metaprofiling.com. He is Argentine by birth and British by adoption, and lives mostly in Brooklyn, New York.

The Talent Delusion

The New Psychology of Human Potential

Tomas Chamorro-Premuzic, Ph.D.

piatkus

PIATKUS

First published in Great Britain in 2017 by Piatkus

Copyright © Tomas Chamorro-Premuzic 2017

3 5 7 9 10 8 6 4 2

A CIP catalogue record for this book
is available from the British Library.

ISBN 978-0-349-41248-1

Typeset in Sabon by M Rules

Printed and bound in Great Britain by
Clays Ltd, St Ives plc

Papers used by Piatkus are from well-managed forests
and other responsible sources.

Piatkus
An imprint of
Little, Brown Book Group
Carmelite House
50 Victoria Embankment
London EC4Y 0DZ

An Hachette UK Company
www.hachette.co.uk

www.improvementzone.co.uk

to Isabelle

CONTENTS

ACKNOWLEDGEMENTS

It would be difficult to mention all the people who in one way or another contributed to this book, but I am very grateful to all of them.

In particular, I would like to thank my two academic mentors, Adrian Furnham and Robert Hogan, for leading me into the exciting (but chaotic) world of talent and shaping much of my thinking in this and other areas. Someone once said that 'talent imitates, but genius steals'. Although I'm not a genius, I have had enough talent to steal voraciously from these two maestros, and will continue to do so. So, thank you – and sorry! – Adrian and RT.

I am also grateful to my media editors: the incredible Sarah Green-Carmichael at *Harvard Business Review*, the bionic Rich Bellis at *Fast Company*, the sardonic Kate Bassett at *Management Today*, and the wonderful Adam Davidi at the *Guardian*. This book evolved from many articles you have helped me create, and many ideas you agreed to pilot, curate and vet. It is because of you that this book pretty much wrote itself.

I also thank many of my friends and colleagues who, despite their very busy schedules (and my short notice), were kind enough to provide helpful feedback on the first draft of this book: Mike Haffenden and Gillian Pillans at the Corporate Research Forum; Adam Yearsley at Red Bull; Peter Steinlauf at Edmunds; and Dave Winsborough at Hogan X. I wish all reviewers were as prompt, constructive and knowledgeable.

I'm grateful to my agent, Giles Anderson, for co-creating the footprint for this book and finding a nice home for it; and to the rather marvellous people at Little, Brown, in particular Zoe and Jillian. A special thanks goes to Meri Pentikainen, for being the smartest and most cynical book editor I ever met. I hope we can work together again.

Finally – and I know this is unusual – I would like to thank Singapore Airlines, where most of this book was written. Unlike most airlines, you clearly don't need to read this book, but I will make sure you get a copy, anyway. I could not have hoped for a better office at 30,000 feet.

PREFACE

All organisations have problems, and they nearly always concern people. How to manage them; whom to hire, fire or promote; and how to motivate, develop and retain them. Psychology, the science of understanding people, should be a pivotal tool for solving these problems, yet most organisations play it by ear. As a result, billions are wasted on futile interventions to attract and retain the right people in key roles, and most people remain disenchanted with their careers. The effects are felt by everyone. Employees want better jobs and better leaders; leaders want better employees; organisations and entire economies under-achieve. McKinsey first introduced the notion of a war for talent, the idea that since people are *the* critical asset of organisations, organisations' success depends on attracting, motivating and retaining top employees, in 1997 – yet, nearly twenty years on, most organisations' ability to identify and nurture human potential remains limited.

I consider myself lucky. My career choices have been fairly improvised. For example, the reason I decided to study psychology at university was that it was the only subject I found

vaguely interesting – and easy – at school, not least because the
final assignment was to write an essay on *One Flew Over the
Cuckoo's Nest* (the Jack Nicholson movie, rather than the book).
I liked the film. Expressing my views was fun and painless. And
my teacher told me I had a natural talent for psychology. I don't
think she was a great talent spotter, but I do remember listening
to her because the idea of getting a university degree without
having to do too much work was quite appealing. At university, I
became obsessed with Sigmund Freud and Jacques Lacan, whose
theories made for great bar conversations in the late hours of the
Buenos Aires night until I realised they were pure metaphysical
masturbation.

I decided I needed a way out – a return to reality – so I moved
to London and embraced British empiricism. Data became my
new best friend. The only problem was that psychometrics and
personality assessment provided few opportunities to emerge
from the depths of academic psychology and into the real world
of business, where I ultimately wanted to live. Yet by the time I
had finished my Ph.D. the war for talent was in full swing, and
demand for the science of personality was booming. Since then a
great deal of my time has been devoted to creating scientifically
credible tools for evaluating, predicting and explaining human
behaviour. Hogan Assessment Systems, the company I'm proud
to lead, is a major arms manufacturer in the war for talent:
our focus is the development of tools for understanding people,
especially their talents.

I know most people aren't as lucky. Even when they have
talent, and they live in places where opportunities abound, they
struggle to find the right careers. As a result, they end up staying
in meaningless jobs for many years, underperforming and alienated, or compulsively switching from one job to the next. Work

ends up being a burden and the main source of their miseries, so the only joy they have left is succeeding in their personal lives. On the other hand, employers keep lamenting their inability to find the right people for critical roles, which makes job markets inefficient.

We all play a role in the war for talent. Organisations are the countries, their CEOs are the generals, human resource (HR) leaders the lieutenants, and independent consultants and coaches are the mercenaries and soldiers. But, infiltrated among all these groups are many toxic agents – the uninformed and misinformed – who corrupt the state of affairs and turn this conflict into a dirty war. To be fair, most of the people contributing to the war for talent are well-intentioned, but in following unscientific and populist advice they unwittingly add to the crisis. Then there are the actual thought anarchists, who proactively create the intellectual chaos that makes thinking about talent an amateurish activity. This book is an attempt to combat these populist agents of irrationality. Its main ammunition is science, which, as Adam Smith noted, 'is the great antidote to the poison of enthusiasm and superstition'. It is not that science provides the ultimate truth on any issues, but that it is a powerful weapon for eliminating misconceptions and debunking myths. As Thomas Schofield observed: 'science is not about finding the truth at all, but about finding better ways of being wrong'.[1]

In order to bridge the gap between the psychological science of talent and real-world talent malpractices, this book aims to educate HR practitioners and leaders on critical talent matters in light of some of the latest research in this area. To this end, it will explain the current challenges pertaining to employee selection, development and engagement; how best to define and evaluate talent; how to detect and inhibit toxic employee behaviours; and

how to motivate employees to perform to the best of their capabilities. This book digests the evidence drawn from key academic
studies to provide theory-based and data-driven recommendations on how to fix organisations' talent problems. I have written
this book for practitioners, but since the topics discussed in
it are arguably of broader interest, it may also appeal to any
reader who is curious about human potential at work. In fact, it
is hoped that anyone interested in the psychology of talent may
refer to this book as a trustworthy and enjoyable alternative to
the talent delusion, the nonsensical feel-good writings commonly
published on the subject of human potential.

My main intention with this book is to be critical and constructive but not adversarial. However, given the lack of critical
thinking that characterises mainstream coverage of talent-related
issues, some of my arguments may seem controversial. I will
therefore provide as much scientific evidence in support of my
points as I possibly can; more than is common in non-academic
books. If you believe in data, there is no better source of evidence
than peer-reviewed academic journals, because of their focus on
thorough and carefully executed studies and their attention to
impartiality and conflicts of interest. Another important element
of peer-reviewed articles is that they adhere to the main scientific method, which is to advance knowledge incrementally by
building on previous knowledge and providing a clear basis for
refuting findings. Conversely, white papers published by commercial enterprises fail to meet scientific standards, are rarely
replicated by academic studies and, deliberately or not, ignore
the more robust body of evidence that exists in peer-reviewed
journals. This explains the proliferation of fads and buzzwords
that manage to not only survive the critical eye of evidence-based
practitioners and scientists, but also become shiny new objects

with cult-like followings in the world of HR. So long as talent management practitioners continue to rely only on their common sense and intuition to judge the quality of such ideas, progress will be slow, trivial and tedious.

If the purpose of war is to produce peace, how can we end the war for talent? What are the conditions we need to put in place so that the majority of organisations can staff key jobs more effectively and upgrade the collective potential and output of their workforce? How do we enable the majority of people to unleash their full potential and enjoy meaningful and rewarding careers? There is no magic or simple answer to these questions. However, improving our ability to understand, predict and manage talent is a necessary step for achieving some progress.

Tomas Chamorro-Premuzic, Ph.D.
New York, August 2016

'In all affairs it's a healthy thing now and then to hang a question mark on the things you have long taken for granted.'

BERTRAND RUSSELL

'The greatest enemy of knowledge is not ignorance, it is the illusion of knowledge.'

STEPHEN HAWKING

'Science is the belief in the ignorance of experts.'

RICHARD FEYMAN

CHAPTER 1

The war ~~for~~ on talent

This chapter provides an update on the war for talent, a term coined almost 20 years ago to denote the growing importance of people as a central asset of organisations. As the chapter will show, talent is hotter as a topic today than it ever has been, and there is clear consensus among leading organisations and thinkers that attracting, developing and engaging top employees is the utmost priority for any aspiring business. Yet, paradoxically, most companies feel ill-equipped to address these challenges, and many macro-economic indicators suggest that the war for talent is being lost rather than won. First, most people dislike their jobs. Second, most people are passive job seekers, hoping for better career prospects. Third, a growing number of people are tempted into self-employment, mostly because of their unhappy experiences with their current jobs. And finally, there has been a steady increase in entrepreneurial intentions even in countries where job opportunities abound. In order to reverse this unfortunate set of circumstances and win the war for – rather than on – talent, it is necessary to improve our understanding of the science of talent, and the first step is to come to terms with the bitter truth about our feckless quest for unlocking human potential.

* * *

Nearly twenty years have now passed since McKinsey, a leading management consulting firm, first introduced the idea of a war for talent, suggesting that the future success of organisations would be largely dependent on their ability to attract and retain top employees, particularly for senior roles.[1] In other words, human capital – people – ought to be considered a major organisational asset, and businesses more capable of managing people should be expected to outperform their rivals. That this suggestion has turned into a well-known management cliché is testimony, not so much to McKinsey's influence, as to their ability to spot a tipping point in the transition of human resources (HR) practices: from more bureaucratic, legal and process-based, to more strategic, influential and content-driven. The key contribution of HR, then, is not to avoid personnel problems or staff-related disputes, but to turn people into engines of growth and productivity by leveraging and upgrading their talents. In effect, McKinsey's war for talent put HR at the centre of organisational effectiveness, at least in theory.

Talent is now a sexy word. We all want to have it, show it and get more of it, even if we are not necessarily able to evaluate it, either in ourselves or others. We are living in the age of talent.

Discussions about the topic inundate popular and business forums, and a substantial portion of our lives is dedicated to cultivating, unlocking and monetising our talents. We are now studying more than we ever did, and, consequently, spending more to get educated than we ever have done. In the UK 72 per cent of graduates will not be able to pay back their student loans.[2] In the US outstanding student loans exceed the trillion-dollar mark,[3] making student debt larger than credit card debt, and marginally lower than car debt.[4] On a recent US flight I overheard the steward say that he was spending $6K (around £4.5K) per month on his daughter's university degree. That was probably twice his salary, and these stories are not unusual in America, which is (still) the epicentre of the war for talent.

Meanwhile, companies spend over $300 billion on employee training programmes, though only 5 per cent of that is spent on developing top talent, such as senior leaders.[5] As Figure 1 overleaf shows, there has been an almost exponential increase in budgets dedicated to the leadership development industry, which has virtually trebled since the talent war formally started a couple of decades ago.[6] And yet during that same time period, confidence in the leadership development industry has plummeted. If we consider that leadership development concerns the crème-de-la-crème of talent management – resourceful interventions to empower elite performers in top organisations – it is clear that we have a long way to go before our interest in talent is translated into an effective and reputable activity.

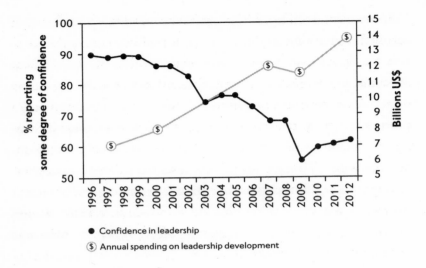

Figure 1: Confidence in the leadership industry as a function of money spent on leadership development

But where does the idea of a war for talent actually come from? McKinsey's original argument was based on two correct observations. First, the fact that in any organisation a small percentage of individuals – the top talent – will be disproportionately responsible for its success.[7] More specifically, McKinsey noted that a substantial amount of variability in corporate output (e.g., productivity, innovation, revenues, profits, etc.) can be explained by the performance of a fairly small number of executives. Second, the idea that because these elite workers are in limited supply, organisations are playing a zero-sum game where competition for top talent will be as fierce as for gold, oil or silver. It is no coincidence, then, that the word 'talent' was originally used to refer to a unit of measurement for silver.[8] For example, in the biblical parable of the talents, 'a talent of silver' was exchanged for a person's labour and the quantity of talents paid depended on the person's ability (Matthew 25).

Subsequent definitions of talent have tended to vary somewhat across different time periods. In the thirteenth century the word was frequently used to refer to a person's inclination or general psychological disposition. In the fifteenth century, the focus was on mental endowment and innate ability, and by the seventeenth century the term referred primarily to an extraordinary capability – being gifted, possessing exceptional faculties, mental or otherwise.[9] This idea is still represented in most definitions of talent today, as they tend to highlight some degree of exceptionality or innate brilliance – Marie Curie in science, Roger Federer in tennis, Amy Winehouse in music and Warren Buffett in business, for example.

Despite the obvious fact that our talents are context-specific, it is possible to draw comparisons between different *types* of talent by evaluating how rare or outstanding they are within a given talent category, vis-à-vis the rest of the population. Hence the idea that Warren Buffett may be regarded as the Roger Federer of business is more intuitive than it perhaps should be. At the same time, evaluations of talent are never entirely objective, which is why they make for passionate pub discussions and prolonged dinner debates that are hardly ever settled by a Google or Wikipedia search. Was Michael Jordan more talented than LeBron James? Was Mozart more talented than Bach? Do Justin Bieber and Miley Cyrus have any musical talent? Unlike in mathematics, there are no definitive answers to these questions, but that does not mean that the issue of talent is entirely subjective. For instance, there are fairly objective methods to demonstrate that I am less talented than Stephen Hawking or Angela Merkel. Ultimately, talent is just an explanation for someone's exceptional level of achievement, one that emphasises ability over and above luck or effort.

Even though the parameters for evaluating talent have historically focused on formal qualifications and educational credentials,[10] the connection between the number of people with university degrees and the number of talented people has declined dramatically in the past century, not least because of the democratisation of higher education. In many industrialised countries, almost 50 per cent of the population will earn a university degree in the next few years. In the US, the percentage of the population attaining some kind of college education increased from 17 per cent in 1980 to almost 60 per cent in 2014.[11] The value of academic titles has been diluted, and employers rarely see fresh graduates as having the necessary skills or expertise to perform well on the job. A Master's degree today is like having a Bachelor's degree in the past; and a Ph.D. is as common today as a Master's was 20 or 30 years ago (except it makes you overqualified). People with higher degrees are seen as hyper-trainable creatures, so their qualifications are a mere confirmation that these candidates have the potential to acquire relevant information and solve real-world problems ... *if* they continue to develop. It is not that employers don't trust formal academic credentials, but that their value is mostly confined to rank-ordering candidates on achievements that are only loosely related to the expertise they need to perform well in their actual jobs.

So where is the war for talent today? On the one hand, organisations clearly believe that talent is important. For instance, 74 per cent of organisations, and 83 per cent of large enterprises, see effective talent management practices as a critical strategic goal.[12] On the other hand, it is also true that most organisations are struggling with talent issues. In a recent global survey of over 1,000 board members,[13] fewer than 20 per cent of respondents said their companies were doing a good job attracting, hiring, developing, rewarding, retaining or firing talent, or aligning talent management practices with their business strategies. To put this into perspective, imagine if 80 per cent of organisations said that technology was a fundamental component of their businesses but only 20 per cent of organisations reported that their technology worked. It is one thing to value something because you reap its benefits, and a very different thing to value something because you don't.

For other areas of talent management, such as leveraging diversity, the situation is even worse, with fewer than 7 per cent of respondents deeming their practices effective, and all these activities being rated more poorly in Europe and Asia than the US. Bearing in mind that these data come from some of the most successful companies in the world, it is conceivable that the picture is even gloomier for the more average organisations out there – small, unknown, remote and unsuccessful corporations that are usually not the first choice of driven and talented employees rarely take part in surveys about good practice and have less advanced talent management practices.

Thus in many ways it appears that the war for talent has become the war *on* talent: instead of attracting and retaining talented employees, most organisations seem to repel them. Four global macro-economic trends support this idea:

1. *The disengagement epidemic*: the fact that most people are disenchanted with their jobs, or even alienated by them.

2. *The rise of the passive job seeker*: the fact that most people are open to new job opportunities, if not hoping for them.

3. *The growing appeal of self-employment*: the fact that, even in good economic times, people quit their jobs to work for themselves, or supplement their full-time jobs with freelance activities.

4. *The rise of entrepreneurship*: the fact that entrepreneurship has become one of the most desirable career paths, despite the minimal odds of success.

These trends are symptomatic of our talent problems – they exist because we are losing the war *for* talent, but winning the war *on* talent. Indeed, talented people are treated more like an enemy than the commodity being fought for, even if the intention of employers is actually the reverse. The following sections will discuss each of these problems in greater detail.

THE DISENGAGEMENT EPIDEMIC

Morgan is a 32-year-old accountant from Bristol who has worked at the same law firm for over a decade. Although she is good at her job, she has mastered the art of performing it with minimal effort, so most of her day is spent on non-work-related activities, such as browsing shopping sites, planning her next holiday and being on Facebook. Morgan knows that there are probably more exciting jobs out there, but at the end of the day her job pays the bills and it is relatively stress-free. Furthermore, if Morgan waits a bit longer she may be considered for promotion even if her productivity remains the same – after all, she has been with her employer for a while and the other candidates are more junior than her.

Sally, on the other hand, is an IT consultant from Birmingham who has just started a new job in a media firm. Although it has taken her some time to find this position she is very excited by it and wakes up full of enthusiasm and energy every morning before her alarm goes off. At work Sally is one of the first to arrive, and she is not only rapidly learning the ins-and-outs of her job, but also of the wider organisation. Sally has already joined the company's strategy team and she is quickly forging important collaboration networks within and outside the organisation. She is so immersed in her role that she tends to work until quite late without really feeling that she is putting in so many hours.

Which of these two individuals would you rather employ? Unless you are desperate for an accountant, you would probably want to hire Sally rather Morgan. This reflects a broader reality in the world of work, which is that people like Sally are in high demand, whereas there is an over-supply of people like Morgan.

Although employee engagement, a person's level of passion and involvement with work, is a critical driver of individual performance and organisational effectiveness,[14] most organisations employ only a minority of engaged employees. In other words, employees are generally disengaged at work; yet the return on investment (ROI) from engagement has been clearly documented, so companies have every incentive to engage their workforces. For instance, Best Buy estimates that a 0.1 per cent increase in employee engagement levels translates into an additional $100,000 in store revenues. Sisco, a global food-service giant, increased employee retention rates from 65 to 85 per cent by boosting engagement, saving the company $50 million in hiring and training costs.[15] Such examples suggest that engagement is a barometer for the war for talent, yet when you look at typical engagement levels around the world the picture is rather bleaker.

As Jeffrey Pfeffer summarised in his 2015 book, *Leadership BS*, global engagement surveys, which are usually conducted by human capital firms to monitor levels of satisfaction at work, consistently show that a majority of employees are not engaged. For example, Nielsen and the Conference Board report that 47 per cent of employees are satisfied with their job: down from 61 per cent 25 years ago. Right Management reports that in the US and Canada only 19 per cent of employees are satisfied. In a worldwide survey of over 30,000 people, Mercer reports that between 30 and 56 per cent of employees want to quit their jobs. And in a recent survey of over 142 countries, Gallup reports that only 13 per cent of employees are properly engaged, while 24 per cent are actively disengaged. In fact, for the past 10 years, Gallup's worldwide surveys estimate that 70 per cent of employees are either not engaged or are actively disengaged at work.[16]

Admittedly, these data are sometimes disputed, and for good reasons. First, categorical distinctions between 'engaged' and 'disengaged' are, by definition, arbitrary. In fact, some engagement companies, Gallup included, define being engaged as agreeing with all the statements of their engagement surveys, making it very easy, from a statistical standpoint, to fall in the 'not engaged' or 'disengaged' camps. In reality, there is no clear-cut line between engagement and disengagement, just like there is no dividing line between 'tall' and 'short', 'thin' and 'fat', 'smart' and 'stupid'. Everything that can be quantified is a matter of degree, and the use of adjectives to classify people's engagement levels does not reflect any meaningful cut-off points in their performance. What matters is the distribution of engagement levels and the fact that those at the top or to the right of the curve are more productive. In that sense, categorical measures of engagement are as objective as categorical measures of economic variables. For instance, the OECD, United Nations and the World Bank consider someone as 'poor' if they live on less than $2 a day, not because someone living on $2.01 is not poor, but because, in order to allocate resources and monitor the success of interventions, it helps to group people into general categories.

Secondly, since most of the firms that sell engagement surveys also sell services designed to improve engagement, one does not have to be overly cynical to infer that these companies are not incentivised to tell their clients that things are going well. It's a bit like taking your car to the mechanic and asking him* if everything is OK, or phoning a new insurance agent to ask him if you are covered for everything.

That said, there are few reasons – and not much data – to believe that the average person in the world is happy with their job. You only need to type 'my job is' into Google to get a sense of how most people feel about their jobs:

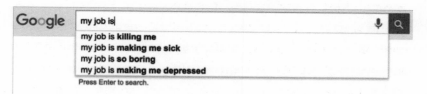

I invite you to try this for yourself, and see if anything has changed. The likely answer is 'no'. In a similar vein, Gallup's

---

* I am not a sexist. Nor do I think that all mechanics are male. However, throughout this book I use 'him' instead of 'him/her' or 'him or her' because it is less tiring for readers.

data on engagement have remained almost constant for the past decade: only 3 in 10 employees like their jobs.

In the US, the economic cost of disengagement has been estimated at $400 billion per year.[17] This figure is obtained by calculating the average productivity difference between disengaged and engaged employees and scaling it up to a national level. However, scientific studies have highlighted a wide range of other negative outcomes associated with low engagement levels. Most notably, disengagement increases turnover intentions,[18] as well as the likelihood to display counterproductive work behaviours (CWBs), such as staff abuse, rule-bending and theft.[19] American companies lose $50 billion a year because of employee theft,[20] and the Enron and WorldCom scandals alone cost the US economy $40 billion.[21] On the other hand, employee turnover, which is associated with a number of problems such as separation cost, replacement fees, morale damage, training fees and productivity losses due to adaptation time for new candidates,[22] costs companies between 10 and 30 per cent of the employees' annual salary, and even more for senior or highly specialised roles,[23] not least because companies will usually pay for the services of an executive search firm, too. Thus people who are less engaged at work can be expected to be less productive, more antisocial and stand a higher chance of leaving, and all this costs companies and the wider economy a great deal of money.

Clearly, some organisations are winning the engagement battle. Unsurprisingly, they tend to be the same companies that have performed well on other key areas of the war for talent. When we look at 'best places to work' rankings or mass-volume, open-source, crowd-sourced engagement scores, such as Glassdoor (www.glassdoor.com), we see the same usual suspects at the top of the chart every year. But the truth is that for every

Facebook, Airbnb, or Bain & Co. there are millions of organisations where the vast majority of employees are disenchanted,
alienated and fed up. Since the war for talent is mainly about
people, the global engagement figures suggest that people are
probably experiencing it as a war *on* them, rather than *for* them.

THE RISE OF THE PASSIVE JOB SEEKER

Gone are the days of lifelong jobs. For at least three decades
developed job markets have been characterised by shorter job
tenure, more frequent job switches and less certain career tra-
jectories. This trend has been primarily driven by organisations'
inability to predict future talent needs, but there's an element of
self-fulfilling prophecy here given that organisations have partly
caused employees to become less loyal to their employers.[24] That
is, it is largely *because* companies are now less able (or willing)
to provide long-term employment prospects that employees, in
particular those who are talented and therefore better able to
land desirable offers from other employers, are less committed
to them. As a result, since the 1980s organisations have taken
less responsibility for their employees' future careers, and expect
them to proactively manage their own destiny. And, in response,
employees have had to adapt, equating jobs to an ephemeral
holiday romance or one-night stand, rather than a long-lasting
marriage.[25]

This sea change should not be interpreted as a fundamental
psychological switch in the mind-set of employees. In fact, the
desire for stability is a universal human need,[26] which means
that people will always want to make their environments as predictable and as familiar as they possibly can, not least because

the alternative is stressful. Dozens of psychological studies have documented the negative effects of job instability (both objective and subjective) on individuals' physical and mental wellbeing.[27] Of course, this does not mean that all individuals are equally affected by the prospect of not knowing what their future careers may look like. For some people, such as those with low tradition and security values, a predictable and stable career may be psychological torture and lead to boredom and alienation. These individuals are often found in creative and entrepreneurial careers, where job security is lower. But they are the exception rather than the norm, much like extreme sensation-seekers (adrenalin junkies) are an anomaly in the wider population that strives to create mental safety in all areas of life. Indeed, most people are not interested in skydiving, rollercoaster riding or swimming with sharks, and they would also rather know what their careers will look like in ten years' time.

And yet, despite the fact that in industrialised economies unemployment rates are generally low, a majority of people are still passive job seekers. They may not be actively looking for a job – e.g., by researching openings, sending their CVs, filling out application forms or going to job interviews – but they are nonetheless open to new opportunities. They may set up job alerts on websites, go to casual networking events and keep their LinkedIn page up-to-date, even when they already have a job. These passive job seekers, who now include the majority of employed individuals in developed economies, are believed to represent around 75 per cent of the full-time workforce.[28] In a similar vein, LinkedIn estimates that close to 60 per cent of its 450 million users (two-thirds of whom live outside the US) are passively but eagerly waiting for better career opportunities, with another 25 per cent actively searching.[29]

If the ubiquity of passive job seeking does not alarm you, it is because we have become habituated to the widespread deficits in employee motivation, engagement and loyalty that characterise the average workplace today. As Jean-Paul Sartre said, the worst part of evil is that one gets used to it. This presents a paradoxical situation: in an age where most organisations are clearly worried about boosting their workforce's productivity, and unleashing its true potential,[30] employees are dreaming of better job opportunities elsewhere. In the realm of romantic relationships, this would equate to 75 per cent of married people being hopeful of finding a better spouse. Even if they weren't actively looking for one, they would be open to such an opportunity. Such a scenario would surely be considered symptomatic of a marital dissatisfaction epidemic, though people are generally less willing to put up with a bad relationship than a bad job ...

An additional problem is that externally hired workers take a long time to adjust to a new company. Their job performance during the first three years tends to be lower than for existing employees, and they are also more likely to leave the company voluntarily or be fired.[31] Large-scale meta-analyses indicate a positive correlation between job tenure and job performance, as well as between job tenure and organisational citizenship behaviours.[32] It is noteworthy that these effects are still significant after controlling for age, so loyalty does pay off for organisations. Thus organisations generally lose out when their employees leave, and when new ones arrive.

Unfortunately, the situation is not much better among senior employees, who, one would think, should be less incentivised to move jobs. After all, they are already successful and well paid, resembling happily married people in the realm of relationships. Yet company executives typically change employers every three or four years, and half admit to being interested in a new job when asked by executive search firms.[33] This explains why the executive search industry – professional recruiters dedicated to headhunting and placing senior leaders and other elite employees – is booming.[34] In contrast, in the 1950s only a minority of executives were chosen from outside a company, and the vast majority started their careers with the same employer. This change creates a clear problem for corporations that, on the one hand, have every incentive to invest their learning and development budgets on their most senior staff members, yet, on the other hand, get insufficient loyalty and commitment from them. However, as Warren Buffett noted,[35] the only thing worse than training your people and have them leave is not training them and have them stay.

Over the past 30 years, organisations have experienced an unprecedented increase in dismissals and external hiring for entry-level, mid-level and senior employees. According to Towers Watson, a global HR firm, half of employers feel they are unable to retain their top performers, and 55 per cent feel incapable of retaining their high-potential employees or those in critical job roles.[36] Unsurprisingly, research shows that losing elite workers hurts firms substantially more than losing average employees.[37]

The past ten years have witnessed an explosion of websites and apps dedicated to the enhancement of passive job seeking.[38] Whenever new technologies grow in popularity, it is tempting to assume that they are the root cause of newly observed, or more frequently manifested, human behaviours (e.g., Facebook has made us more sociable, Wikipedia more knowledgeable and smartphones more narcissistic). However, new technological resources are just catering to a demand that was already there, albeit often tacitly. Professional networking sites and career management apps are simply technology's answer to the problem of disengaged and disillusioned employees, a problem that presented a clear opportunity for innovations in that space. Much like in the online and mobile dating industry, the explicit goal of these innovations is to bridge the gap between supply and demand by making the market more efficient and boosting consumers' satisfaction with their choices. However, as with online and mobile dating apps, career-management apps succeed when they don't fully solve individuals' problems, and a certain amount of dissatisfaction re-emerges after a while. Thus LinkedIn and related sites, just like Tinder in the world of dating, make it easier to find desirable alternatives, but they also make it harder to be fully satisfied with those options because they keep presenting more and more choices, increasing people's temptation and keeping demand alive.[39] The more choice we have, the harder it is to choose and to be happy with our decision, and the easier it is to think that the grass is greener elsewhere.

THE GROWING APPEAL OF SELF-EMPLOYMENT

Having employees hop between organisations every few years is already problematic enough, but the fact that they are also willing to abandon traditional employment altogether, preferring instead to work for themselves, is even more concerning, not least because it worsens the talent supply problem for everyone. As you may have noted, many people now work for themselves even though they are perfectly able to be employed full-time by someone else, and you probably know people who have recently abandoned a corporate career in favour of self-employment – if you are reading this book, there is a significant probability that you fall into this bracket, since a great number of HR professionals are self-employed.

In developed economies it is usually highly educated, top-earning professionals who are more likely to enter voluntary self-employment,[40] complement their full-time jobs with other freelance activities and take on second or even third jobs.[41] In the US, which is not particularly high on the self-employment rankings, around 40 per cent of people are expected to have been self-employed at some point of their lives by 2020. Furthermore, even when macro-economic indicators fail to reveal a substantial change in absolute levels of self-employment or freelance activity, it is clear that the appeal of self-employment has increased over the past decades. By the same token, recent academic reviews show that, in an unexpected historical reversal from previous years, migrants to the US from more affluent and developed countries end up self-employed more often than their counterparts from poorer, less developed nations.[42]

Historically, it was predominantly high unemployment rates that caused population-wide increases in self-employment,[43] and this is still the case in many parts of the world. This well-known economic phenomenon, referred to as the *refuge effect*, predicts that most people will choose to work for themselves only when they don't have any other options.[44] The historical consequence was that self-employed individuals tended to lose out more when they were less qualified, particularly in terms of earnings, than full-time employees.[45] However, the past two decades have seen self-employment rates remain high, or even rise, even when economic conditions are strong. For instance, Britain saw a steep increase in self-employment activity in the immediate aftermath of the 2008 financial meltdown. Yet despite being out of recession for over seven years, and unemployment rates falling to around 5 per cent, there are 700,000 more self-employed people in Britain now than in 2008.[46] Furthermore, across developed countries, including OECD members, there is no longer a clear connection between self-employment and unemployment rates.[47]

All this explains why the self-employed economy, which is based on the premise of talent on demand, has been hailed as the industrial revolution of our age. This influential part of the workforce has been described as the 'the Freelance Nation, the Rise of the Creative Class and the e-conomy, with the "e" standing for electronic, entrepreneurial, or perhaps eclectic'.[48] As *The Economist* noted:

> Whether it's selling your crafts on Etsy or Ebay ... or accommodating tourists in your spare room via Airbnb (perhaps also commuters in your driveway via JustPark), the world of work appears to be changing.[49]

Of course, people are pushed into self-employment for multiple reasons.[50] Gallup's research explores why people actually leave their jobs. Contrary to popular belief, the number one reason is not poor pay or a lack of opportunities, but employees' experience with their direct line manager. As the saying goes, people join companies but quit their bosses. Meta-analytic reviews show that the most common reasons for leaving a job are stress, lack of career opportunities, lack of autonomy and leadership issues – which play a big part in controlling the first three.[51] No wonder, then, that people enter self-employment in order to be their own boss, for this is the best way to avoid having one. Although there are no independent peer-reviewed articles on this issue, it is conceivable that a large proportion of happily self-employed individuals around the developed world have been pushed into their current careers, albeit accidentally of course, by incompetent or unbearable managers. In other words, a good part of the self-employment economy is fuelled by bad bosses, which suggests that working for yourself is a good antidote to the stressful experiences caused by inept leaders.

It is also noteworthy that although self-employment does not generally contribute to economic growth, it does seem to pay off at the individual level. On average, self-employed people work longer hours – about 6 per cent more in the UK[52] – and worry more, often to earn less, yet they are still more satisfied with their jobs and lives than employed individuals are,[53] in part because they feel in control of their careers.[54] It is therefore no wonder that a high percentage of full-time employees report that they would rather be self-employed.[55] Most people would probably be quite happy to take a 15 per cent pay cut if it meant getting rid of their direct line manager. It seems, then, that instead of just fighting the war for talent with each other, organisations are also fighting a war on talent by collectively pushing skilled individuals into independent careers.

To the degree that organisations get better at identifying and engaging key employees, fewer talented people will be tempted into self-employment, and the talent pool of the freelance or gig economy will be mainly comprised of unskilled workers. There will always be exceptions, of course, as certain industries, such as agriculture, construction and professional services, will continue to rely on contract workers for a large proportion of their workforce. However, when talented people are driven into self-employment – as is the case in developing or undeveloped economies – the war for talent is clearly being lost. Consider the case of Argentina, my country of origin. Anyone who visits Buenos Aires will probably be impressed by the fact that the average taxi driver – and it's the same in Greece or South Africa – will speak more than one language, will have a professional degree and will be more tuned into current affairs than a typical Ivy League student is. Yet these data only indicate that the country has managed to mismanage its talent; that despite investing a substantial amount of resources into educating its population (or being able to attract highly skilled migrants from neighbouring countries), there are no opportunities for them other than self-employment or jobs for which they are overqualified. In other words, any influx of skilled individuals into the self-employment or freelance economy is symptomatic of an underutilised supply of talent, a talent surplus that implies a waste of human resources due to government incompetence. It is akin to having lots of natural resources – gold, oil, gas, etc. – but being a poor nation.

Fortunately, talent wants to be free. To the degree that people have skills, abilities or sought-after competencies, they will eventually find a way to translate them into useful services, products and labour – even if organisations are unable to unleash them or benefit from them. This effect is most visible in the rise of entrepreneurship and start-up activity rates.

THE RISE OF ENTREPRENEURSHIP

In the 15 years I have been teaching MBAs, I have noticed a significant change in students' vocational aspirations and career intentions. Fifteen years ago, most aspired to work for companies like JP Morgan, Deloitte or IBM. Ten years ago they wanted to join the likes of Google, Apple and Amazon. Today, most want to start their own business, not least because of the popular glamorisation of entrepreneurship as a career choice that enables people to emulate the lives of iconic self-made billionaires, such as Steve Jobs, Elon Musk or Mark Zuckerberg. Thus *Forbes* hailed the 'rise of the global entrepreneurial class',[56] noting that entrepreneurs are the 'new rock stars'.[57] *Entrepreneur* magazine described entrepreneurs as 'heroes'.[58] And, in a line I wish I'd coined (but can still steal), *Harvard Business Review* pronounced the 'rise of entrepreneurship porn'.[59]

Underlying this hype is the crude reality surrounding entrepreneurship – one that contrasts rather starkly with the usual myths about the profession. As documented very compellingly in Scott A. Shane's classic 2008 book *The Illusions of Entrepreneurship*, most entrepreneurs fail, few of their businesses ever grow and the vast majority would be better off if they had chosen traditional employment alternatives. This is not surprising given the wide range of skills and abilities that are needed to succeed in entrepreneurial ventures, from acting as 'inventors, investors, accountants, facilitators, organisational change specialists, leaders, technologists, marketing specialists, and top salespeople'.[60] In addition, research suggests that entrepreneurial talent is multifaceted because, to be effective, entrepreneurs need to display a number of personality qualities, such as a high need for achievement, autonomy, innovativeness and stress tolerance, that rarely coexist. Thus after a comprehensive review of the subject, Shane noted that the typical entrepreneur is just an unsuccessful business owner.

Of course, there is still an upside to entrepreneurial aspirations, namely the potential to reduce unemployment.[61] When the economy is down, people need to be creative and entrepreneurial to explore opportunities and use untapped resources. In doing so they transition from being unemployed or underemployed, to being self-employed, or a small business owner, helping the market to auto-correct. Furthermore, at any given time entrepreneurs contribute to economic equilibrium by closing the gap between supply and demand.[62] Yet, even in countries admired for their entrepreneurial success, only 1 per cent of people are employed in businesses that are less than two years old, compared to around 60 per cent of people who work in organisations that are over ten years old.[63] Accordingly, the benefits of entrepreneurship are mostly confined to the individual. For the market, the benefits are less palpable.

Nonetheless, interest in entrepreneurship is booming. In 2008, when Shane published his seminal book, there were 37 million Google search hits for 'entrepreneur'. As of 2016, there are now 173 million. Likewise the number of formal education programmes on entrepreneurship has increased from just a handful in the 1970s to over 1,600 now.[64] Each year in the US, more people launch businesses than get married or have kids. Forbes estimates that over half a million new businesses are launched in America every month.[65] However, America is less entrepreneurial today than it was in 1910, when a bigger percentage of the population started their own business. Peruvians and Turks are almost four times more likely to launch a business than Americans, not least because they have fewer opportunities to be employed. It is for this very reason that the most talented individuals in Silicon Valley are now more drawn to large corporations – e.g., Google, Facebook, Apple – than to more entrepreneurial ventures.

Much as in the case of self-employment, people launch their own business mainly to avoid working for others, and the very small number of individuals who succeed at growing their businesses are almost always employed by another organisation before they launch their start-up. In that sense, one could say that their new venture was incubated in, and to some degree funded by, someone else's business. Research shows that entrepreneurial employees – precisely the type of people companies need to retain if they are interested in innovating – are more likely to leave their current organisation to launch a new company.[66]

One of the possible reasons is that people with an entrepreneurial mind-set – nonconformist, innovative and disruptive individuals – are less tolerant of (and less tolerated by) incompetent management. In other words, the small minority of individuals who actually do have what it takes to succeed in entrepreneurial ventures would be a critical asset for big organisations, yet managers and leaders are often unwilling to put up with their difficult personalities and big egos. While it is hard to blame employees for being unable to cope with incompetent or obnoxious managers, managers must understand that there are good reasons for putting up with difficult employees when they are talented, in particular when they have the potential to contribute to innovation and growth for the business. Conversely, if all managers want is people who are well-behaved and conform, they will end up with an army of 'yes men' but their company will die a slow and stagnating death. As *The Economist* noted:

> Conventional talent management schemes fail because they rarely accommodate: mavericks and outsiders who are creative and innovative in their thinking but do not perform well using traditional appraisal measures.[67]

This phenomenon, which I have labelled 'accidental growth leadership', consists of bad bosses contributing to innovation, unintentionally and otherwise, by expelling or repelling creative talent from their teams and organisations. It is a rarely discussed form of talent drain that is more disruptive than people think. As Max Marmer noted in a *Harvard Business Review* article:

> instead of applying their talents to a company that is actually poised to solve an important problem and become a transformational company, they build another vapid iPhone app that nobody wants. As a result, many potentially transformational startups are inflicted with dysfunctional teams as a result of the depleted hiring pool.[68]

This obsession for ditching bigger firms in favour of launching 'the next big thing', no matter how mundane and trivial one's idea may be, has been successfully satirised in the HBO TV show *Silicon Valley*, where smart but socially clueless youngsters reject better career opportunities and risk everything they have to pursue their improbable entrepreneurial ambitions.

Research shows that entrepreneurs are generally more overconfident than the overall population, with a substantial proportion of business owners believing that their chances of success are 100 per cent. Although this explains why they are more likely to take risks, such as launching a business, over-confidence has negative rather than positive effects on business performance. Thus the more overconfident you are, the more likely you are to become an entrepreneur, but, at the same time, the less likely you are to succeed at it.[69]

Millennials – people born between the early 1980s and early 2000s – are particularly interested in being entrepreneurs. For example, data from 53 different countries indicates that almost 50 per cent of entrepreneurs worldwide are between 18 and 25 years old.[70] This is important for two reasons. First, in most countries millennials are already the dominant generation in work, and according to most estimates they will represent half of the global workforce by 2020, and 75 per cent by 2025. Following nature, the original succession plan was for them to replace ageing and retiring employees, but if a large number of millennials decide to launch their own businesses, who will fill the vacant positions in larger organisations? Second, millennials are generally less interested in hard work, more interested in fun and more individualistic than other generations.[71] Scientific studies also show that narcissism, a personality trait characterised by unrealistically positive self-views, overconfidence and a sense of entitlement, has been on the rise for some time and is higher in millennials than other generations.[72] This set of attributes suggests that millennials may be more ill-equipped for entrepreneurial activities than past generations, even if such ventures have higher appeal to them.

In brief, despite unprecedented professional and lay interest in talent – as well as vast amounts of money squandered on trying to win the talent war – the outlook is far from optimistic. Most people dislike their jobs, which explains why they are hoping for better opportunities, and increasingly open to the riskier and less profitable options of self-employment and entrepreneurship. It appears that the war for talent is just a delusion, but the war on talent is a reality.

In order to win the war for talent, HR must be a driver of organisational effectiveness, an engine of business growth and productivity. And the best way to achieve this is by improving companies' ability to attract, manage and retain valuable people. Yet there are few reasons to have confidence in HR's ability to deliver these pivotal talent management functions. Part of the problem is that real-world HR practitioners, though passionate about talent, are often clueless about how to define it. What do we really mean by talent? How is it manifested at work? And what effective ways do we have to truly work out whether some people have talent or not? The next chapter will answer these questions.

CHAPTER 2

Defining talent

This chapter provides four simple definitions for understanding talent. The first is the rule of the vital few, which posits that, in any organisation or group of individuals, a minority of people will be responsible for most of the collective output. The second is the maximum performance rule, which states that a person's talent can be gauged when he is trying to do his best. The third is the effortless performance rule, which asserts that if a person has talent he will be able to achieve the same level of performance as a less talented individual despite exerting lower levels of effort, because performance is ability plus motivation. The fourth states that talent is personality in the right place, in that a person will display talent if he finds the right context – or role – for his natural dispositions and default behavioural tendencies. As the chapter notes, these four generic principles can be applied in any field, profession or industry to get a quick sense of a person's talent vis-à-vis a normative group. Once this is achieved, organisations can move on to the next key step, which is to establish what specific qualities they ought to assess in order to predict talent, and how they can do this.

* * *

Muhammad Ali was the greatest boxer of all time, and one of the best athletes in modern history. Like most champions, Ali's talent was the by-product of nurture and nature: raw innate qualities that were harnessed through a combination of critical environmental experiences. Consider the fact that Ali's decision to go into boxing was triggered fairly early on in life, when he was nine years old, for rather arbitrary reasons. The already temperamental and combative Ali had his bicycle stolen, and when he pledged to revenge himself by giving the thief a good beating, a local gym instructor advised him to first learn how to box. Luckily for the thief, Ali never found him. Instead he knocked out most of the men who stood in front of him in the ring. Boxing is not the most common of careers, though, as Ali himself noted: 'It's just a job. Grass grows, birds fly, waves pound the sand. I beat people up.'

Clearly, the vast majority of bicycle thefts don't produce boxing champions, or any type of elite athlete. However, it is possible that without this specific catalyst the young Ali would have ventured into a different career. It is also likely that the instructor who advised Ali to take up boxing would have identified some early signs of talent, or at least potential, in the young boy. But no matter how naturally endowed you are, you will only develop exceptional skills if you have the right training and practice. Like Ali, any exceptional performer you know has made a successful bet on their potential, and has effectively cultivated his talent.

But what is talent?

Talent is not a simple phenomenon: it cannot be observed directly (i.e. what colour is it, how big is it, can we put it under the microscope?), and the signals we use to infer it are often elusive and ambiguous. As the Roman playwright Plautus pointed out: 'The greatest talents often lie buried out of sight.' And yet if we can't understand what talent is, even through some simplified definitions, it will be impossible to measure it, let alone manage it. Just like you cannot fight the war on drugs without first defining what you mean by drugs, or embark on a quest for gold without a clear sense of what gold actually looks like, the business of talent can only be effective if we first establish what talent is and is not.

Clearly, there's no lack of popular definitions for talent, but most of these definitions are wrong or confusing. Common problems defining talent concern mistaking performance for potential, overestimating how many people are talented and failing to acknowledge consequential ability differences between different people, which leads to overemphasising luck or hard work. Here are just a few examples highlighting misleading, yet widely endorsed, conceptions of talent:

Talent is persistence ... there's no such thing as not having enough talent ... persistence is talent, really. Just sticking with it. Talent is not stopping.[1]

We all have talents. In varying directions of varying types. Some common to all. Others all of our own.[2]

Talent reflects how you're hard-wired. That's what sets the concept apart from that of knowledge or skills.[3]

Although I chose these statements arbitrarily, they are representative of the common confusion surrounding the notion of talent. The first statement by equating talent to self-discipline and motivation, which, as will be seen, are largely separate from talent as drivers of performance and accomplishments; the second by endorsing the populist view – adored by the positive psychology movement and the self-help industry – that we are all talented in our own way (according to this view, the idea that some individuals may be more valuable than others is actually questionable); and the third statement, though somewhat more sensible, by assuming that talent is a fixed entity, and that it therefore cannot be developed.

In addition to these misconceptions, there are those who maintain that we ought to refrain from defining talent altogether. The most common reason for this argument is the notion that any attempt to classify someone as talented – or untalented – is driven by prejudiced motives.[4] Why, proponents of this argument ask, pigeonhole people into such deterministic categories instead of acknowledging that everyone is just different or unique, as opposed to better or worse? Can't we just embrace psychological diversity and accept that, since we are unable to predict performance with absolute accuracy, we should avoid betting against anyone? After all, even if some people appear to have more potential than others, there are always the hidden gems, the dark horses or raw talents who are yet to blossom but who would be unfairly discriminated against if we decided to designate other people as talented.

There are, of course, plenty of geniuses who flew under the radar for much of their lives, and would have no doubt benefited from a more open mind in those who were tasked with judging their talents. This list includes the eminent Albert Einstein, who was average at school and had to work as a patent clerk for years because he was unable to get a university job. And Winston Churchill, who had the lowest grades in his class and never made it to upper school. Not to mention J. K. Rowling, who, before publishing her first Harry Potter book, had worked as a teacher and spent some time on income support. Few would have predicted that she would eventually sell over 400 million books and amass a $1 billion fortune. In short, why do we even need the notion of talent?

There are three important reasons. First, although individual behaviour is not entirely predictable, it is also not random. That is, if you observe any person long enough you will realise that there are consistent patterns in the way they behave, even across different situations. These patterns make that person's probability to behave in certain ways different from other people's. Second, high-stake decisions about people's careers cannot be left to chance. Just like doctors would not be helping their patients by assuming that they are all equally healthy (or unhealthy), employers and HR practitioners would not help their employees by assuming they are equally talented – and for sure they would not help their businesses either, since ending up with less talented people *is* a disadvantage. And third, in order to develop your talents, you need first to be able to assess them. In other words, you must realise what you have and lack in order to get better. For instance, if I wanted to become an opera singer, it would be enormously helpful for me to realise that I have very limited talent for singing, so that I can work ten times harder to accomplish my goal (or just pick a more feasible goal).

Needless to say, laypeople would continue to make implicit evaluations of their own and others' talents even if HR professionals refrained from assessing their talent. Research shows that we all judge others' talents, even after very brief interactions[5] and in the presence of very superficial data. As the saying goes, there is no second chance for a first good impression. Although these inferences are based on prejudiced attitudes and stereotypes, they are often accurate. For example, studies show that laypeople can estimate with relative accuracy how talented managers are just by looking at their photographs.[6] Unsurprisingly, the motivation to infer talent is even greater among professionals, such as HR people, recruiters and interviewers. It is therefore hypocritical to pretend to ignore talent differences between people, and to maintain that the world would be better off if we abandoned the quest to judge how talented people are. The fact of the matter is that we do care a great deal about talent; we do need to know how talented people are, and so do they.

How, then, should talent be defined? The basic premise of this book is quite simple, namely that talent is an attribution, albeit an indispensable one. In other words, any notion of talent is ultimately a social construction of sorts, artificially created in order to make a future prediction about an individual's performance on a task, job or role. Yet at the same time, in order to be accurate, that prediction should not be based on an arbitrary notion of talent but on key individual differentiators – relevant attributes that can help us distinguish between better and worse future performers, as well as quantify the degree of effort that has accompanied each performance instance.

To that end, the next sections outline the four basic principles, or rules, of talent. These rules can be used to classify talent across any domain of work, career and occupation.

1. THE RULE OF THE 'VITAL FEW'

From an output or productivity perspective, the essence of talent is easy to grasp. There is a universal rule in economics that predicts that in any organisation, 20 per cent of the workforce will account for 80 per cent of the output, and the other 80 per cent of the workforce will account for the remaining 20 per cent of output.[7] By the same token, 20 per cent of the workforce tends to account for 80 per cent of the problems, and vice-versa. This law is the so-called Pareto effect, also known as the rule of the vital few, which states that a relatively small number of group members is usually responsible for a large number of consequences or aggregate effects[8] – a model of distribution found in virtually any area of performance. And in the real world of work, this distribution is often more 90/10 than 80/20, though that is not always observable through clear metrics since organisations often lack objective performance data on their employees.

So, who are the talented employees? The answer is straightforward: the 20 per cent that account for 80 per cent of productivity, or the minority of individuals that drive the biggest portion of a company's success. In this way, the rule of the vital few provides an elegant measure to connect individual behaviours with organisational outcomes; one that can also be used to quantify the potential or actual value of each employee.

There are many organisational applications of Pareto's law, most notably the 80/20 rule for managing one's own performance – i.e. focus most of your energies on the few tasks that yield the most and don't invest too much time on the vast majority of tasks that don't. However, 80/20 thinking is remarkably absent from everyday talent management approaches. One of the reasons for this is the political incorrectness of telling people that they are part of the bottom 80 per cent. Another reason is the difficulty, particularly for managers, of accepting that most people in an organisation contribute relatively little, even when you look at their cumulative output.

In essence, Pareto's law is a principle of unequal distribution, and its application to talent is rather obvious – namely that talent is not equally distributed in the overall population. Yet to most people, including managers, the 80/20 rule is counterintuitive because it marks a departure from the commonly accepted notion of the normal distribution (Gaussian 'bell curve'), which posits that the majority of people are average or close to average. Although most things, including physical and mental traits, are indeed normally distributed, it is also true that their cumulative effects on performance-related outcomes are unevenly dependent on the output of a minority. In other words, we may live in a world of normal distributions, but the far right end of the tail in the bell curve has far more impact than the 60–70 per cent of cases congregated under the main body of the bell. As the physicist and Nobel laureate P. W. Anderson observed: 'Much of the real world is controlled as much by the "tails" of distributions as means or averages: by the exceptional, not the commonplace; by the catastrophe, not the steady drop ... We need to free ourselves from "average" thinking.'[9]

An equally important implication of the Pareto effect concerns the sub-division of the bottom 80 per cent into two groups, namely the B and C groups (with the A group being the top 20 per cent) – see Figure 2 overleaf. The B group consists of the 30 per cent of cases directly to the left of the A group, and it accounts for 10 per cent of output, while the C group con-sists of the bottom 50 per cent and accounts for the remaining

10 per cent of output.[10] This idea was first hypothesised by Plato, who believed that people came in three classes: gold, silver and bronze.

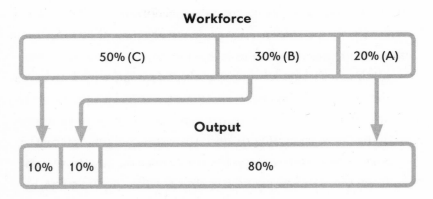

Figure 2: The three tiers of productivity

Crucially, the Pareto effect also suggests that nobody can be better off without someone else being worse off: if an employee improves and joins the top 20 per cent, it necessarily means that someone else drops into the bottom 80 per cent.[11] Thus organisations should not aim to eliminate or alter their Pareto distribution, which will always be found, but rather to ensure that their top 20 per cent ('the vital few') are as productive as possible, and more productive than their competitors' top 20 per cent. A secondary, but still important, goal is to make their bottom 80 per cent performers ('the trivial many') as effective as they can, and more effective than their competitors' bottom 80 per cent.

Many top firms around the world have in place talent management processes that are congruent with the rule of the vital few. For example, General Electric divides its workforce into three sub-groups that signal how promising they are. Hindustan

Unilever and Novartis identify a small percentage of 'high-flyers' early on and invest a great deal of time and money in developing their leadership potential.[12] Note that their focus is not to make everyone better, but to further develop those who are already great. In summary, defining talent according to Pareto's law enables organisations to adopt exclusive talent management programmes, focused on the vital few.[13]

All this said, it is also true that elitism can have its drawbacks. As *The Economist* notes:

> In their rush to classify people, companies can miss potential stars. Those who are singled out for special treatment can become too full of themselves. But the first problem can be fixed by flexibility: people who are average in one job can become stars in another. And people who become too smug can be discarded.[14]

2. THE 'MAXIMUM PERFORMANCE' RULE

'A problem is a chance to do your best.'

DUKE ELLINGTON

Another way to define talent is by focusing on an individual's best or top output. That is, what someone can do when they are highly motivated and trying hard under optimal conditions. This rule equates talent to an individual's *maximum performance*, defined as 'the level of performance in a given domain that one can produce on demand for a short period if one chooses to exert maximum effort'.[15] This definition is so intuitive that it is almost unnecessary to discuss it further. Whether we are trying

to work out how good someone is at singing, running or thinking, the behaviours we focus on to make our inferences will be
meaningful and informative only if we can safely assume that
they are accompanied by high doses of effort. If the person is
truly trying to do their best, then we can conclude that their performance is indicative of talent, but if they are not bothered or
not making an effort, then our guess will be as good as flipping
a coin. Thus, despite the fact that talent is a conceptual rather
than observable entity, when someone performs to their best,
their behaviour provides the clearest and most direct window
to that person's talents.

The origins of the maximum performance rule come from
the old idea that, in order to understand human behaviour, it is
necessary to take into account the context in which it occurs,
as well as its underlying motives. This idea is based on two
key assumptions. First, that when describing what people are
like – e.g., how they differ from others, how they stand out and
in what ways they are unique – one can focus either on what
they can do or what they typically do.[16] In other words, is the
main issue how my performance differs from yours most of the
time, or just when we are both trying to do our best (which
may happen only occasionally)? And second, that differences
in performance are a function of both ability (talent) and effort
(motivation), though the proportional influence of these two
factors on performance varies from one person to another, as
well as from task to task. Talent will be the key differentiator
between people's performance when they are highly motivated
to do well; motivation will be the key differentiator when they
are similarly talented. Therefore, talent sets the upper limits to
maximum performance, revealing the best you can do when you
are trying to do your best.

Psychologists have also defined the circumstances that should ideally be present for performance to be classified as maximum.[17] There are three particular conditions:

a. people should be asked to do their best;

b. they should know that their performance will be evaluated; and

c. the duration in performance should be sufficiently long to allow for a reliable measure to be obtained, but not so long as to produce performance drops (e.g., due to fatigue, boredom, or the difficulty of sustaining one's best for a long time).

Consider the case of running, in particular running speed – a very concrete and easily definable skill (albeit not obviously central to most modern jobs or organisational competency models). Suppose we are trying to evaluate how fast you can run. The best way to figure this out would be to create the conditions for maximum performance, which would involve (a) asking you, and ideally also incentivising you, to run as fast as you can; (b) telling you that your running speed will be measured; and (c) constraining your performance interval to a specific amount of time or distance (e.g., run as fast as you can for 1 minute, or run 300 metres as fast as you can). It is possible that a single trial would not reveal what your running speed ability is, but after a few attempts we would probably start seeing homogeneous results in your performance, as well as observing your top speed, or something close to it. And that would enable us to estimate your running talent.

Importantly, whatever your top speed may be, it would not

imply that you usually run at that speed. Indeed, your typical performance – what you do most of the time – may be completely unrelated to your maximum performance. By the same token, it would be foolish to infer someone's running speed by observing how fast they usually run, or walk. Now, this does not mean that we can never infer how talented someone is from his typical performance. When professional musicians, athletes or actors train, their performances will still exceed those of 99 per cent of the population, even though they are saving their best for when it actually matters.

What, then, can we say about typical performance? It represents mostly enduring situations 'in which performers are not aware of any performance evaluation or instruction to invest effort'.[18] Under typical performance conditions motivation is usually lower, mostly because individuals feel that they are not being observed and that their actions will not be the target of consequential decisions (e.g., rewards, punishments, promotions). The more motivated people are, the less their typical and maximum performance will differ. To a large degree, our personality determines how frequently we will try to engage in maximum performance efforts. This explains why ethical employees, who are more self-disciplined and conscientious, tend to perform to their maximum level more often.[19] Likewise, people with high recognition and achievement needs tend to have higher standards and therefore maintain maximum levels of performance more often. This can be seen not just at the individual, but also at the cultural level: for example, Eastern cultures are more collectivistic and respectful of formal rules and authority, so they tend to slack less.[20] Studies also reveal that openness to new experiences, a trait related to higher levels of curiosity, inquisitiveness and aesthetic sensitivity, is correlated to a person's maximum performance, whereas neuroticism, a trait related to emotional sensitivity, tendency to anxiety and negativity, relates to their typical performance, albeit negatively.[21]

For most people, typical performance merely reflects low-stakes output or 'eco mode' performance. A common example is 'social loafing', the tendency for people to slack during team assignments because they expect other team members to do their work.[22] Social loafing is the productivity equivalent of the bystander effect, in which people fail to engage in prosocial behaviour because the presence of others dilutes their own sense of responsibility – if other people are also watching, why should I act? The larger the group, the less interesting the task, the less individuals care about the group, and the more performance is judged at the collective rather than individual level, the more likely it is that individuals will engage in social loafing, and the more their typical and maximum performance will differ. At the same time, when people don't feel sufficiently competent, when tasks are hard, or when the pressure to do one's best may be too stressful, individuals may underperform under maximum performance conditions vis-à-vis their typical performance.[23] This is fairly common during high-stake activities such as job interviews or employee selection tests, in particular when individuals are nervous or of an anxious disposition.[24]

Given that managers often make critical decisions about employees based on their maximum performance, particularly in the context of personnel selection, it would be helpful if people's maximum performance had some relationship with their typical performance. Consider the case of selection interviews, aptitude tests and job simulations, all of which are widely employed in recruitment and staffing. The value of these methods depends primarily on their ability to predict candidates' future performance. However, since typical and maximum performance are only weakly correlated – their overlap is less than 20 per cent[25] – their main utility is in forecasting what people *could* do, rather than what they *will* do most of the time. Studies have shown that aptitude tests used in the selection process, such as IQ or intelligence tests, are most useful when the goal is to predict job performance under maximum performance conditions, but not so much under typical performance conditions.[26]

Thus if you want to know who your best employees are, the answer will differ depending on whether you focus on people's maximum or typical performance.[27] When the focus is on the former, the answer will relate to employees' talent; when the focus is on the latter, what is primarily at stake is motivation. Likewise a person's leadership potential will be manifested differently under typical and maximum performance conditions.[28] Even when people think of the worst bosses they ever had, they will still be able to recall certain moments when those awful bosses displayed some talent and expertise.

Perhaps the biggest advantage of the maximum vs. typical performance distinction is that it enables us to account for the familiar cases of underachievement. When the best a person can produce is impressive, to the point of putting them in the top 5 or 10 per cent in a group, there is no questioning the person's talent. However, if such levels of performance are rarely replicated, then we can safely assume that the person is underperforming. Many great athletes fall into this category. They are talented enough to become professionals, and even break into the top 100 of their sport's world rankings. Furthermore, they are often talented enough to beat athletes in the top 10, as well as occasionally record wins against the number 1 player. Yet their inability to repeat this often, and their tendency to show much poorer levels of performance in a typical tournament, turn them into a case of wasted talent. By the same token, in any field of achievement there are people who fail to live up to their expectations because their maximum performance isn't displayed frequently enough.

3. THE 'EFFORTLESS PERFORMANCE' RULE

'What I lack in talent, I compensate with my willingness to grind it out. That's the secret of my life.'

GUY KAWASAKI

Although the 80/20 – 'vital few' – and 'maximum performance' rules provide us with two elegant criteria to judge talent, they are focused on past behaviours, or what individuals have already done. The 80/20 rule classifies people as talented if their output puts them in the top 20 per cent, and the maximum performance rule posits that people are as talented as their personal best. However, a comprehensive view of talent should also be able to account for cases in which individuals have not yet shown the best they can do. This would include people who, though not part of the vital few, have the potential to be part of that group, together with people who have not yet reached their maximum performance, and may therefore be more talented than they seem – at least judging from their past performance.

One way to overcome this limitation is to consider how much effort a person has put into achieving their personal best. As already noted, performance is a function of effort (motivation) and talent (ability).[29] This notion was popularised in Malcolm Gladwell's *Outliers*: 'achievement is talent plus preparation', though under the false premise that preparation matters much more than talent. It is fair to say that, much like Malcolm Gladwell, people generally adhere to the principle that exceptional achievement is 99 per cent perspiration, yet this idea is sheer wishful thinking, particularly when people uphold meritocratic ideals (i.e., if you work hard you will definitely make it). There is a common bias that drives people to attend selectively to evidence highlighting the role that effort and motivation play in success, while downplaying, if not ignoring, evidence for the effects of talent.

Likewise, there is no shortage of exceptional achievers who attribute their own success merely to hard work, if not also 'luck'. For example, when Charles Saatchi, the founder of the world's biggest advertising agency, was once asked how he took his company to industry number one in record time, he responded: 'There is no answer or formula I can offer. We worked brutally hard, and got blindingly lucky.'[30] Although there are no reasons to doubt that hard work played a key role in determining Saatchi's success, it is more feasible that talent – rather than luck – was the key ingredient.

Indeed, since clear performance differences between people remain even when they are well matched on effort, there has to be some personal quality that explains individual differences in performance beyond motivation. In other words, you can put people through the same training and preparation, and have them equally motivated, and yet their output will rarely be the same. There is extensive evidence for the fact that even among people who have invested 10,000 hours of practice or training in developing expertise, achievement and knowledge differences between them remain.[31] Therefore, when two people exert the same level of effort, the more talented individual will perform to a higher level. And when two people perform to the same level, the more talented individual has exerted less effort to reach that level.

If performance is talent plus effort, then talent is performance minus effort. In other words, talent is effortless performance. What this means is that when a person achieves the same level of performance by making less of an effort than their colleague, they are more talented. It is, in fact, the person's very talent that is driving their performance. They are not relying on effort, hence talent must be the key factor at play. This simple formula can explain the familiar cases of raw talent: individuals who, without much practice or preparation, achieve remarkable levels of performance. They are most clearly epitomised by early child prodigies – individuals who, before the age of ten, perform at a professional level[32] – because the effects of practice are clearly insufficient to explain their accomplishments. Consider the case of Bobby Fisher, who started playing chess at the age of six and became US national champion at the age of fifteen. Or Mozart, who published his first musical composition at the age of five. Or Jeremy Bentham, who was accepted at Oxford at the age of twelve.

The effects of talent on achievement are also noticeable during the performance instance. If you watch any expert or professional while they are executing their work, you will be able to observe a sense of mastery that highlights effortless performance. Whether it's Luis Suárez scoring a goal, Serena Williams hitting a serve, Nina Simone singing, or Meryl Streep acting, talented people in any field are known for displaying not just outstanding, but seemingly effortless, performances. The German philosopher Martin Heidegger attributed this ability to their expertise, which he defined as the capacity to ignore the irrelevant aspects of a situation. Thus when experts look at a problem they are able *not* to pay attention to all the irrelevant elements of the situation. Conversely, when amateurs or novices approach the same problem it will seem a lot more complex to them, because they will focus on aspects of the situation that are not relevant, and therefore will waste mental resources and so require more effort. Accordingly, the 'talent = performance – effort' formula is also useful for working out what your own talents are. If something comes very easily to you, then you are probably talented at it – or at least you have the potential to develop those talents faster than others.

While it may seem nice to make everyone think that they can achieve anything they want if they try hard enough, there are two big problems with this. The first is that achievement motivation is not as malleable as we like to think. You cannot suddenly turn into a very driven or highly achieving person, just because you want to. Rather, work ethic and drive are largely dispositional, and therefore are influenced by an array of factors and events that occur in our early years (and even before we are born). The second problem is that even if you manage to dedicate a great deal of time and energy to a cause – because you are motivated and determined to succeed at it – that does not guarantee exceptional levels of performance. In fact, some people work exceptionally hard in life without achieving even average levels of performance. Moreover, even if individuals of low motivation had the choice to become extremely driven people, they would probably reject that choice if they understood how hard they would have to work and how ascetic their lives would be, and that such discipline would by no means guarantee their success. Most people don't want to achieve; they want to *have* achieved.

4. THE 'PERSONALITY IN THE RIGHT PLACE' RULE

'The talent is in the choices.'

ROBERT DE NIRO

Another way to think of talent is as personality in the right place. By 'personality' I mean an individual's typical tendencies or default predispositions, including his values, interests, skills and usual behavioural patterns[33] – in other words, everything we normally mean when we talk about what a particular person is like. When these attributes are matched to the right task, context or environment, they will represent important career weapons for the individual, as well as crucial performance drivers for the organisation. Conversely, if there is a poor match the employee will be at best irrelevant, and at worst counterproductive.

Personality can also be understood as a 'strategic function for responding to life situations'.[34] Depending on your personality, you will be more or less able to respond effectively to different situations. That is, your natural behavioural tendencies may be an asset with regard to certain jobs, but not others. This idea is represented in one of the main tenets of scientific personnel selection, which is that in order to predict and effectively influence an individual's job performance, one should focus on the qualities or attributes that are important with regards to the specific job one is trying to fill.[35] In other words, if you want to understand what talent for a given role entails then the most important issue is to identify the specific behaviours that enhance performance in that role.

The next critical question is which individuals are more likely to display those behaviours. This logic holds when the criteria are specific tasks (e.g., driving, selling, negotiating), as well as when predicting success in broad occupations (e.g., banker, psychologist, HR director and so on). Professional domains differ from each other in terms of the critical attributes that their high-performers display, but it is generally the case that highly accomplished individuals have found the right niche for their natural inclinations or default patterns of behaviour: a suitable home or career ecosystem for their personality.

Successful individuals are deemed talented because of their relative ability to adapt to their environment, but only because they have ended up in environments that make their person-alities assets rather than hindrances. This is true even when their personalities consist of fairly undesirable characteristics. For example, thanks to her narcissism and attention-seeking behaviour Kim Kardashian has a clear talent for being famous, especially in an age where, if your goal is to be famous, it is pretty much disadvantageous to have any other talents. Likewise, Donald Trump – the Kim Kardashian of politics – excels in polit-ical debates because of his ability to entertain the crowds with his seemingly spontaneous, controversial and absurd statements. Since US presidential campaigns have been reduced to reality TV shows, and given that many voters are disenchanted with tra-ditional politicians, Trump's personality is *in the right place* – it is an asset and a career weapon.

If you are too intellectually snobbish to consider Donald Trump or Kim Kardashian as talented (which I could under-stand), here are a few less extreme examples to illustrate that talent is largely personality in the right place:

- Many accomplished entrepreneurs, including self-made billionaires, were corporate misfits and failed to make it in large organisations. Steve Jobs was once fired from his own company, and the co-founder of WhatsApp, which was acquired by Facebook for almost $20 billion, had been previously rejected by Facebook when he applied for a job.[36]

- Oprah Winfrey was fired from her first journalism job as a TV anchor for being 'too emotional' and 'overly invested' in her stories.[37] That same style propelled her to become one of the most successful TV presenters of all time, contributing to her net worth of $3 billion.

- Before enrolling in Cambridge to begin his academic career as one of the most influential scientists of all time, Sir Isaac Newton was put in charge of his family farm and failed miserably.[38]

By the same token, many outstanding people are unlikely to be top performers outside their own field of competence. For example, would you hire Usain Bolt as your IT manager, Adele as your accountant, or Angela Merkel as a stand-up comedian? If you wouldn't, that is not because they couldn't do those jobs – they are probably capable of learning them – but because their talents would be wasted in such roles. Mega-successful companies such as Google regularly evaluate where to place their low-performing employees so they are better matched to a role's demands – and their performance improves.[39]

It is therefore not surprising that most, if not all, talent management interventions are attempts to increase person–role fit, defined as 'the degree of compatibility or match between individuals and some aspect of their work environment'.[40] If they aren't, they should be! For instance, selection interventions ought to maximise the fit between job applicants and the job they are hired for: 'the right person for the right job' is the most important goal staffing decisions must try to accomplish. Likewise, leadership development interventions aim to enhance the fit between leaders and their teams, or between leaders and their organisation's goals. Finally, interventions designed to boost employee engagement are mainly focused on increasing the fit between employees and the organisation, in particular its culture and climate,[41] defined as 'the subconscious assumptions, shared meanings, and ways of interpreting things that pervade in an organisation', and employees' perceptions of 'the way things are around here'.[42]

In addition, hundreds of scientific studies show that employees perform better when their personalities are compatible with the tasks required by their jobs.[43] For instance, emotionally stable people perform well in jobs that involve working in stressful environments and making decisions under pressure (e.g., investment banker, neurosurgeon, firefighter), but more anxious individuals do well in contexts where pessimistic thinking, attention to detail and hyper-alertness are assets (e.g., air traffic controller, health and safety officer, academic research). On the other hand, friendly and outgoing people do well in jobs that require a great deal of interaction with others, particularly where they have to build trust and maintain relationships (e.g., PR officer, customer service agent, teacher, nurse), but stand-offish people have an advantage in jobs that require tough decision-making and straight-talking (e.g., army general, CFO, football manager). Finally, extraversion is advantageous if the job requires a great deal of networking and public speaking (e.g., politician, estate agent, stand-up comedian), but introversion will be more useful when the job requires working independently and concentrating for long periods of time (e.g., librarian, software developer, auditor). Importantly, the effects of personality–job fit have also been found in longitudinal studies. For example, every standard deviation increase in adolescent extraversion is associated with a 7 per cent increase in adult salaries for managers, a 4 per cent increase in salary for sales and services professionals and a 2 per cent decrease in the salary of other professionals.[44]

In short, talent is largely a function of being in the right place. But this does not imply that talented people are just lucky. Rather, they manage to make smarter career choices by deliberately picking environments that turn their typical dispositions and default behavioural tendencies into effective career enhancers. Inevitably, this requires high levels of self-awareness. If you don't understand what you are like, you will only end up in the right job by accident. This highlights the importance of measuring talent, in both oneself and others. Unless we can effectively identify what specific talents people have, it will be difficult to find suitable roles for them.

CHAPTER 3

Measuring talent

This chapter examines the two critical questions pertaining to the measurement of talent: namely, *what* should we assess, and *how* should we do it? Even if talent is rationally defined, it is important to break it down into its key components in order to actually measure it. If we cannot measure it, we won't be able to manage it. As this chapter shows, the 'what' of talent concerns three basic elements: being *Rewarding* to deal with, *Able* to do the job and *Willing* to work hard (or RAW). In other words, in any job, role and organisation, more talented individuals are generally more endowed with these three advantageous qualities – likeability, ability and drive – than their less talented colleagues. As for the 'how' question, the chapter shows that there are several well-established and scientifically defensible methodologies for quantifying the degree of talent individuals possess, e.g., structured job interviews, prolonged assessments,

IQ tests and personality assessments. When the right qualities are targeted, and the correct methods are used appropriately, it is possible to make rather accurate predictions about an individual's probability to display high performance levels in any particular job. Thus the science of talent is reliable and predictive; the problem is how infrequently it is applied in real-world work settings.

* * *

The science of personnel selection is over a hundred years old yet decision-makers still tend to play it by ear, or believe in tools that have little academic rigour. When managers are asked how they go about identifying talent, their most common response is 'I know it when I see it', or 'well, you just know'. Yet there is conclusive evidence indicating that decisions based on intuition are almost always biased (and therefore less effective) than those based on data or actual evidence. An important reason why talent isn't measured more scientifically is the belief that rigorous tests are difficult and time-consuming to administer, and that subjective evaluations seem to do the job 'just fine'. However, there is a well-established return on investment for academically defensible methods, and a high cost for trusting one's own instincts. This is problematic: if you start your talent management programmes without the ability to identify talent, you will not get very far.

One of the main causes of this problem is the fact that few organisations are good at measuring job performance; and if you cannot distinguish between the best employees and the rest, it will be difficult to identify the qualities that top performers possess. This is disappointing, because there is no shortage of tools or proven methods for quantifying a workforce's output and productivity. Indeed, few criteria have been studied more extensively than job performance.[1] Although much of this research has focused on individuals, it provides the foundations for understanding team and organisational performance, which makes individual job performance 'the basic building block on which the entire economy is based'.[2]

An individual's overall job performance is the sum of actions linked to the pursuit of organisational effectiveness. Being able to measure this accurately is essential for making good talent decisions, such as whom to hire, promote or fire. From a legal standpoint, talent management decisions rest on their ability to evaluate performance objectively. Thus, in an ideal world, we would quantify each employee's contribution to the organisation's goals. In the real world, however, the most widely used measure of job performance is the supervisor's opinion of it.[3] This represents a very unreliable measure of job performance. Consider that, on average, two supervisors rating the same employee correlate at around .5, implying only 25% overlap between their evaluations.[4] In other words, if two managers are asked to rate ten employees, their views would be different for at least seven of those employees.

As if this weren't subjective enough, supervisors' ratings are often combined with self-ratings of performance by the candidate! For example, traditional performance reviews require employees to recap their year's accomplishments against some previously agreed goals, and supervisors use this information to determine whether employees have met, exceeded or failed to meet expectations. At times, and this is probably the best-case scenario, there are some objective measures to evaluate people's performance. These enable supervisors to compare employees' achievements with their initial goals, as well as with the achievements of other employees. Yet the main factor usually determining the outcome of performance reviews is how much supervisors like the appraised employees, which partly depends on how good employees are at marketing their own achievements. Unsurprisingly, performance evaluations are contaminated by organisational politics, and are seen as unfair by most employees. Research shows that even when supervisors are able to evaluate employees' performance accurately, they are not necessarily motivated to do so.[5] Thus a recent review concluded:

> Poor quality, contaminated, and mis- or underspecified measures of performance hinder our capacity to advance our understanding of the true importance of individual differences as predictors. Although more data are now tracked by organisations on individual performance, we are still limited in our capacity to predict because of the challenge of obtaining accurate and complete assessments of individual behaviour at work.[6]

To make matters worse, even when companies manage to measure job performance reliably, they cannot always assume it is a valid talent signal or accurate indicator of future performance. When jobs are complex, there is a great deal of within-subject variability in job performance, such that an individual's maximum performance will rarely be observed (even when performance is measured objectively).[7] Furthermore, although past behaviour is generally a good predictor of future behaviour, when employees change roles and the new role requires a significantly different set of skills, dispositions and abilities, past performance is unlikely to predict future performance. A report by the Corporate Leadership Council indicated that only 29 per cent of high-performing employees across almost 60 companies, from 15 different industries and 29 countries, could also be considered 'high potentials', in terms of their ability to perform exceptionally at the next level of the organisation or in critical company roles. And yet, most organisations still promote people on the basis of their past performance, not least because they find it harder to justify decisions based on things people have not yet done but are instead likely to do in the future – even when the data back up those predictions.[8] As a result, good performers think they deserve a promotion even when they don't have potential, and people with potential are easily ignored when they have not been performing well in their current (less relevant) role.

This is why, as the famous Peter principle predicts, people are eventually promoted to their own level of incompetence. Thanks to the pervasive bias of emphasising past performance over talent, not to mention the fact that past performance is rarely measured properly, employees are generally promoted until they reach a stage where they are no longer worthy of promotion because their performance sucks or they stagnate. Thus for most people who have been employed sufficiently long enough, potential is where they are minus one level – because they should have stayed in their previous role, where their maximum performance was reached. This is particularly salient when people are promoted from individual contributor to management roles, where people skills become a more critical component of performance than technical expertise.

Once you establish reliable parameters to quantify people's performance, it is fairly straightforward to measure talent. Examining precisely how top performers differ from the rest is a pretty direct way to identify the core components of talent with regards to a given role, and a great deal of scientific research has been devoted to this issue. These efforts have essentially focused on answering those two key questions: *what* should we assess and *how*?[9] The next section examines the first question.

THE 'WHAT' QUESTION: THE RAW INGREDIENTS OF TALENT

The vast majority of problems that talent identification must solve boil down to the following question: what exactly should you measure? To some degree, the answer will depend on the specific job or role we have in mind. Indeed, few people would disagree with the idea that, since performance is largely dependent on the context, task or role, it is pretty pointless to try to produce a universal model of talent. Accordingly, the *what* question of talent should be determined by the specific elements of each job, and we should not expect the same individual to be deemed talented across different settings or professional contexts.

Alternatively, we could opt for a pragmatic solution, which is to classify all jobs according to a generic model of vocational interests. John Holland's theory of professional interests is one of the most robust frameworks in vocational psychology, and specifies six major types of jobs: realistic, investigative, artistic, social, enterprising and conventional.[10] These major job types require not only different interests, but different skills and dispositions. Moreover, the six types can also be used to describe people, and matching people and jobs will tend to boost performance.[11]

If we wanted to be more specific, we could zoom into some common job titles (e.g., CEO, sales manager, accountant, fundraiser); there are over 1,000 catalogued for the US alone. Or you could examine jobs at the most granular level, regarding each of the roughly 4 billion workers in the world as individuals with a unique job, for no two jobs are exactly the same. When I applied for my first academic post, due to my non-EU-citizen status the university had to prove to the UK government that nobody in the entire European Union was better suited for the job than me. And despite the fact that I was still a junior candidate, the university managed to show that none of the 400 million EU citizens was a better candidate for the job than I was because my profile fitted the job requirements exactly, down to the last biographical detail. If you really want to make the case, then every job is unique.

Yet just like individuals, organisations overestimate their uniqueness. Sure, every job is different and there are billions of jobs and millions of companies. But at the same time talented employees tend to share certain universal characteristics, which makes them surprisingly similar across different jobs, companies and industries. By the same token, most organisations have their own model of talent and invest a great deal of time and money outlining the specific facets or qualities they want in employees, but all models look remarkably similar once we overcome the differences in terminology – e.g., 'agile' versus 'adaptable', 'driven' versus 'motivated' and 'inspires others' versus 'team-builder'. As the joke goes, a camel is a horse designed by a committee. My colleagues and I have shown[12] that all competencies can ultimately be reduced to three fundamental buckets of talent, which represent the raw ingredients of individual differences in employability and career success. The term 'raw' is appropriate, not only for emphasising the potential contribution that these talent qualities make to an individual's achievements – providing the recipe for success – but also as an acronym for these key components, namely: *rewarding*, *able* and *willing*. Hence we referred to this as the RAW model of talent.

Thus individuals who score highly on all RAW components

will stand a much stronger chance of being top performers and succeeding in their careers. They will be much more likely to be part of the 'vital few', to deliver effortless and exceptional performance, and to be 'in the right place' for a variety of jobs. Although there is no abundance of people who unequivocally display all three components of the RAW model, those who do are probably doing pretty well, and not just in their careers but life in general. People who have two of the three RAW components are probably employed, even when economic times are tough. Unless the unemployment rate is effectively zero, people who display just one of the three RAW ingredients are probably unemployed. And people who have none are probably unemployable: if you are inept, irritating *and* lazy you will not be able to get or keep any job.

Each element of the RAW model can be regarded as a unique bucket of talent. Now let us examine this in more detail.

Rewarding

The first RAW ingredient of talent is a person's likeability or how rewarding they are to deal with. This core element of talent includes what psychologists usually refer to as organisational citizenship:

> discretionary behaviour, not necessarily part of a job description, that promotes the effective functioning of the organisation via being co-operative, helping other people, tolerating less-than-ideal working conditions, going well beyond minimal requirements, identifying with the organisation's goals, and participating voluntarily in organisational governance and administration.[13]

It is a function of personality and concerns intrapersonal skills (managing yourself) and interpersonal skills (managing others), both of which are captured by the concept of emotional intelligence (EQ).

Some people may be rewarding to deal with because of their charisma and likeability, which does not imply that they are interested in engaging in prosocial behaviours or good citizenship. In fact, many individuals with accentuated 'dark side' personality characteristics, such as Machiavellianism, narcissism and psychopathy, may at times seem rewarding to deal with because of their ability to engage in tactics of manipulation or display mischievous charm and social skills.

What is clear is that, in a world where most talent decisions are made by people who follow their intuition, likeability pays off. As the great Dale Carnegie once remarked, 'when dealing with people remember that you are dealing, not with creatures of logic, but with creatures of emotion'. Thus, other things being equal, more likeable people will have a higher probability of succeeding in their careers, and can therefore be considered more talented, particularly when people skills are a key ingredient of job performance. And, let's face it, they almost always are. Even academics, accountants and software engineers benefit from knowing how to deal with people, and not just via email.

Able

The second RAW ingredient of talent is a person's ability to do the job. The sub-components of ability are *expertise*, which covers the specific aspects of talent (domain or job-related knowledge, experience and skills), and *intelligence*, which includes learning ability and reasoning potential (both of these are key determinants of expertise acquisition).

What talented people need to know depends on their field or occupation. At the same time, it is also true that high-performers in any field tend to have more expertise than their low-performing counterparts. Expertise covers the hard skills or technical knowledge we tend to include in our CVs or LinkedIn profiles, as well as academic and educational credentials, which are simply badges – some more credible than others – for our expertise.

Expertise is an umbrella term that encompasses all the job-related subject matters in the world. If you don't have it, even the best personality in the world won't save you. Nor will a high IQ. This is so obvious that it seems unnecessary to state it, but the mainstream emphasis on soft skills is now so strong that you would be forgiven for thinking that expertise is trivial. Likewise, an examination of the scientific literature on talent reveals a considerable neglect of the topic of expertise, particularly in comparison to competencies, IQ, personality and motivation. Again, the smartest, most motivated and likeable person in the world will fail at any job if he doesn't have the necessary expertise to do that job. Even if the person flying your plane has a great sense of humour, a high IQ and a strong work ethic, you would probably still want them to be a qualified pilot. Likewise, you wouldn't want someone with great critical-thinking skills, charisma and drive to perform root canal surgery on you if they are not a dentist ...

Of course, expertise can be critical without necessarily being job-specific. For example, if you want to work in Japan you will probably need to speak Japanese, but knowledge of Japanese is not particular to any job (you will need it whether you are a doctor, waiter, or politician, so long as you are in Japan). As Wittgenstein famously stated: 'The limits of my language mean the limits of my world.' By the same token, a minimum level of physical fitness, basic IT skills and adequate communication skills are all part of expertise, though they are mostly generic rather than job-specific skills.

Leaving expertise aside, no other factor matters more in relation to ability than general intelligence (IQ).[14] This may surprise you, not least because IQ tests seem very abstract at face value, especially compared to tests designed to evaluate job-specific knowledge and expertise. Yet, at a time of growing criticism of the lack of replication in psychology,[15] few findings are as consistent and robust as the positive correlation between IQ scores and job performance. So much so that it is virtually impossible to find a well-designed academic study where that correlation is zero. As one would expect, the link between IQ and performance is particularly strong when jobs are highly complex (e.g., professor of mathematics or software engineer rather than warehouse operator or window cleaner). However, there are very few job categories where IQ is unrelated to performance – one such rare area is professional athletics, with IQ tests failing to predict the performance of American football players in the NFL.[16] Thus general intelligence is a core ingredient of talent across most professional domains.

Willing

The third RAW ingredient of talent is a person's willingness to work hard, or their general motivation. This factor has been widely explored in psychology – almost as much as intelligence. But unlike IQ, motivation is confined to the realm of personality, where it is generally referred to as ambition, drive or

conscientiousness.[17] Whereas intelligence determines the degree
to which a person is able to do a job, motivation determines a
person's work ethic, drive or willingness to work hard. In that
respect, work ethic is essentially a talent accelerator.[18] The more
of it you have, the more your talent will grow. As already noted,
talent may be regarded as effortless performance, in the sense
that talented people need to work less to achieve the same result
as their less talented peers. Yet at the same time the potential
talent someone has is largely dependent on their willingness
to work hard. Accordingly, while talent is performance minus
effort, potential may be best conceptualised as talent *plus* effort.
In other words, how much talent you are *likely* to develop
depends on the talent you already have and the work you are
willing to put in to develop more.

It has been said that models are either accurate or useful,
but rarely both at the same time. The RAW model provides
a simplified account of the determinants of workplace talent.
Rather than covering all the potential qualities in detail, its goal
is to underline the core dimensions that provide the grammar
or syntax of workplace talent. Despite the universality of the
RAW model, it is important that organisations strive to achieve
a healthy degree of diversity, defined as the distribution of personal qualities across teams and the organisation.[19] Much like
teams, companies benefit when their people possess different
skills, knowledge and expertise. These dispositional differences
between team and organisational members – i.e., variety in how
they think, feel and act – will be an asset, so long as they do not
result in friction or clashes between people because the differences are too large to allow for a synergy.

Now that we have established what the core qualities of talent
are, let us examine how they can be measured.

THE 'HOW' QUESTION:
TALENT IDENTIFICATION TOOLS

Although the most common method for spotting talent is intuition, there are many better alternatives, including well-established scientific tools. Most large organisations tend to employ at least some of these methods, though often in small doses rather than for the majority of employees. These talent identification tools have been around for many decades, and there is a substantial body of scientific evidence demonstrating their accuracy. This evidence consists primarily of empirical studies correlating scores on these tools with subsequent measures of job performance. For example, a company may be interested in screening 100 job applicants using an intelligence test. How can they know whether that method can help them end up with better employees? By checking whether, among current employees, those with higher scores on that test tend to perform better on the job. To this end, it is useful to understand correlations, the main statistical parameter for evaluating the relationship between two variables – i.e., the potential score and the performance score.

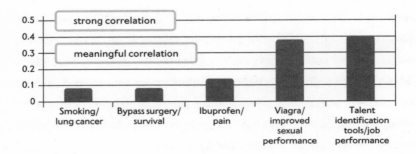

Figure 3: The correlation scores of five pairs of variables

Correlations range from 0 to 1, with 0 signalling no association between two variables (they are totally unrelated), and 1 signalling a perfect association between two variables (they are totally interdependent). In the social sciences, correlations higher than .30 are generally considered meaningful, and even lower correlations can be statistically significant and have visible effects. For example, consider the following correlations commonly found in the medical sciences (shown in Figure 3): the correlation between Ibuprofen consumption and pain reduction is .14; the correlation between smoking and developing lung cancer within 25 years of smoking is .08; the correlation between bypass surgery and survival rate is .08; and the correlation between Viagra and improved sexual functioning is .38. The correlation between scientifically robust talent identification tools and job performance is around .40, which means that talent identification tools are stronger than Viagra (though not for the same purpose).[20] Let us now discuss some of these tools.

Job interviews

Regardless of the job, type and size of organisation, no talent identification method has been as widely used as the job interview – the Royal Navy used interviews as early as 1800. It is almost unthinkable today that a person is offered a job without previously going through some form of interview,[21] and this has probably been the case since the beginnings of employment. Furthermore, job interviews are often the only method used for evaluating a candidate, and when used in conjunction with other methods they are generally the final and decisive hurdle applicants need to pass. Given their popularity, plenty of data have accumulated to examine the accuracy of interviews to predict work performance.

There are at least 15 different meta-analytic syntheses on the validity of job interviews published in academic research journals. These studies show that *structured* interviews are very useful to predict future job performance, with meta-analytic correlations of .51 reported.[22] In comparison, unstructured interviews, which do not have a set of predefined rules for scoring or classifying answers and observations in a reliable and standardised manner, are considerably less accurate (correlations of .38). In addition, unstructured interviews tend to increase the probability of biased judgements, that is, inferences about talent based on job-irrelevant qualities (e.g., race, gender, age and disabilities). For example, research suggests that initial impressions during informal interactions with the candidate, including the type of handshake, influence interviewers' decisions.[23]

But what do interviews actually assess? Content analyses of interview questions indicate that a significant proportion of them focus on evaluating candidates' intelligence[24] and personality, particularly aspects of conscientiousness, such as work ethic, reliability, achievement motivation and proactivity.[25] For instance, the following question may be used to evaluate a candidate's proactivity, i.e., the tendency to improve the status quo and facilitate positive change:

> Tell me about a time when you were involved in a project that resulted in a positive change? What role did you play in this project? How did you facilitate the change? What actions did you take to overcome the challenges along the way?[26]

Unlike personality tests, the answers to interview questions are unstructured and therefore are subject to the interviewer's interpretation. In well-designed structured interviews there are generally *a priori* guidelines or scoring criteria to evaluate all answers. The potential qualities that interviews may evaluate are so varied and wide-ranging that it is impossible to generalise about what interviews assess.[27] From a practical standpoint, however, it is sufficient if interviews predict job performance.

Assessment centres

Another widely used methodology for evaluating talent is the assessment centre.[28] This method, which was pioneered by the German military in the early twentieth century, requires candidates to perform a series of tasks that can be seen as snapshots of the actual role they are being considered for. Assessment centres are based on an old psychological adage, namely that past performance is a good predictor of future performance. Different exercises and simulations are designed to enable a direct observation of a candidate's ability to perform on the job. In some instances, assessment centres focus on candidates' ability to perform job-relevant tasks, but they may also be used to infer candidates' work ethic and likeability – particularly in exercises requiring interpersonal interaction with other candidates. If time and money aren't issues, assessment centres are hard to beat as a talent identification method. It is as simple as saying that if you want to work out whether someone will be good at a given job, then you can just make him do that job and see. This common-sense idea has been supported by several meta-analytic studies, which estimated the validity of assessment centres at .54 (higher than any other assessment method).[29] It is also noteworthy that job applicants tend to regard assessment centres as fairer than other talent identification methods.[30] The only disadvantage is that they are expensive and time-consuming to run: imagine flying in over a hundred international candidates for a given role and putting each of them through a four-hour assessment process.

IQ tests

One of psychology's most significant contributions to talent identification is the invention of cognitive ability or IQ tests. As a study has concluded:

> validities of cognitive ability tests are substantial and useful across industries, job families, and even cultures. In other words, validity generalises at useful levels. Data from large-scale meta-analyses leave little doubt that, although not the sole determinant of job performance, in many – and perhaps most – settings it is the single best predictor for personnel selection.[31]

One of the main reasons for the importance of IQ tests as a talent identification tool is that they evaluate how quickly people learn, and how well they respond to training. Thousands of academic studies have shown that IQ tests predict both job and training performance. Although typical correlations between IQ tests and job performance are around .20,[32] when job performance is measured objectively they can expect to reach correlations of .50.[33] This implies that over 25 per cent of the variability in employees' performance may be due to their intelligence, and that for every standard deviation increase in IQ individuals may be expected to increase their job performance by .5 of a standard deviation.[34] To put this into perspective, if someone's IQ is higher than that of 80 per cent of the population, his job performance will probably be higher than 65 per cent of the population's. If someone's IQ is lower than that of 80 per cent of the population, his job performance will probably be lower than 65 per cent of the population's.

It is also noteworthy that although there is more to job performance than IQ, once a candidate's IQ is taken into account other talent identification methods become weaker predictors of their job performance.[35] The main reason is that many of the other methods tend to overlap somewhat with IQ tests, though this is not the case with personality tests. And, contrary to Malcolm Gladwell's claim,[36] even among highly educated professionals, such as lawyers, accountants and doctors, there is not just high variability in IQ scores, but higher scores predict higher levels of performance and success.[37] What this means is that you can take a group of extremely smart people and the smartest people in that group will tend to outperform their very smart (but not as smart) counterparts.

Moreover, higher IQ scores are also predictive of job performance at the team level: teams with higher average IQ scores tend to perform better.[38] Although this seems like a truism, it should be noted that few organisations take IQ scores into account when building teams, yet there is arguably no better predictor of effective team performance than the average intelligence level of the team. Likewise, when organisations move employees to new teams – whether junior or senior – disregarding their intelligence level may lead to potential cases of misfits. People work better with others when they have similar levels of intelligence (whether they are high, average or low).

IQ tests are also practical to administer as they yield virtually the same result when completed remotely.[39] This makes them highly cost-effective, particularly vis-à-vis interviews or assessment centres. Moreover, there is no better way to evaluate a person's intelligence than via IQ tests. Thus after a seminal review of evidence, psychologists suggested that, in the US, using IQ tests for selection would translate into yearly economic gains of $35 billion (in today's money).[40]

That is not to say that IQ tests are infallible. First, they can underestimate people's intelligence when they underperform due to nerves, pressure or anxiety, which is quite common in high-stake settings, when most IQ tests are administered (few people take them for fun).[41] For example, experimental studies show that the mere presence of red ink on an IQ test decreases test-takers' performance on the test.[42] Secondly, practice improves people's performance, and it is not uncommon for people to retake an IQ test more than once when applying for a job.[43] However, these two distortions are less problematic than people think. People who panic during an IQ test are also likely to choke under real-world pressure; and people who are motivated enough to retake a test and improve their performance are probably more driven, which is a desirable quality for any job. Thus even when IQ tests fail to measure intelligence correctly (or 'purely'), they may still effectively predict job performance because they also measure other facets of talent, such as emotional stability and conscientiousness.

That said, a big problem with IQ tests is that they often have adverse impact on some demographic groups, particularly poorer and less educated people.[44] For instance, recent research shows that children from less privileged backgrounds already perform worse on IQ tests at the age of two, and that these small initial differences are accentuated dramatically by the time they are sixteen.[45] This is ironic given that intelligence tests were invented to increase meritocracy, rather than augment inequality. In the

US, there are also significant score differences between ethnic groups, with white people doing better than African Americans and Hispanics but worse than Asians. These differences are reflected in college admission tests, which overlap substantially with IQ tests and can therefore be considered unofficial intelligence tests. Some groups, such as East Asians, score so highly that universities have been forced to introduce caps against them to enable other groups to be accepted more widely. As for gender, differences in IQ are mostly negligible, with small advantages reported for women on verbal tests.[46]

Personality assessments

Personality assessments come in many shapes, but the majority involve self-report exercises where candidates are required to rate a series of self-referential statements or answer a range of set questions about their typical preferences and behaviours. Unlike IQ tests, personality assessments have no objectively correct or incorrect answers. Instead, people's responses are compared to a normative group or benchmark, which is then used to compute scores on various scales or dimensions, commonly described as 'traits'. In essence, the mechanics underlying these assessments are based on working out what individuals who answer in specific ways generally do or look like. On average, personality traits correlate with job performance and other career-related outcomes at around .30,[47] though there is great variability depending on the trait and role examined. When outcomes are measured reliably, the right personality attributes are selected (e.g., extraversion for sales performance, creativity for advertising jobs, conscientiousness for projects requiring attention to detail) and scientifically defensible personality measures are used, the multiple correlation between relevant personality scores and outcomes can be as high as .50,[48] including for leadership positions.[49]

Although there is a fair amount of resistance to the use of personality assessments for talent identification purposes, laypeople assess their own and others' personalities on a regular basis, though using very different criteria than the ones used by scientists.[50] To laypeople, the main criterion to evaluate the accuracy of a personality profile is whether they intuitively agree with the results. Yet 50 years of psychological research show that self-perceptions are inaccurate and inflated, as our unconscious desire to feel good about ourselves is much more powerful than our interest in reality.[51] As for judgements of other people's personalities, laypeople tend to make quick and intuitive inferences based on appearance and initial interactions, and subsequently ignore any evidence that contradicts their initial impressions.[52] It therefore appears that people's prejudices about personality assessments are based on their own prejudiced assessments of personality.

Since personality assessments are predominantly based on self-reports, it can seem logical to assume that respondents will fool the test by either lying or 'faking good', particularly in high-stake situations such as job applications, promotion rounds, etc. Although this view underpins the most common argument against the use of personality assessments as talent identification tools, it is completely unfounded. As a matter of fact, there is a large body of academic research that addresses the issue of faking, with over 7,000 published studies on the subject.[53] What do these studies suggest?

First, when tests are properly designed and validated, candidates will struggle to guess what different questions assess, or work out how they should be answered, making deliberate manipulation quite ineffective. For instance, in a robust and scientifically valid personality assessment, the statement 'I choose a different route to work every day' may primarily relate to a candidate's creativity, while the statement 'Strangers are quick to recognise my amazing creative talents' may capture how arrogant or self-deceived a candidate is (rather than whether he is creative). Secondly, robust personality assessments deliberately *invite* a certain degree of dishonesty, without necessarily condemning it.[54] The underlying premise is simple: in important real-life situations, like a job interview, it is far more adaptive and desirable to present a favourable persona that is slightly fake than to be honest but antisocial. So, if you are asked whether you enjoy working with people, it may be honest to say 'No', but that will also highlight an important lack of social skills and may cause the candidate to come across as unrewarding to deal with. On the other hand, people who say 'Yes' may be lying, but they will probably be socially astute enough to understand that it is important to make an effort in order to work well with others, and that a certain element of faking good is also needed in the real world. As a result, both answers (Yes and No) will predict the relevant behaviours, regardless of whether people were being honest or not. What matters is not what people think, but what they actually do.

This point has been addressed extensively by studies on *impression management*, defined as any deliberate attempt to generate a positive image during social interactions.[55] Traditionally, psychologists viewed all impression management as a nuisance or distortion of the talent components different assessment methods are trying to gauge.[56] However, since most jobs involve dealing with people and in all those instances it is important that one creates a favourable impression, whether they are clients, colleagues, bosses or subordinates, impression management is a job-relevant skill and a relevant signal rather than 'noise'. As the above example shows, this is most clearly illustrated by the opposite case scenario, namely people who are unable to engage in impression management, both during talent identification instances and at their actual jobs.

Unsurprisingly, numerous studies have found that impression management is positively related to a wide range of desirable workplace variables, such as employee motivation, organisational citizenship, social skills and general job competence, as well as negatively related to counterproductive work behaviours (CWBs).[57] It can therefore be concluded that people who are better at impression management are generally more talented – and make better potential hires – than those who are less capable of managing impressions, not least because they have more talent for getting along with people.

It is therefore unsurprising that properly designed personality assessments predict future work performance when they are administered in high-stake settings, such as personnel selection contexts, where candidates have every incentive to lie and portray themselves in an unrealistic and rosy way.[58] It's a bit like going on a first date with someone who asks you all the right questions and knows exactly how to decipher your answers: it does not matter if you exaggerate or lie, so long as your answers still predict what you are likely to do in the future. Thus an honest answer is not one that you believe in, but one that predicts how you will behave.

There are also people who object to the use of personality assessment in selection purely on the basis that these tests may be 'unfair', meaning that some people will not get job offers because their answers may render them unsuitable. However, when personality assessments are used appropriately the scores are indicative of real job potential (e.g., a person's ability to sell insurance, drive a bus, or manage a hotel effectively), so the only unfair thing would be to offer the job to candidates with inadequate profiles or scores. Moreover, unlike IQ tests,[59] personality tests do not harm the chances of applicants from ethnic minorities or people from underprivileged demographic groups. In short, for over a hundred years psychologists have been developing a wide range of scientific personality assessments that describe, explain and predict human behaviour. Organisations, managers and employees all benefit from understanding how people work, what their interests and values are, whether they will fit into a team and how much potential they have for a role.

Other 'old-school' methods

Although the vast majority of academic articles evaluating talent identification tools focus on interviews, IQ tests and personality assessments, a few other 'classics' deserve consideration.

Biodata
The first of such methods is *biodata*, which refers to the evaluation of candidates' personal histories or biographies, and in particular their past career records, as potential markers of talent. Meta-analyses report validities of around .30 for the correlation between biodata and both job and training performance.[60] Furthermore, biodata is also a valid predictor of employee turnover, though HR practitioners are usually sceptical about this and see their own intuition as more accurate.[61] In theory, biodata can encompass all sorts of variables, but in

most cases it will exclude personality and attitudinal information, focusing instead on actual biographical events. The two main ways of processing biodata are the 'a-theoretical method', which determines the chosen biodata markers based on their statistical associations with desirable outcomes, and the 'rational method', which tries to combine biodata variables in a way that is conceptually meaningful and reveals the 'why' underlying the relationship between past data and future behaviours.

Traditionally, biodata is obtained via self-reports, though technology has enabled organisations to obtain records of employees' behaviours without relying on questionnaires. Much like assessment centres, biodata is cemented in the idea that past behaviour predicts future behaviour. People are pretty consistent, and if the right historical signals are captured it is possible to make fairly accurate forecasts about future workplace behaviour. That is, the probability of displaying talent will differ according to individuals' past accomplishments and life experiences.

The CV
Another old-school method to gauge talent is the CV (or résumé), which is mainly important because it contains information on the relevant hard skills, expertise and experience candidates have. In an age when many people have a significant portion of their CVs available online – via sites such as LinkedIn – it is less likely that candidates can get away with fake claims about their past achievements, as there are multiple witnesses online. Studies show that employers and recruiters often use résumés to make inferences about candidates' personalities (and quite effectively so when the recruiters are trained).[62] Unfortunately, most of the academic research on CVs has focused on exploring how they are evaluated or perceived by employers and recruiters, as opposed

to quantifying their actual ability to predict future performance.

However, some of the key pieces of information reported in CVs, such as educational credentials, experience and competencies, have been examined in relation to actual job performance. For example, a meta-analysis showed candidates' educational level predicts their job-related task performance, as well as being positively related to employee creativity and organisational citizenship behaviours, and as negatively related to CWBs. Despite the fact that academic qualifications are now more common than they ever have been, more educated employees still get paid more, are promoted and developed more often, and have higher levels of job mobility and satisfaction.[63] It is therefore unsurprising that most organisations see a link between a person's educational level and their talent. Organisations expect experience and qualifications to translate into higher returns for the organisation, so they compensate employees differently based on their CVs.[64]

It is also noteworthy that the same individual qualities that contribute to better CV credentials (e.g., academic performance and educational attainment, occupational status and quality of previous employers) tend also to contribute to higher levels of job performance. Thus throughout life, an individual's generic talent qualities (RAW ingredients) affect different achievement milestones through similar processes, which explains the continuity of career success in a person's life. Some people generally succeed, while others generally stay unsuccessful.

'The 360'

Another popular methodology for evaluating talent is the *360-degree feedback survey*, also known as multisource or multirater feedback. This method consists of asking co-workers, subordinates and bosses to provide ratings on an individual's performance, and getting that individual to self-assess using the same ratings.[65] The most common use of 360s is as a source of feedback in developmental reviews, particularly with managers and leaders. In this context, 360s can help individuals increase their self-awareness, i.e., understand how other people see them.[66] However, the information 360s provide is equally useful for internal talent identification, as there is arguably no better way to obtain a comprehensive measure of someone's performance or reputation at work, in particular when jobs are complex or when they involve dealing with a large number of employees. It is hard to think of a better measure of a leader's performance than a 360, especially ratings by the leader's subordinates (upward feedback).[67] Many organisations pay attention to the results of 360s when deciding on promotions, pay and succession planning.[68]

It is also obvious that 360s should provide more reliable data on candidates' performance than single source ratings do. Even when different assessors don't converge much in their views of the target's performance, their average rating tends to be more predictive of future performance than any of the individual ratings.[69] It is also noteworthy that when the ratings from different sources overlap too much it defeats the purpose of actually gathering ratings from different sources – why bother, if you can just do with one? Unsurprisingly, the predictive validity of 360s increases when different raters provide more diverse perspectives on the rated candidate, not least because the average profile will provide a more complete picture of the person, covering a wider repertoire of behaviours and multiple facets of the candidate's reputation. Peers, supervisors and subordinates tend to see the target in somewhat different ways, not because they differ in accuracy, but mostly because they witness different elements of the target's performance. It's as if you were described by your closest friends, work colleagues and relatives: they would all provide slightly different views of you, reflecting what you do in different settings. All this explains why 360s have become a widely used tool to evaluate the performance of employees and, in particular, leaders. And by comparing people's self-ratings with other people's ratings of them, 360s can also be used effectively to assess individuals' self-awareness. Leaders who rate themselves closely to how others rate them tend to be more effective, showing that self-awareness translates into higher leadership performance.[70]

The situational judgement test

Another tool that has gained popularity in the past few decades is the *situational judgement test* (SJT), which in some ways is a hybrid of an intelligence and a personality test. Reviews suggest that SJTs tend to assess three main types of attributes: knowledge/skills; interpersonal/social competence (including teamwork and leadership potential); and other personality traits (e.g., drive, openness to experience, adjustment).[71]

SJTs present candidates with a series of vignettes consisting of work-related scenarios. Candidates are asked what they either would or should do in such scenarios, and their responses are used to evaluate either job-relevant expertise or dispositional qualities that affect job performance. Here's an example of an SJT scenario:

Imagine that you're a hotel concierge, and a guest asks you to make a dinner reservation at a specific restaurant. You know the place fairly well, and previous guests have given you negative feedback about it. But this guest seems very excited about the prospect of eating there and has not asked for your opinion. What do you do?

A. Congratulate the guest on his or her choice and make the booking.
B. Make the booking without providing your opinion.
C. Offer a couple of alternatives, explaining that they are probably better.
D. Share your opinion and say that several guests have been disappointed with the restaurant.
E. Pretend the restaurant is fully booked and offer to find an alternative.[72]

If this scenario were used to evaluate suitability for a hotel customer service role, it would probably highlight not only candidates' knowledge of reception etiquette, but also some generic and relevant aspects of their personality, e.g., social skills, honesty, altruism. Although there is no objectively correct answer, some answers would be indicative of higher levels of competence. Thus candidates who pick C or D would be deemed more competent than those who select A or B, which would make the guest unhappy. Option E would probably be considered dishonest and somewhat extreme.

As this chapter has shown, there are two key questions in relation to the measurement of talent, namely what qualities should be assessed and how. The *what* question can be addressed by the RAW ingredients of talent, because in any job it is better to have individuals who are more rewarding to deal with, more able and willing to work hard. In other words, ability, likeability and drive will always matter, and there is little else that really matters regardless of job or role. As for the *how* question, there are four well-established methods of talent identification which align with what the science of personnel selection prescribes, namely structured interviews, assessment centres, intelligence tests and personality assessments, as well as additional tools, such as biodata, the CV, 360s and SJTs. With the right framework and appropriate methods, the likelihood of ending up with the right person for each role will increase substantially, though attracting talent is just the first step – the second is to engage it.

Thus there is no excuse for playing it by ear. Instead of relying on their intuition – no matter how experienced and confident they are – leaders and talent management practitioners will make better personnel selection decisions if they base their talent-related evaluations on established tools and methodologies, and if they focus on meaningful attributes. No talent management intervention will be effective unless it starts with an accurate evaluation of the candidate, and the methods discussed in this chapter can facilitate just that.

CHAPTER 4

Engaging talent

This chapter discusses the importance of workplace motivation, and what organisations can do to ensure that employees are enthusiastic and eager to give it their all. Over the past 10 years these issues have been widely articulated through the concept of employee engagement, which refers to individuals' level of energy and enthusiasm at work. As this chapter shows, the practice of gathering diagnostic organisational data on employee engagement is now mainstream among big organisations. Yet, despite an acknowledgement that engagement matters – and conclusive academic evidence for the positive consequences of higher engagement, and the negative consequences of lower engagement – there is a lot of room for improvement. This chapter suggests that the best way for boosting engagement is to align employees' values – their drives and goals – with the culture of the organisation. This requires paying attention to the values of leaders, as they play a major role in shaping the culture of their organisation.

* * *

Imagine a hypothetical scenario where two companies are staffed by equally talented individuals. Both companies are in the same sector and they are also comparable in size and operate in the same market. Would we expect these companies to perform similarly? Probably, unless there are critical differences in motivation. That is, if one of the two companies has managed to make key jobs more relevant and meaningful to its employees, then that company could generally be expected to outperform the other, not least because its employees will be more motivated to go the extra mile.

There is a solid body of scientific evidence on employee engagement. Since the concept was first introduced in management psychology in the early 1990s,[1] a wide range of academic research papers has been published. What these studies suggest is intuitive: people will love their jobs more if they are treated fairly, if they are challenged, and when they have some freedom to meet those challenges. That means that finding the right people for the right roles is not just a matter of matching them in terms of skills, but also in values and interests. In this way performance drives engagement as much as engagement drives performance, which means that people will love their jobs more when they are given the chance to perform highly and feel proud about what they do at work.

Thus two critical issues in talent management concern the ability to place people in the right roles and to ensure that their typical performance is as close to their maximum performance as possible. In other words, savvy talent management practitioners must figure out how to find the right person for each role, and then how to squeeze the best out of them on a regular basis.

To achieve this, it is not sufficient to identify a person's talents and match those talents to the job. In addition, one must ensure that the person's interests or goals can actually be satisfied by the job in question. It is possible for someone to have the necessary skillset to perform well in a job or role, but be utterly devoid of motivation to do so. Therefore, winning the war for talent is as much about finding competent individuals for critical jobs as making those jobs appealing to them.

Although this makes intuitive sense, we can test whether and to what degree motivational differences actually matter. To this end, most large organisations around the world monitor the average level of motivation of their workforce by running annual or bi-annual engagement surveys. For example, the New York-based company Sirota Intelligence Survey has surveyed millions of employees from hundreds of businesses, including Shell, Unilever and Amazon, over the past three decades. Their data provide invaluable insights on the impact of motivation on performance and productivity. As one would predict, businesses do better when their employees are more engaged, and the same company will experience an increase in revenues and profits after employee engagement levels go up, and vice-versa. Moreover, Sirota's data can be used to compare the performance of companies in the same sector and of similar size and demographics. In other words, actual data can be used to simulate a real-life experiment where we control for the key predictors of employee productivity while assessing the impact of changes in motivation.

This pattern of results is also mirrored by the wider academic literature, as meta-analytic studies show that employees perform better, stay on the job and with their employer longer, and display fewer CWBs when their interests and values are congruent with their roles and the values of the organisation.[2] This explains why there is so much interest in employee engagement.

Engagement is not really a new concept. Its precursor – job satisfaction – has been studied in psychology for decades, and several large-scale studies and meta-analyses demonstrate the benefits of higher job satisfaction for a wide range of individual and organisational performance outcomes, not to mention physical and psychological wellbeing.[3] However, a conceptual distinction has been made between both constructs, based on the idea that job satisfaction is merely an attitude or mental concept – how you *think* of your job – whereas engagement also involves an emotional and behavioural component – how your job makes you *feel* and what your job makes you *do*.[4] Thus engagement is job satisfaction plus feeling and action.

As one would expect, engagement is good for both the individual and the organisation. A wide range of studies have been conducted in this area and the results consistently demonstrate (a) negative correlations between engagement and undesirable outcomes, and (b) positive correlations between engagement and desirable outcomes.

For example, engagement has been negatively associated with turnover intentions, actual staff turnover, counterproductive work behaviours (e.g., bullying, antisocial behaviour, abusive management, loafing) and burnout. In fact, the negative association between burnout and engagement is so strong that engagement is often regarded as the reverse of burnout. Imagine a line representing a continuum going from engagement at one end to burnout at the other. Burnout is not just problematic for the individual, it also disrupts teams, organisations and entire economies. That is, the adverse effects of burnout transcend organisational boundaries and represent a cross-national epidemic. For example, an estimated 20 per cent of employees in the European Union are reported to suffer from work-related stress, costing their economies many billions of euros in lost productivity and health-related expenses.[5]

With regards to the positive consequences of engagement, they range from motivation and wellbeing to actual performance and productivity. For example, engaged individuals are generally healthier, report better work–life balance (even when they work harder!) and are more persistent and driven at work. This is reflected not just in better individual performance and higher productivity rates, but also in more positive organisational citizenship behaviours. In other words, engaged employees are not just more valuable to their employers because of their work-related output, but also because they are better colleagues and have a more favourable impact on other employees. Thus the positive effects of engagement are often contagious, and in the case of leadership they trickle down to engage employees and subordinates.

Many studies document the effects of engagement on organisational variables, such as business-unit performance, profits and customer loyalty. For example, a widely cited meta-analysis linked increases in employee engagement with collective productivity and profitability gains, as well as improvements in customer satisfaction ratings. This evidence highlights the bottom-up effects of engagement on organisational effectiveness: aggregate gains in employee engagement translate into more desirable organisational measures. Another tranche of studies quantified top-down effects of engagement, or how increases in supervisors', managers' and senior leaders' engagement favourably affected employees' motivation, loyalty, productivity and performance. As one would expect, direct supervisors – first line managers – have the biggest impact on employees' engagement levels because of their proximity to them. However, senior leaders indirectly affect the engagement levels of all employees by setting strategy and shaping culture. Indeed, meta-analytic studies show that leadership is one of the strongest causes of variability in team engagement levels.[6]

Despite the pervasive benefits of higher engagement levels, it is noteworthy that the relationship between engagement and job performance is considerably stronger in individualistic than in collectivistic cultures.[7] Thus collectivistic cultures, which are more other-oriented and prioritise group over and above individual welfare, will see fewer returns on productivity by increasing employee engagement than individualistic cultures will.

ALL PEOPLE WANT THE SAME, EXCEPT WHEN THEY DON'T

What do employees actually want from work? There is often a difference between what people want and what they need; for example, throughout the free world almost half of marriages end in divorce, yet most were the product of what people (apparently) wanted. Therefore, it is important to pay attention not just to what people want, but also what they need from work. In other words, what are the basic psychological motives or needs that individuals strive to fulfil via their jobs and careers? Furthermore, what are the causes and consequences of attaining those needs, and of failing to do so? Last, but not least, how do people's needs differ, and what are the potential consequences of such differences?

The answers to these questions are articulated by the socio-analytic theory of personality,[8] which explains the importance of individual values – people's psychological drivers – as determinants of employee engagement and organisational effectiveness. The theory's underlying premise is simple: understanding what people want can help us predict and explain where they will fit in at work, which will enable us to predict their engagement level, and, in turn, their team and business performance. In other words, if you want to predict people's level of enthusiasm and involvement at work, you need to first work out whether their values and drives are likely to be fulfilled by their jobs. This can be done on a generic or a personalised level. Let us start with the generic level.

Universal values, drives and motives

Based on an evolutionary and anthropological analysis of human behaviour, socio-analytic theory identifies three major elements that characterise human life from its early beginnings to current times, and will probably continue to do so for as long as human life exists. First, the fact that humans have always lived in groups. Second, the fact that every group or social unit has always had a hierarchy – and it always will. Whether formal or informal, this hierarchy determines the unequal allocation of power, decision-making and influence in a group. This can be seen most clearly in traditional organisations, such as the Church or the army, but there is really no group or organisation without a hierarchy. Comparable structures were present even in small groups during prehistory, as there has never been a group without a leader. (Holacracy, the idea that groups and organisations can have fully distributed leadership and effectively function without a leader, is a populist myth, a PR fad aimed at selling the idea that everybody can be in charge because nobody is in charge.) It is for this reason that the collapse of leaders – whether in politics, business or sports – generates anarchic vacuums that result in the immediate struggle for power among other members of the group. And third, the fact that no form of human civilisation can exist without a system of meaning, a symbolic universe that enables individuals to make sense of the world. In the beginning, that system was represented by the informal precursors to religion, such as morality, superstition and shamanism. Then religion and philosophy emerged. Then it was science. Note that these different lenses through which individuals view and make sense of the world are not mutually exclusive. At any given time there are multiple systems of meaning that coexist in the same group, organisation, or culture – and they are often in direct tension or competition. This explains the ubiquity of fights between different ideologies, religions and scientific paradigms, and why some may ridicule Scientology but not Christianity, while for others it is the other way around.

The significance of these three universal principles of human life is that they have shaped our fundamental needs: the need to *get along* with others; the need to *get ahead* of others; and the need to *find and impose meaning*.[9] In every area of life, including work, we will try to fulfil these fundamental master motives. Indeed, we are the offspring of social animals that have to manage the tension between competition and collaboration, and we have a natural craving for understanding the world which has led to the development of complex systems of truth and our passionate desire to refute and shut down competing systems.

The first two motives – getting ahead and getting along – were discussed extensively by Freud, who compared humans to hedgehogs in winter. In the cold, hedgehogs must get close to each other to warm up. But if they get too close, things become a bit prickly as they poke each other with their spines. So they need to separate again, but then they get cold. What Freud meant is that though we are inherently social animals, we are also quite antisocial, because we want to compete with others to climb to the top of the group hierarchy and be in charge.[10] Mastering this tension between cooperation and competition is critical. We need to get along to get ahead, but if we focus too much on getting along we may end up not getting ahead, and if we focus too much on getting ahead, we may end up not getting along.

Accordingly, the answer to the question of what people need from work is as follows: first, people need *affiliation*, or the possibility to bond with others and experience a sense of camaraderie and companionship; secondly, people need *achievement*, or the opportunity to compete with and outperform others; and thirdly, people need work to provide themselves with a sense of purpose and *meaning*. Therefore, people will engage at work if they can fulfil their desire to get along, get ahead and find meaning. Failure to do so is demotivating at best, and alienating at worst.

Given that most individuals are not engaged at work, it is safe to assume that organisations are largely failing to make their jobs appealing to employees, probably because of their inability to fulfil people's need for affiliation, achievement and meaning. This is also consistent with the rise of passive job seeking, and the growing interest in self-employment and entrepreneurship. Ironically, the 'gig' economy may be providing people with more meaningful careers than traditional employment choices. Yet in order to improve, organisations must shift from a generic to an individual focus on human needs. That is, if companies want to engage employees, they must first understand how *each* employee fulfils his personal needs for affiliation, achievement and meaning. Clearly, one size does not fit all, so organisations and managers must learn to decode employees' personal values, drives and motives.

Personal Values, Drives and Motives

Although we all have the same needs – to get along, get ahead and find meaning – we don't want them in the same way. There are, in fact, multiple avenues for fulfilling our core needs, which is why it is important to decode what individual employees and leaders need.

Table 1 provides a summary of the main values, drivers and motives outlined by socio-analytic theory. The 10 values in the left-hand column (recognition, power, commerce, etc.) may be regarded as the coordinates of purpose, and when they are matched to the right jobs, careers and organisational cultures they will result in higher levels of employee engagement and performance. The values are connected to sets of corresponding interests and drivers, which ultimately link to a master motive.

Table 1: The Socio-analytic Model of Values, Interests and Motives

Value	Interests & Drivers	Master Motive
Recognition	Being known, appreciated and famous; standing out	
Power	Influencing others, competing, winning	Getting ahead
Commerce	Money, profits, business, finances, investments	

Value	Interests & Drivers	Master Motive
Hedonism	Fun, variety, pleasure, excitement, thrill	Getting along
Affiliation	Social interaction, meeting people, networking	
Altruism	Helping others, improving the world, social justice	
Tradition	Morality, high standards, principles, rules	
Security	Order and predictability, structure, safety, certainty	Finding meaning
Aesthetics	Intuition, style, experience, creativity	
Science	Facts, logic, technology, data, knowledge	

As shown, the main values determining how and why people attempt to *get ahead* are recognition, power and commerce. These values are often referred to as 'status drivers' and they explain individual differences in people's willingness to compete with others, climb up the group hierarchy to occupy positions of power, pursue financial rewards and accomplish things that may be admired and recognised by others.

The next four values, namely hedonism, affiliation, altruism and tradition, concern people's desire to *get along*, or their social or affiliation motives. They explain why some people are particularly driven to seek joyful and pleasurable activities, connect with others and meet new people, engage in prosocial ventures to improve the lives of others, and respect established norms and traditions.

Finally, the last three values – security, aesthetics and science – explain individual differences in how people make sense of the world and *find meaning*. In particular, they describe the degree to which people need to minimise uncertainty and ambiguity, and to make sense of the world via more intuitive/holistic or factual/analytical means.

Each of these 10 values is normally distributed in the overall population, such that individuals may score low, average or high on them. High scores mean that the person will experience a strong drive or urge to fulfil that value, and that they will feel frustrated or empty when that value cannot be fulfilled. Low scores indicate that the person will be repelled by that value, and motivated to achieve the exact opposite. On average, people score highly on two or three values, though it is possible for them to have many high scores, possibly on all values. Such individuals will be particularly hard to please because they have so many drivers and interests to satisfy; they may often appear quite frantic or manic.

Unsurprisingly, personal values also impact on leadership: what leaders want determines how they lead and what culture they create in their organisations. If you think of the people who run the organisation where you work, and understand what makes them tick, you will get a good sense of why the culture is what it is. Leaders' core beliefs and needs shape their management and leadership styles and determine the team players they select, the climate they create in their teams, the decisions they make, and the behaviours and values they reward and punish. Leadership is ultimately about influencing others, and the values of leaders impregnate teams with meaning.[11] Individuals who share the values of the leader will be more engaged, and find more meaning and purpose in their jobs, than those who do not.

Now let us examine the key implications that personal values have with regards to leadership.

Getting ahead values

Leaders who are driven by recognition will create a culture of achievement, and will reward individuals who work hard and are competitive. However, their own recognition drive may lead to an inability to admit mistakes and a tendency to take credit for other people's achievements. It is not rare for leaders to compete with their own subordinates, which can lead to them rewarding only people who are not a threat. Although such leaders are often confident communicators who handle pressure and criticism well, they may be too focused on themselves to pay attention to their subordinates. The key to effective leadership is building a high-performing team, which means managing the tension between subordinates' desire for getting ahead and getting along. José Mourinho, the current manager of Manchester United football club, exemplifies this value well. Every team he has managed ended up winning trophies, and most of the players he managed described him as the best manager they ever had. When high-recognition people transition from individual contributors to leadership roles, they must learn to achieve *through* their teams, and collaborate rather than compete with them. This requires getting along (with each other) in order to get ahead (of rival teams or organisations).

Things are fairly similar for leaders who are driven by power, except their focus will be on competition and control, rather than on being respected and admired. The power value is the strongest determinant of whether an employee is even interested in managing others and becoming a leader, and it also determines how happy individuals will be when they have to relinquish control to others. Unsurprisingly, leaders with a high power drive are often seen as strong, competent and visionary. Yet they often clash with other power-driven individuals. Vladimir Putin represents this value well, and many political analysts have argued that, after being ruled by tough and powerful leaders for so many years (first by tsars, then communist dictators), it is understandable that Russians like their leaders to be strong.

As for leaders who value commerce, they will tend to create a culture that is centred round profits and revenues, and where frugality and cost control are rewarded. Such leaders, who are ideal for managing sales and consulting operations, will value employees who are entrepreneurial and opportunistic, as these individuals have the ability to create strong financial returns for the organisation. Commercial leaders are typically seen as hardworking, pragmatic and business-savvy. They keep up with market trends and are quick to make sense of financial data. Their style will generally be direct, and they will tend to be task-oriented and focus on the bottom line. Jeff Bezos, the maverick founder and CEO of Amazon, is a great example of a high commerce leader. Before launching Amazon, Bezos was already known as a quantitative Wunderkind in the finance world, and most of the projects Amazon touches turn to gold.[12] With yearly revenues of over $100 billion, Amazon is a true colossus of the internet – the digital version of Walmart, a company it tries to emulate. And, much like Walmart, a key element of its high commerce culture concerns being extremely careful with money.

Getting along values
Leaders with high hedonism scores focus mostly on instilling a fun-loving culture where employees are expected to play hard. This does not mean that they should not work hard, and hedonism and commerce values often coexist, not just in a manager,

but also in an organisation's culture. But, whereas commerce concerns getting ahead, hedonism is more related to getting along. Hedonistic cultures will not just tolerate but will also reward organisational manifestations of collective fun, excitement seeking and enjoyment. In spite of not being a great case study of a competent political leader, there is no question that Silvio Berlusconi displayed good talent for business leadership, which explains his personal net worth of around $8 billion. More importantly, even Berlusconi's critics would agree that he is a hedonistic leader. From his humorous TV and parliamentary appearances to his 'bunga bunga' parties, he is as far removed from a serious politician as anyone – except perhaps Donald Trump – can be. And although common sense may dictate that everybody is interested in having fun at work and in finding a job that enables them to work on pleasurable and interesting tasks, that is certainly not the case. People with low hedonism scores will be quite happy to have jobs that are neither interesting nor fun, and they will not expect to enjoy themselves at work.

On the other hand, people driven by affiliation will expect work to provide them with a great many opportunities to enrich their social life and have rewarding and diverse connections with work colleagues. Likewise, leaders with high affiliation needs will usually create sociable work environments and reward employees who are outgoing, gregarious and good at networking. Such a profile is obviously a good fit for sales, customer-service, PR and entertainment jobs, but counterproductive for jobs that require a great deal of independent working and deprive individuals of opportunities to connect with others. Oprah Winfrey, with her telegenic charisma and remarkable people skills, exemplifies this value well.

As for altruism, leaders who espouse this value have a strong interest in helping others and working on projects that have the potential to make a difference in the world and to improve the lives of those who need it most. Such leaders will tend to instil a culture where ethical and prosocial behaviours are rewarded, while condemning crooked and dishonest acts. It is not surprising that altruistic leaders are themselves a reference or focal point for employees with altruistic values, who look up to them to fulfil their own need for 'doing good' at work. Indeed, when altruistic individuals perceive their work environments, employers, or leaders as selfish, they will experience a strong cognitive dissonance and seek to address this value-based discrepancy by switching to more moral and ethical careers. Pope Francis, the current leader of the Catholic Church, personifies the altruism value.

The final value in the *getting along* cluster is tradition, and leaders who display it tend to have a high degree of respect for authority, rules and processes. They value the status quo and will tend to uphold very clear-cut beliefs about what is right and what is wrong, avoiding relativity and ambiguity in favour of categorical thinking and clear principles. This will tend to lead to the creation of work environments that are generally strict and formal, where social relations must conform to a well-defined etiquette and where authority is generally respected. Traditional leaders are the exact opposite of progressive and unconventional leaders, and they like things to be fairly predictable, rule-bound and routine-based. Perhaps the biggest organisational advantage of high tradition leaders is that they are generally concerned with quality and reputation, so they tend to impose high standards on their employees. Indeed, few expressions capture the essence of high tradition better than the adage: 'If a job is worth doing, it is worth doing properly'. A good example of a leader who values tradition is Gordon Ramsay, the celebrity chef. His militaristic approach to running a kitchen puts consistent quality at the top of the agenda – with strict rules put in place in the pursuit of that goal.

Finding meaning values

Leaders with a high security value tend to be cautious and promote risk-avoiding behaviours in their teams. Checking details, foreseeing potential problems and preparing for the worst are some of the key adaptive habits of leaders who value security. The popular German adage, apparently inspired by Lenin – '*Vertrauen ist gut, Kontrolle ist besser*' ('Trust is good, supervision is better') – sums up the values of high security leaders well. As does its English equivalent, 'Better safe than sorry'. Such leaders are well suited to instil a culture of safety and minimising uncertainty. By the same token, they will not cope well with adventurous risk-taking, unexpected change and unpredictability. Indeed, improvisation and spontaneity are to secure leaders what stress and pressure are to anxious people. Lee Kuan Yew, the founding father and long-time ruler of Singapore, embodied this value. Although his policies made Singapore one of the most dynamic and entrepreneurial economies in the world, they were based on careful and calculated top-down planning, and an obsession for reducing uncertainty.

Those leaders who value aesthetics will try to promote a culture of ideas and innovation, get their teams excited about new products, and pay a great deal of attention to style, sometimes even more than they pay to substance. Accordingly, they will tend to be guided by intuition and prioritise their feelings about facts over and above the actual facts themselves. These leaders will also tend to be more unpredictable, eccentric and disinterested in processes, and can sometimes be lacking in pragmatism.

Richard Branson, the flamboyant founder of Virgin, embodies this value well. A leader who is full of ideas, and more interested in launching new ventures than in running or growing them (which he leaves to others), he has always led by intuition. Branson's approach is all about ideas, experimentation and innovation, and the Virgin brand reflects this in all its services and products.[13] Likewise, Steve Jobs injected a strong sense of aesthetics into a field historically deprived of it – before Apple, technology was rarely stylish. Despite his engineering background, Jobs was famous for his mystical vision quests and for his unrivalled obsession with design and style, which have made Apple the most desirable luxury brand in the world, as well as one of the most successful companies of all time.[14]

In contrast, leaders who value science create environments that cherish the pursuit of knowledge and value data-driven, logical thinking over intuition. They keep up-to-date with technological advances and tend to make objective, fact-based decisions. Their management style is generally cold, analytical and apolitical. Of course, it would be naïve to assume that human beings are ever able to think and act completely objectivity, and this is perhaps the downside of individuals who are strongly driven by science: their tendency to overestimate the power of logic and assume that data and knowledge can always be translated into bullet-proof facts, when they are rarely free from subjectivity and human biases. Sergey Brin and Larry Page, the founders of Google, epitomise this value, and if Google were a person it would probably display the key characteristics of a geek: intelligent, but more interested in technology than people; curious, particularly about complex problems that may seem too abstract to interest the average person; and fully convinced of the power of science and logic to make this a better world.

These values are reflected in the company's main tenet ('There's always more information out there') and vision statement ('To organise the world's information'). Thus people who are driven by science, much like Google, thrive to translate information into knowledge.

THE MEANING OF CULTURE

Having a model for decoding individual values is useful, but only if we are also able to catalogue a person's environment with a similar degree of detail. Indeed, profiling people is at best only half the job – the other half is profiling the work context. Aside from the specific characteristics and features of a person's job or role, the critical determinant of whether the person's values are likely to be fulfilled is the profile of the organisation. You can think of an employee and his employer as two individuals going on a first date. In order to determine the compatibility of this potential couple, we can't just focus on one of them – we need to understand both. Likewise it is not sufficient to know what makes employees tick; we also need to understand what a given employer and organisation represents for them.

When it comes to profiling work contexts, Industrial/Organisational (I/O) psychologists have paid a great deal of attention to the concept of organisational culture, defined as:

the implicit values, beliefs, and assumptions that employees infer guide behaviour, and they base these inferences on the stories, myths, and socialisation experiences they have and the behaviours they observe (especially on the part of leaders) that prove to be useful and promote success.[15]

Culture is critical because it informs us about the type of psychological rewards provided by a person's work environment, and
whether they will match the person's values, drivers and motives.
Although this idea may seem new, it was proposed more than
a hundred years ago in a seminal book on vocational interests,
written by Frank Parsons:

> An occupation out of harmony with the worker's aptitudes
> and capacities means inefficiency, unenthusiastic and perhaps
> distasteful labor, and low pay; while an occupation in har-
> mony with the nature of the man means enthusiasm, love of
> work, and high economic values – superior product, efficient
> service, and good pay.[16]

Another influential psychologist, Edgar Schein, provided a
detailed illustration of how cultures form, what their purpose
is and how they are transmitted. Specifically, Schein noted that
all groups develop on the basis of certain shared assumptions
or principles about the world, as well as their interaction with
it. Organisations are just big groups, and their cultures are the
implicit assumptions that dictate the rules of conduct for its
members. For example, 'basic assumptions determine organisational strategy, objectives, and means chosen to achieve
objectives in adapting to the external environment'.[17] Although
these may evolve over time, once cemented they are fairly stable
and consistent, providing a context for all work behaviours and
the rules of the game for everyday life at work.

In the past two decades, a great deal of academic research has
focused on advancing our understanding and measurement of
culture. One interesting, but rarely discussed, issue is that there
are different layers of culture operating in any organisation; and

measuring some layers is easier than measuring others. In this respect, Schein postulated the existence of three major dimensions of culture, which can be illustrated by three concentric circles.[18]

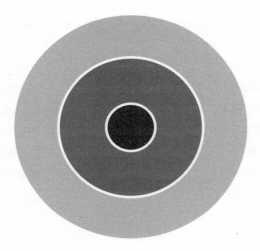

Figure 4: In Schein's three dimensions of culture the outer layer represents artefacts, the middle layer espoused values, and the inner layer underlying assumptions.

The outer layer – cultural *artefacts* – includes such things as habits, language, dress code and urban legends. They are easily observable by any visitors to the organisation, and are to a firm's culture what behaviour is to an individual's values and personality. However, like individuals' behaviour, they are also ambiguous in the sense that their underlying causes are hard to observe directly, and therefore are easily misinterpreted. The second, middle layer – *espoused values* – concerns the explicit cultural precepts formulated by managers and leaders. This is the stuff that tends to feature in organisations' mission statements and represents their ideal self. The third, inner layer – *underlying assumptions* – concerns the organisational life or the secret life of the organisation. This dimension of culture is the least visible but most influential; it dictates the real rules of social interaction in organisations and represents their actual self. In-depth interviews with representative members of the organisation – particularly employees rather than leaders – are needed to assess this level of culture.

But how does organisational culture relate to individual-level values? Various meta-analyses have examined this question.[19] As one would predict, some cultures are more compatible with one's values than others. For example, hierarchical cultures, which expect employees to behave according to predefined processes and well-established rules, will suit employees who value tradition and security. Market cultures, which reward people for achieving clear organisational goals, such as growing revenues and profits, will suit employees who value commerce and recognition. So-called 'ad hoc-racies', which focus on innovation and change and have an informal hierarchy, will suit employees with low security and high aesthetic values. And clan cultures, which promote collaboration and loyalty, will suit people with high hedonism and affiliation needs.

Unfortunately, in the real world of work most organisations do a poor job at evaluating their culture. Instead, their core cultural attributes tend to be the product of arbitrary brainstorming sessions by their marketing and PR teams, with minimal input from HR. When one looks at the recurrence of certain values in the website descriptions of organisations, it seems that company values are a mere reflection of what organisations *would like to be*, rather than what they actually are. For instance, most organisations describe themselves as having a culture of innovation, diversity and corporate social responsibility. However, when one asks the people who work there whether these attributes truly reflect the company culture, they will often react with cynicism and surprise, and provide a very different take on things. There is typically a mismatch between the cultures of organisations, as seen and desired by their leaders, and how they are perceived or lived by their employees. Some scholars have therefore conceptualised organisational *climate* as the subjective experience of culture. 'Climate' has been defined as the 'meanings people attach to interrelated bundles of experiences they have at work'.[20] For example, do employees perceive that there is a climate of safety, fairness, customer service or innovation in their firms? This is what climate surveys attempt to address when they assess employees' perceptions of these and other critical organisational issues.

Clearly, if organisations are unable to measure their cultures effectively, it will be hard for them to work out where their cultures originate. As my colleagues and I have suggested, an evolutionary framework can be used to explain how cultures originate,[21] not just at an organisational but also at a national level.[22] That is, culture can be conceptualised as the product of the values of the elite. When small groups become organisations, the values of the founders represent the cultural DNA of the organisation. As organisations mature, their leaders and influential figures shape the formal and informal rules of interaction via their own values. Thus the shared values of dominant individuals impregnate the culture of organisations, enabling leaders to impose meaning on their followers. The same logic applies to more macro versions of culture, such as national culture. Indeed, the laws, customs and social etiquette that provide the rules of interaction for any encounter between people are the product of those who have accrued power and influence throughout the history of that country. Rulers, land owners, aristocrats, religious, military and intellectual leaders all change and mould the existing culture of a country, reshaping it to their own values. Their legacy is to update and renew the rules of the game, which will in turn be transformed by the next generation of leaders. Culture is therefore dynamic rather than static – it never ceases to evolve.

RETHINKING ENGAGEMENT

No matter how big or small organisations are, and what their cultures are, they will only be effective if they manage to engage their workforce. Despite its popularity in the world of HR, engagement is no fad – it is a critical diagnostic measure and a driver of performance, with real benefits for both employees and employers. However, the popularity of engagement has led to a proliferation of opinions on the subject, not all of them informed, as well as the intellectual dilution of the concept. Rethinking engagement requires a return to its roots, going back to basics.

The concept of employee engagement was first introduced over 25 years ago in a now-seminal article by William Kahn, an American sociologist.[23] To Kahn, the essence of engagement was the notion of a strong psychological identification with work. More specifically, Kahn saw work as role-playing: when people are at work, they play certain roles – embodying an employee, a manager, a leader, a CEO, etc. – just like in other areas of life people have to play certain roles – e.g., husband, friend, wife, student, or parent. In other words, life is fundamentally about role-playing, and the major spheres of life require different roles.

Yet Kahn argued that when people are engaged they are so immersed in their roles that they become unaware of them. Instead, they *become* their roles, which erodes the psychological distance between their work personae and themselves. It is as if no other aspect of their self-concept counts; their job completely defines them. Thus work engagement is about turning a seemingly artificial and transactional role into a meaningful, fulfilling and almost existential experience. Martin Heidegger alluded to this with his concept of mastery, defined as the process whereby individuals extract hidden meaning from work and become 'as one' with their object of work.[24] In a similar vein, the founders of positive psychology put forward the concept of flow as a deeply enjoyable state of task absorption and focus, in which individuals lose their sense of time and unleash their creativity.[25] Flow is, undoubtedly, an extreme manifestation of engagement.

Much research has since been carried out on the causes of engagement, an issue that is important from both a theoretical and practical standpoint: identifying the drivers of engagement may enable us to manipulate or influence it. The causes of engagement fall into two major camps: situational and personal. The most influential situational causes are job resources, feedback and leadership, the latter, of course, being responsible for job resources and feedback. Indeed, leaders influence engagement by giving their employees honest and constructive feedback on their performance, and by providing them with the necessary resources that enable them to perform their job well. It is, however, noteworthy that although engagement drives job performance, job performance also drives engagement.[26] In other words, when employees are able to do their jobs well – to the point that they match or surpass their own expectations and ambitions – they will engage more, be proud of their achievements, and find work more meaningful. This is especially evident when people are employed in jobs that align with their values.

As for the key personal determinants of engagement, the more extraverted, emotionally stable, conscientious, agreeable and open to new experiences people are, the more they will tend to engage.[27] Unfortunately, all employee engagement measures, including annual climate surveys, ignore these important dispositional sources of variance in engagement levels, assuming instead that engagement is merely determined by situational factors. Yet, just like when someone is naturally pessimistic or grumpy they will provide a fairly negative review of a movie, restaurant, or job – even if, by their own standards, they liked it – those who are naturally cynical or negative will seem disengaged even when things are going OK for them. By the same token, natural optimists – people who are emotionally intelligent, positive, even somewhat naïve – will *seem* engaged even though their engagement levels may just reflect that their standards are low and they are easily pleased. We all have friends who are so positive about everything that their recommendations of movies, restaurants, or people cannot be trusted. In short, two people can score 7 out of 10 on the same engagement measure but if one individual is naturally negative and the other naturally positive, their scores should be interpreted differently: the former may be very engaged while the latter may be about to quit his job.

Personal factors affect engagement through different paths. As the above example shows, one way is by affecting people's interpretations of events, which implies that two people in the same organisation or team may see the culture and jobs in very different ways because of their personalities.[28] A second path is via the effects that personality has on how they approach their job, and in turn how they perform it. For instance, more extraverted people will tend to build wider and stronger networks at work, which will result in more job resources (a key situational driver of engagement). Curious employees may invest more time on learning and other activities that develop their expertise, and so make their jobs more interesting. Moreover, a third path through which personal factors influence engagement is the effects that people's personalities have on their colleagues, reports and bosses. The more stable, composed and emotionally intelligent people are, the more rewarding to deal with they will be, which will make their co-workers more engaging in return – making the job more engaging, too. Thus although we tend to think of the person and situation as independent, they are clearly intertwined, such that interactive and reciprocal links between both factors exist. The same situation has different effects on different people, different people interpret the situation in different ways, and different people *craft* different situations, including jobs, according to their personalities.

Contrary to popular belief, leaders don't necessarily engage by being warm and empathetic. Though people skills and caring behaviours are generally a plus, leaders can also engage through a compelling vision and strategy, and by pushing employees to perform to a higher level, holding them accountable and fomenting a culture of achievement.[29] Think of successful military commanders, such as Alexander the Great or Ulysses S. Grant, or top sports managers such as Sir Alex Ferguson or Pat Riley: such leaders are tough and impose high standards on their teams and subordinates; they punish poor performance while also rewarding genuine accomplishments and promoting talented individuals. Perhaps more importantly, great leaders excel at developing their own and other people's talents.

CHAPTER 5

Developing talent

This chapter examines the degree and ways in which talent can be nurtured. Although people can change, they mostly don't. The reason is that change requires self-awareness, effort and persistence. In the absence of extreme life circumstances, people tend to change by becoming amplified or exaggerated versions of their early selves. Yet coaching interventions have achieved positive results as a catalyst of employee performance and talent development. In particular, coaching that is not just focused on strengths but also addresses people's shortcomings or weaknesses tends to boost people's capabilities and turn them into better performers. As this chapter argues, effective coaching is largely about reputation management, in that the goal is to help employees be perceived in a more favourable manner by their co-workers and managers.

* * *

Executive coaching, which focuses on the development of leaders, is a growing industry, and no matter how much potential leaders have they will only be great if they take their own development seriously. One of the worst characteristics a leader can have is being uncoachable, which occurs largely as a result of being immune to negative feedback and failing to accept one's mistakes.

> If you want one year of prosperity, grow grain,
> if you want ten years of prosperity, grow trees,
> if you want a hundred years of prosperity, grow people.
> > Chinese proverb

Although organisations spend much more money and time on training and development than they do on sourcing talent, the reality is that proper selection would make training and development less necessary. But since selection efforts tend to fail, there is always training and development! This makes it necessary to answer a few critical questions about development, such as whether people can change (and if they actually do), and what the key determinants of change are. As we shall see, accurate feedback, self-awareness, the will to change, and the persistence and perseverance to go against one's nature are needed to drive change. Sadly, these elements are rather more elusive than most people think.

Like other psychological qualities, talent is the result of developmental experiences. That said, these experiences interact with certain biological predispositions that make some individuals more likely to acquire talent than others, even when exposed to the same life events and opportunities. What this implies is that, when it comes to talent, the issue is not an either/or choice between nature and nurture, but a combination of both. As scholars have pointed out:

> Asking how much a particular individual's attitudes or traits are due to heredity versus the environment is nonsensical, just like asking whether a leaky basement is caused more by the crack in the foundation or the water outside. In a very real sense, genetic effects are also environmental because they emerge in an environment, and environmental effects are also genetic because they are mediated by biological processes.[1]

In other words, given that there are physical and psychological constrains on talent, which are already manifested early in life and are hard to reverse at will, not everyone is equally likely to become an elite performer. And not everyone is prone to developing talent. Likewise, old age also constrains performance by restricting our talents, though the detrimental effects of age are less pronounced in some individuals than others. And although practice and training cannot explain a great deal of variability in individual differences in achievements, even among expert and elite performers, it is obvious that effort and training do impact the development of talent throughout a person's lifetime.[2]

For example, intelligence, which, as we have seen, is a key component of any form of talent, does develop with age and would never develop without appropriate environmental stimulation.[3] Lock alert babies in a basement and deprive them of intellectual stimulations, and they will grow up to be quite dim. At the same time, early manifestations of intelligence still predict how much adult intelligence people develop later in life, and with a remarkable level of accuracy.[4] For instance, measures of intelligence at the age of 6 predict what a person's intelligence will be at the age of 18, which does not mean that the person has the same level of intelligence at 6 as at 18 years of age, but rather that the person's standing on an age-specific ranking of intelligence is extremely similar during their childhood and their adolescence. In a similar vein, how smart people are relative to others does not change much after the age of 18, and this logic can largely be applied to other areas of talent: where there are visible differences between a person and his age group, the chances are that such differences will be maintained, if not accentuated, later in life.

Yet, as Nietzsche noted, 'every talent must unfold itself in fighting', which is why the will to improve and to get better, though independent of other talents, may be considered a key catalyst of achievement in any area. So much so that it is challenging, if not impossible, to think of any exceptional achiever who, in addition to his talents, did not work remarkably hard.

CAN PEOPLE CHANGE – AND DO THEY?

One of the most intriguing and commonly asked questions in psychology is whether people can change. However, the important question is not whether they can, but if they actually do. Unless we can answer this question properly, it is quite pointless to discuss developmental interventions designed to modify any consequential human quality.

To be sure, change interventions, such as coaching and training programmes, are by definition unnatural: they involve deliberate attempts to break habits and replace them with some new, presumably more effective, behavioural patterns. For example, some people may want to be more creative, productive, or charismatic; others may want to be less volatile, impulsive, or anxious. As such, developmental interventions attempt to produce changes that would otherwise not take place if people were left to their own devices or continued to behave as they normally do. Let us then start by examining the degree to which significant changes happen spontaneously in a person's life, as this question will help us understand the extent to which professional interventions are actually needed. Clearly, if professional change interventions merely produced as much improvement as people could achieve on their own, there would be little point in wasting money on them.

Changes in intelligence

Given its importance as a generic marker of talent across all jobs, it is quite critical to assess the degree to which intelligence tends to change. This question has been explored in hundreds of peer-reviewed articles, which provide compelling evidence for the rank-order stability of intellectual ability across a lifespan. These studies indicate that, after adolescence, there is virtually no change in the position of a person on a bell curve of IQ scores. For example, studies re-testing people on the same IQ tests report test–re-test correlations in the region of .90, which suggests that people's scores rarely shift, and when they do it is probably as a result of measurement errors rather than changes in actual abilities.[5] Even during childhood, when one would expect prominent changes in intellectual abilities due to the impact of schooling, which is focused precisely on developing children's intellectual capabilities, there is almost no rank-order change in children's IQ scores.[6] Slight changes can be found during late adulthood, but mostly because of the presence of individual differences in cognitive decline after the age of 60.[7]

To be sure, training does improve performance on the same test, with practice effects of around .25 of a standard deviation being quite common.[8] But such gains are confined only to the specific test in question – i.e., they do not translate into increases in actual intelligence. The more you practise anything, the better you become at that activity, yet that doesn't mean you will also become better at others. For instance, despite the popularity of brain-training games, there is not much evidence that spending your days solving brain teasers or practising cognitive tests will make you smarter. Lumosity, a leading provider of online brain-training games, recently paid $2 million to settle a complaint over misleading users into thinking that their games boost players' performance at school and work.[9]

Certain aspects of intelligence, such as knowledge or expertise, are obviously influenced by learning, which also depends upon a person's own will and motivation. However, though these crystallised aspects of intelligence may continue to increase even in late adulthood, the more process-based aspects of intelligence (fluid IQ) remain the same or deteriorate.[10] In that sense, human intelligence resembles a personal computer. On the one hand, it gets 'wiser' with age – because it keeps storing more information, files and knowledge. On the other hand, it also gets slower – because its capacity to handle operations and multitask declines. A person's speed of reasoning and problem-solving is largely dependent on their working memory capacity,[11] which is akin to the operational power of a computer (its RAM memory and/or processing speed). It is also noteworthy that the determinants of adult knowledge acquisition – e.g., curiosity, openness to experience and self-discipline – are largely dispositional in nature. Hence they are no more malleable than other major personality traits.

Changes in personality

The next question, therefore, is: what do we know about the stability or variability of personality over time? Since personality encompasses what people *typically* do – e.g., their usual behavioural, emotional and thinking patterns – the stability of personality will set the upper limits to any change intervention. As many practitioners know, this creates something of an intellectual conundrum. On the one hand, there is no better measure of change than improving someone's personality. It would have been nice, for instance, if someone could have turned Hitler into an altruist, Elvis into a health freak, or Bernie Madoff into an honest guy, when they were young – a great deal of suffering would have been avoided. On the other hand, personality is not supposed to change. It represents the essence of our character and all the attributes that make us systematically different from other people. There is a well-known cliché in coaching that states that, though you cannot change someone's personality, you can change their behaviours. Yet, if personality is the sum of a person's behaviours, then changing their behaviours should eventually produce a 'new' personality.

Interestingly, recent research indicates that most people want to change their personality – or at least they would like to if they could, particularly if it required no effort.[12] Indeed, 90 per cent of people are eager to boost their scores on at least one personality dimension. Typically, that entails becoming more extraverted, emotionally stable, conscientious, agreeable, or open to new experiences – particularly in the US, where high scores on these attributes are widely regarded as desirable and low scores are more or less stigmatised. Consider the fact that author Susan Cain has found a rather lucrative career out of championing the benefits of introversion.[13] Only in America can this movement – the 'quiet revolution' – be hailed as brave and controversial! The self-help industry, which in America alone is worth more than $10 billion a year, is largely sustained on people's willingness – and hopes – to change, and that generally involves becoming more talented or desirable. But how much – or little – do people change?

Scientific studies show that personality is neither very malleable, nor set in stone.[14] Although some changes do occur over a person's life, most of these changes are age-related transitions that happen to most people, so they imply more rank-order stability than change. For example, between the ages of 20 and 40 years, people tend to become more socially dominant, conscientious and emotionally stable. Furthermore, most people become more extraverted and open to new experiences during adolescence, but decline in both domains later on in adulthood. During adulthood people tend to become more agreeable, too.[15] In essence, we tend to become more boring – the psychological euphemism for this is 'mature' – as we grow older.[16] And from the age of 30 onwards there is very little change in personality, with substantial stability after the age of 50.[17]

Astonishingly, even extreme life events fail to produce major changes in personality. For example, studies on lottery winners show that, after an initial stage of euphoria, people tend to revert to their baseline levels of positivity or negativity – e.g., when grumpy people win the lottery they are happy for a few weeks, but after that they go back to being as grumpy as they usually are.[18] By the same token, when optimistic or positive people suffer big setbacks – e.g., the death of a relative, job loss, or divorce – it does not take them too long to bounce back. In short, though life experiences affect our behaviours, personality determines how we respond to those experiences, so it is unusual for any episode to create major, longstanding changes in a person's personality.[19]

This explains why personality predicts career success over a 65-year lifespan,[20] political attitudes over 45 years,[21] psychological disorders over 17 years (and from the age of 3),[22] health and mortality risk over 60 years,[23] and why happiness is better predicted by personality[24] and genetic dispositions[25] than by income.[26] Thus, despite the overwhelming number of choices we face every day, and the fact that, unlike squirrels or fish, we are free to choose from a wide repertoire of potential behaviours, we act mostly in predictable ways. Even when our behaviour appears irrational, it is by and large still predictable.[27] Twin studies, which quantify the relationship between genetic relatedness and similarity in psychological attributes (e.g., ability, values, or personality), suggest that there are hereditary factors that contribute to the stability of individual differences throughout the lifespan. Yet these studies also indicate that around 50 per cent of the variability in those attributes is due to environmental factors. The problem is figuring out what these factors actually are, and finding out how to influence them.

It should also be noted that even highly heritable traits can be influenced by choice and experiences. For example, in humans the heritability of adult weight is around .80, which means that a whopping 80 per cent of the variability in weight can be attributed to genetic factors. Although this figure is substantially higher than the heritability of any psychological attribute, anyone can change his genetically predetermined weight by deciding to eat less and exercise more – the issue is that most people don't, and when they do they have trouble maintaining these changes (precisely because of genetics).

More often than not, key environmental influences on personality occur during a person's early life, so it would require a time machine to fix things – think *Back to the Future*. It is also quite common for nurture to act in concert with nature, accentuating predispositions or enhancing existing potential. For example, ambitious people tend to have competitive jobs, and as their jobs become more competitive they tend to become more ambitious as a result. Likewise, extraverts may choose jobs that require a great deal of networking and interpersonal schmoosing. Yet adaptation to those jobs tends to increase their extraversion even further.[28] And so personal qualities, including talent-related traits, are always influenced by both nature and nurture, but often in the same direction, such that nurture ends up amplifying characteristics that were already there to begin with.[29] In that sense, the more people change, the more they become like themselves. By and large, as we grow older we all become exaggerated versions of our earlier selves.

In all, the reviewed evidence suggests that laypeople tend to overestimate the degree to which people change. Sure, people can change, but when people are left to their own devices they mostly don't. This is why when you meet old school friends at those dreaded school reunions, the changes you observe in them are mostly physical rather than mental or behavioural. Yes, they will tend to look older, fatter and balder, but from a personality, values and intelligence perspective, it will seem as if time hasn't passed at all. This makes professional development interventions indispensable. If people are not able to change alone, then surely some help or assistance is needed. The next sections evaluate the effectiveness of such interventions, notably coaching programmes.

TOURING THE WILD WEST OF COACHING

Coaching programmes are the most common attempt to develop people in organisations, and they are particularly popular with leaders. Although there is a growing body of scientific evidence on the effectiveness of coaching interventions, it is hard to extrapolate from academic findings to the realities of the work-place because there is huge variability in the nature of coaching practices, and few people know what really happens behind closed doors during a coaching session.[30] Unsurprisingly, the world of coaching has been described as the Wild West,[31] and for every competent coach there are probably dozens of unqual-ified practitioners who escape scientific scrutiny and survive in business merely thanks to the naivety of their clients. At the same time, the popularity of coaching practices has been increasing globally for the past two decades, with some estimates suggest-ing that the coaching industry now generates over $2 billion a year, twice as much as it did ten years ago.[32]

But what do we even mean by 'coaching'? One definition is: any 'result-oriented, systematic process in which the coach facil-itates the enhancement of life experience and goal-attainment in the personal and/or professional lives of normal, non-clinical clients'.[33] Although this definition is too inclusive, it is none-theless useful to delineate the boundaries of coaching, and help us get a sense of what should *not* be considered coaching: for example, the treatment of clinical symptoms, pathological conditions, any process that is not systematic or result-oriented, or where the practitioner is not concerned with helping clients attain specific goals. The distinction between coaching and clinical practices is important. Even when coaches focus on mitigating maladaptive patterns of behaviours, these are not necessarily abnormal by clinical standards. As the next chapter will explain, most of the potential derailing or dysfunctional behaviours that are targeted through coaching interventions fail to meet the requirements for being deemed clinical or psychopathological, because they are neither statistical outliers nor *fully* disruptive of a person's ability to work or maintain relationships.

Many coaching interventions try to enhance some aspect of EQ – emotional intelligence – such as social, intrapersonal, interpersonal, or soft skills.[34] In that sense, they try to make people more rewarding to deal with, which should generally improve their career success and employability. For example, if you've been told you need to keep your temper under control, show more empathy for others, or be a better listener, what are the odds that coaching can help you achieve this? While no intervention can take a person from 0 to 100 per cent on any of these behaviours, well-designed coaching programmes can easily achieve improvements of 25 per cent. The most comprehensive meta-analytic review of this issue indicated that motivation, coping skills, self-awareness and well-being can all be significantly boosted through coaching. Although such interventions are usually evaluated via self-reports, which tend to overestimate success rates,[35] a review of 46 independent studies suggests that 70 per cent of coaching recipients can be expected to outperform the average person in a control group.[36] This means that, on average, coaching interventions boost job performance drivers by around 20 per cent. Reassuringly, these results tend to be replicated when effectiveness is measured via more valid indicators than self-reports, such as supervisor ratings of task or job performance.[37]

Studies have also examined the impact of stress management programmes, and results suggest that interventions can have effects of over 1 standard deviation, which means that 85 per cent or more of the participants in the coaching group will score above the average level of the control group.[38] Even empathy, a biological trait concerning the ability to understand and feel what other people are feeling, is trainable to a degree. For instance, neuropsychological studies suggest that, with adequate coaching, people can become more prosocial, altruistic and compassionate. Furthermore, even when such interventions are focused on improving work-related outcomes, the benefits of EQ coaching are not just confined to the workplace. They also produce higher levels of happiness, mental and physical health, improved social and marital relationships, and decreased blood levels of cortisol (the major stress-regulation hormone) in other areas of life.[39] These findings are consistent with meta-analytic evidence on the effectiveness of psychotherapy, which reports improvements of around .85 of a standard deviation for various interpersonal and intrapersonal skills.[40]

Despite these encouraging findings, there are two caveats to consider.

First, given the substantial heterogeneity of coaching practices, it may not be too informative to focus on the average effect sizes reported in comprehensive reviews: they are likely to result from a mix of very ineffective and very effective interventions, akin to comparing apples and oranges. As Benjamin Disraeli astutely observed: 'A man eats a loaf of bread, and another man eats nothing; statistics is the science that tells us that each of these men ate half a loaf of bread.'[41] Clearly, some approaches – and some people – are much more likely to succeed than others, and only a few academic studies have evaluated what methods or approaches work best. The most successful sessions follow a cognitive behavioural framework.[42] According to this paradigm, problematic behaviours are primarily driven by irrational or counterproductive beliefs, which coaches can help clients reframe. This leads to more effective behaviours being put in place, and subsequent reinterpretations of reality that are less counterproductive and inaccurate. In addition, attempts to enhance psychological flexibility – the capacity to accept and deal with (as opposed to avoid) unpleasant situations[43] – are also highly effective. Contrary to popular belief, interventions designed to enhance self-esteem or confidence are rarely effective, and often counterproductive.[44]

The second caveat is that, because scientific studies tend to report findings from well-executed and robust interventions (i.e., the standards in academic publishing are higher than in real-world practices), it is perhaps overly optimistic to assume that real-world interventions are as effective as the average intervention examined by scientific studies.

Fundamentally, coaching is not a pure science – it is in part an art. Scientific assessment tools provide robust data so that the coaching session is based on reliable evidence. However, in coaching the science of assessment must give place to the art of intervention, moving from diagnosis and prediction to development and change. As such, the success of coaching will largely depend on the talent and craftsmanship of the coach.

Research suggests that generic characteristics and behaviours of coaches matter more than the coaching method.[45] Thus if you

are interested in predicting the success of a coaching intervention, study the personality of the coach. Personality assessments
are already widely used in coaching and development interventions, but to assess the client.[46] Perhaps it is time for clients to
administer a personality assessment to their potential coaches
before they decide to work with them. Moreover, when coaches
advertise their credentials and experience, they might also want
to include information about their personality – both their bright
and their dark side. Not only would this help clients evaluate
fit and predict success, it would also enable them to deal more
effectively with their coach. All this is also consistent with
clinical psychology studies showing that the personality of the
therapist is often more important than the approach he follows.[47]
Although research has yet to examine these issues in the world
of coaching, one would expect a similar phenomenon to exist:
the closer the bond between coach and client, the more the client
will progress.

It is also clear that some people are much more coachable
than others, and even the best coach and coaching methods will
fail with certain clients (just imagine trying to coach Donald
Trump). People who are less arrogant, more empathetic and
self-aware respond more favourably to coaching interventions,
not least because they are more used to seeking feedback.[48]
Likewise, individuals who are more interested in others' opinions, and worried about disappointing people, are often more
eager to change. Although there is not much research on coachability, evaluating clients' coachability levels at the start of the
sessions can increase the effectiveness of coaching. Furthermore,
given that many coaching engagements are arranged by HR,
even coachable people may not be very open to development.
There is an old joke about how many psychologists it takes to

change a light bulb. Just one – so long as the light bulb *wants* to change.

COACHING AND DEVELOPING LEADERS

Although any attempt to develop workplace talent is important, interventions with leaders are more likely to pay off, not least because of the amount of people, processes and outcomes that leaders control. Thus, when leaders improve there is a spill-over effect that trickles down to the rest of the organisation and creates improvements in the wider workforce.[49] Conversely, developing junior employees or technical experts will only affect their own performance. It is therefore unsurprising that a disproportionate and growing amount of money is spent on developing leaders. In the US, the number of executive coaches has increased exponentially in the past 15 years, from 10,000 in 2002 to 50,000 in 2007, and to almost 100,000 now.[50] A similar increase has been reported for the UK, and the International Coach Federation, the leading international network of professional coaches, reports that its membership has soared globally from merely 1,500 coaches in 1999 to almost 25,000 now.[51]

Executive coaching, the most common developmental intervention for leaders, has been defined as a one-on-one session between a professional coach and a leader – usually a senior executive. Originally, the focus of such sessions was to rescue talented leaders who were in trouble.[52] However, in recent years the scope of executive coaching has been expanded considerably, with the aim now being to 'enhance the coachee's change through self-awareness and learning, and ultimately contribute to individual and organisational success'.[53] This is particularly important given that most leaders are feedback deprived,[54] and yet the only way they can improve is by being aware of their potential and performance; studies show that increases in self-awareness correlate with improvements in subsequent job performance.[55]

Although the recipients of executive coaching fall into many different categories, there are four major groups:[56]

a. *People who are valuable, but at risk of derailing*: As the next chapter will show, a company's top people are sometimes the most problematic. Just like 20% of people tend to account for 80% of the productivity, 20% of people tend to create 80% of the problems – and they are often the same as the 'vital few' who perform best. Thus, to ensure that your most valuable people keep contributing to the best of their capabilities, you need to help them avoid problems. Coaching people around the dark side of their personality can help you achieve this (there's more on this in the next chapter).

b. *High potentials*: These are individuals who, mostly because of their previous performance, have been identified as key future contributors to the organisation. They may not be leaders yet, but they have the potential to be. In some cases, they may merely be considered rough-cut diamonds,[57] and their designation may have resulted not from their previous performance but from a thorough evaluation of their actual potential (for example, through psychometric tests). This group is an important recipient of coaching because, in order to make the successful transition from individual contributor/top employee to effective manager or leader of others, it is necessary to develop good people skills. From Silicon Valley to Wall Street to professional sports, there is no shortage of examples of people who were great individual contributors but who failed to become good leaders. Coaching can address this by training and developing leadership skills. This explains why big companies, such as General Electric, spend over $1 billion a year on training and development programmes for their elite workers. Likewise, Novartis and HSBC send their high-potential employees to offsite development programmes, not only to train them on content but also to create strong bonds and networks between the potential future leaders of the organisation.

c. *Newly hired/promoted*: Any new job requires a period of adaptation, as well as learning new skills and acquiring some new experience. Coaching can help to speed up this process by targeting specific developmental needs and equipping clients with the necessary skills to perform well in their new roles. Many companies speak of 'stretch assignments' or 'baptisms by fire'. P&G implements accelerator experiences and crucible roles for their new appointees. The most coveted posts are foreign, as they help young managers understand the intricacies and practicalities of running a big business, and put specialists through experiences that require them to deal with a wide range of problems. Other tough tests include building a business in an isolated village (a popular challenge at Hindustan Unilever) or turning around a failing division.

d. *Expatriates*: As organisations grow, they become more global, and the world of talent is now more international and connected than it was 10 or 20 years ago. This means more cross-border mobility and a higher number of expatriate employees. Coaching can be used effectively to prepare people for their expatriate experiences, enhancing their global mind-set and preparing them for the new culture. This is particularly important since in big corporations there are likely to be many sub-cultures in different locations: e.g., IBM Argentina is not a replica of IBM US, and Microsoft UK is very different, in cultural terms, from Microsoft China. In addition to preparing people for this cultural transition, coaching expats is important for helping them cope with the more personal aspects of the move: e.g., leaving a family behind, living on their own, or adjusting to less stable political or social environments (e.g., a UN employee who moves from Vienna to Kinshasa, or a Deloitte manager who moves from London to Manila).

Beyond executive coaching, organisations also deploy group interventions to boost leaders' potential and increase their effectiveness. Interventions designed to enhance leaders' expertise or knowledge are highly effective, with average gains of over 1 standard deviation reported in systematic reviews.[58] Similarly, meta-analyses suggest that the average training intervention will boost learning, performance and effective behaviours by over .60 of a standard deviation.[59] Most training programmes consist of the communication of proven approaches to solve known problems, although many of the problems leaders must solve in their everyday lives are ill-defined and unpredictable.[60]

And yet, despite the steady increase in resources dedicated to improving leaders, and the fact that the leadership development industry is worth billions, the efficacy of leadership development programmes is in question as much as ever, and confidence in the industry as a whole keeps declining. In light of the compelling scientific evidence for the effectiveness of well-designed programmes, one can only conclude that what goes on in the real world of organisations must be substantially different from what scientists and evidence-based practitioners advocate. There are obviously exceptions, such as big and innovative multinationals that have managed to adopt science-driven methods to develop stellar leaders, not only for themselves, but also for others. For example, some of P&G's illustrious alumni include Meg Whitman (Hewlett Packard), Scott Cook (Intuit) and Jim McNerney (Boeing).

Another point that deserves consideration, and highlights a gap between what is and what should be, is who the client is. As reviewers have noted, in coaching 'it isn't always clear whether the client is the person being coached or someone else in the organisation – perhaps someone higher up the management ladder or someone in the human resources department'.[61] Most coaches behave as though the client were the coachee, but what is good for the coachee is not always good for the organisation (their bosses, subordinates, peers, or clients). In fact, some of the most sought-after coaches in the world have made stellar careers out of helping their clients – i.e., the people being coached – stay out of trouble, and advance in the organisational ranks. For coachees, then, coaches become trusted advisors who care about advancing their career, even if success comes at the detriment of the organisation. (Think of Tony Soprano using his personal therapist to become a more successful Mafioso.) In a logical world, coaching would produce improvements in the coachee that are also beneficial to the major client or stakeholder (i.e., HR, the senior leadership, the coachee's team, or the organisation). In the real world, however, what is good for the coachee is not always good for the organisation.

STRENGTHS-BASED COACHING

Among the wide range of coaching approaches that exist, one paradigm has clearly stood out during the past 15 years, namely the 'strengths approach' to coaching. Although definitions vary – and there is also large variability in approaches among different strengths coaches – the central idea of this movement is that behavioural change interventions will be more successful when we ignore the coachee's potential or actual faults. Thus the main idea of the strengths approach is that, instead of worrying about addressing our weaknesses, we should capitalise on our natural tendencies and build on what we are already good at.

Strengths-based coaching has a cult-like following among HR and talent management professionals. For example, a Google search reveals almost 50 million hits for 'strengths coaching'. Most of these lead to websites that provide coaching services, or praise the virtues of this method. Likewise, Amazon lists over 8,000 books on the subject, including Gallup's bestselling book on their StrengthsFinder method, which is reportedly used by 1.6 million employees per year and almost all of the Fortune 500 companies. Furthermore, there have been reports that some organisations are even planning to eliminate negative feedback from their performance appraisals, and the word 'weakness' has more or less become taboo among HR practitioners, who prefer to refer to them as 'opportunities' or 'challenges'. Although there are no signs that HR's fascination with strengths is likely to disappear, there are five main reasons why evidence-driven practitioners should stay away from it.

First, the strengths approach to coaching is *not* grounded in science. That is, there is no single peer-reviewed article – published in a reputable scientific journal – that provides evidence that developmental interventions will be more effective when they don't take into consideration people's weaknesses. And while absence of evidence does not necessarily confirm evidence of absence, it is noteworthy that the main thesis of the strengths approach is in conflict with well-established academic findings on the benefits of negative feedback,[62] which highlights people's faults, for improving performance. This point is crucial, because the pioneers of the strengths movement stated that traditional development and training programmes – which pay attention to people's faults – are doomed, yet, as the scientific meta-analyses discussed in this chapter show, such programmes improve behaviours by up to 1 standard deviation. How does this compare to a strengths-based intervention? We simply don't know, unless we base our knowledge on practitioners' self-evaluations, or on the promises of strengths vendors. In addition, it is clear that in order to be effective, leaders must learn to develop new strengths, rather than just relying on the strengths they already possess.

Second, the strengths approach claims to help individuals to identify their key competencies, talents and career weapons, yet practitioners fail to provide any normative data on how strong people are vis-à-vis a group or population benchmark. Instead, the approach is based on the premise that a person's top strengths are his own best qualities, regardless of how they compare to other people's. In other words, strengths are defined as the characteristics that enable a person to perform to their personal best.[63] However, most people's personal best is just the population average, and for many people it is even worse. Imagine that someone is not very hard-working, but that that person is even less creative, and less socially skilled than he is hard-working. Would that make that person hard-working? Not really – that person would be uncreative, socially inept and lazy! And in order to help that person perform better, it is probably useful to let them know that they are handicapped in all three areas, as opposed to pretending that they are hard-working (because they are even weaker in the other two domains). Thus, if we are serious about evaluating people's strengths – or any domain of talent – non-normative feedback is useless.

Third, the strengths movement maintains that every employee deserves to be developed, because everybody has potential and is talented (though in their own ways). However, given that top performers are many times more valuable than the rest,[64] organisations would be ill-advised to spend money on developing all employees. In other words, the highest return on investment will come from developing only top performers or high-potential employees, while the presumed 'strengths' of the rest will be of marginal value to the organisation. Thus, in a world of limited resources, businesses should focus their learning and development budgets on the 20 per cent of people who are responsible for 80 per cent of the revenues, profits or output.

Fourth, everything is better in moderation – the only exception is moderation itself. Indeed, even positive qualities have adverse effects when they are manifested or expressed in large quantities. Psychologists refer to this as the 'too much of a good thing' effect,[65] and the implication is that working on your strengths can turn potential assets into career disadvantages. For instance, attention to detail can become counterproductive perfectionism and OCD-like procrastination. Confidence may turn into arrogance, reckless risk-taking and hubristic overconfidence. Ambition may become greed, and imagination may turn into odd eccentricity. As the next chapter will show, there is no shortage of competent leaders – individuals with clear strengths – who will nevertheless derail because they are careless about their toxic tendencies. It has been estimated that almost half of all Fortune 100 firms may engage in counterproductive or unethical activities that are bad enough to feature in the press.

Fifth, although initially the strengths movement attempted to compensate for an excessive historical emphasis on negativity, the imbalance today is in the opposite direction. Indeed, as the popularity of positive psychology and strengths attests, there is now a disproportionate focus on positivity. This focus is in stark contrast with the realities of management practices and the world of work that most people seem to experience. As Jeffrey Pfeffer noted, organisations are full of unsatisfied

> employees who do not trust their leaders; leaders at all levels lose their jobs at an increasingly fast pace ... and the leadership industry has failed and continues to fail in its task of producing leaders who are effective and successful.[66]

It is therefore intellectually irresponsible, not to mention out of sync with reality, to adopt as our overarching framework a paradigm that is happy to ignore our shortcomings and understate our potential flaws. Like the wider popular literature on leadership, which has been hijacked by the self-help industry, the strengths movement seems to exude an inexplicable degree of optimism, which, as Voltaire's Candide noted, 'is the obstinacy of maintaining that everything is best when it is worst.'

SELF-AWARENESS AND
REPUTATION MANAGEMENT

The most generalisable feature of good coaching interventions is that they enhance clients' self-awareness. Although definitions of self-awareness vary, they usually involve knowing one's strengths and limitations. A more specific, and arguably actionable, take on self-awareness focuses on enhancing people's knowledge of how they affect others. This view is rooted in the interpersonal tradition of social psychology, which sees others as a major source of meaning and identity for the self.[67] Accordingly, healthy self-views are shaped by others' views of us, and others' views of us are shaped by our behaviours. In other words, our egos must reflect our reputation. To know yourself is to know what others think of you, because others are better able to observe your behaviours than you are yourself. Supporting this thesis, research shows that leaders who describe themselves more closely to how others describe them tend to be more effective.[68] Conversely, self-deluded leaders, e.g., Sepp Blatter, Cristina Kirchner, or Tony Blair, will find it harder to get valuable feedback from others to improve. While these examples may be extreme, most of us are at least somewhat unaware of how others see us, and this is especially true of managers. It is indeed astonishing how many smart and driven individuals fail to evaluate their own actions objectively.

People are generally unaware of their abilities,[69] and

self-estimates of performance are generally too lenient to be accurate.[70] Moreover, meta-analytic studies show that people are also unaware of how self-aware they are, and the correlation between self- and other-ratings of EQ, a major marker of self-awareness, is lower than for IQ and other abilities.[71] While many factors need to converge to boost our self-awareness, the most important is accurate feedback. So much so, that coaching is often defined as a systematic feedback intervention,[72] and studies show that coaching is substantially enhanced when more frequent and accurate feedback is given.[73] Large quantitative syntheses suggest that the average feedback intervention will improve performance by almost half a standard deviation, though 30 per cent of real-world interventions actually worsen performance.[74] Thus feedback is key to enhancing one's self-awareness and gaining more insights into one's own strengths and weaknesses, but when feedback is unclear or inaccurate – particularly if it just tells people what they want to hear – it can do more harm than good.

Unfortunately, we are not naturally predisposed towards seeking feedback, neither at work nor in other contexts of life. First, because we tend to overestimate our self-knowledge, particularly when we have little of it. And secondly, because in most cultures – especially in the Western world – seeking feedback is often seen as a sign of weakness. Likewise, not requesting feedback may make us seem confident in our performance, which helps us fake competence and, in turn, get ahead in our careers.

Clearly, some people are more comfortable with feedback than others. Research indicates that there are consistent individual differences in people's willingness to seek feedback at work. The older, more established and experienced people are, the less likely they are to request feedback from others.[75] Conversely, curious and open individuals, people with a strong learning motivation, and people who are slightly under-confident and more self-critical will be more likely to ask others to report on their own performance. Unsurprisingly, there are also individual differences in dispositional self-awareness, meaning that some people are naturally better able to understand how others see them and how they affect other people.

Although less than 15 per cent of organisations evaluate the effectiveness of their coaching initiatives, there is strong evidence that robust assessment methods, such as scientifically valid personality assessments and 360-degree surveys, produce the best outcomes. For example, a controlled experimental study of 1,361 managers in a global corporation showed that feedback-based coaching increased managers' propensity to seek advice, and improved their subsequent performance (as judged by their direct reports) one year later.[76] It is therefore good news that the use of 360-degree feedback is now fairly common across industries, as no other tool can provide a more direct route to enhancing self-awareness. If you want to understand how your behaviour impacts on others there is no better way to achieve this than to examine their anonymous views on you.[77] Much like in TripAdvisor, IMDb, or Amazon user reviews, some opinions will be more reflective of the person doing the rating than the target. Yet when most people are pointing out the same issues, there is surely something going on and it would be foolish for recipients to ignore it. Studies also indicate that individuals with a strong natural tendency to monitor their own behaviour are not rated significantly higher on 360s, suggesting that 360 ratings are unaffected by targets' deliberate attempts to fake impressions or deceive others.[78]

In addition, 360-degree feedback is an invaluable tool to

measure the effectiveness of change interventions. Given that 360s tend to focus on a wide range of work-related behaviours, and that some of those behaviours will be the very focus of coaching and developmental interventions, re-administering the same 360 at a second point in time is an effective method for quantifying change. It is not uncommon for individuals, including leaders, to attempt to measure change by retaking the same personality assessment over and over again. Although valid personality assessments are unlikely to change from one time to the next, particularly within a five-year timeframe and in the absence of extreme life circumstances, if people have managed to change critical aspects of their behaviours, this will be reflected in their 360 evaluations, much like changes in weight will be reflected on the same set of scales. Thus the role of coaching or behavioural change interventions is to *in*validate personality assessments: when coaching works, the predictions of performance made by valid personality assessments will be nullified because the candidate's natural tendencies and default habits are suppressed by his deliberate effort to change.

The figure on page 139 illustrates how feedback interventions can be maximised for effective coaching programmes. The model shown is based on my own company's development framework, though similar models have been used and validated by the wider academic community.[79]

As the diagram shows, the cycle begins with the process of building awareness. Via the use of 360s and valid personality assessments, which provide feedback on performance and potential, respectively, individuals identify blind spots between their self-views and how they are viewed by others, as well as gaps between their ideal and actual self. It is no accident that

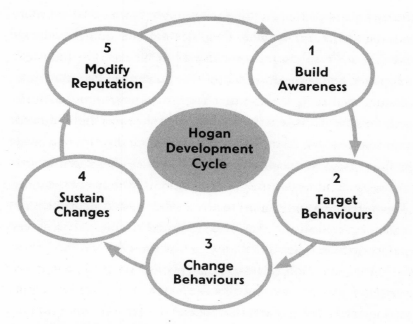

Figure 5: The Hogan development framework

the term 'coach' also means 'carriage', for the main goal of the coach is to *transport* individuals from where they are to where they want to be.[80] The second step in the process is to target specific behaviours that need to be modified. This involves setting relevant goals, and aligning personal career objectives with organisational outcomes. In essence, this stage of the process requires working out what the client needs to change in order to be more effective (or satisfied) at work. The third stage concerns the actual change: starting new behaviours and stopping old ones; replacing toxic habits with effective ones. Although it is always tempting to aim high, well-cemented habits are hard to break, while new habits take significant time and effort to form. Thus targeting a few critical behaviours with persistence and dedication will pay off more than attempting a whole personality transplant. The fourth stage is arguably the hardest one: sustaining changes over time. Consider the fact that the average New Year's resolution is broken within the first few months.[81] However, the reward for those who succeed is big, namely to modify their reputation so that they are perceived more favourably by others – this is the final stage of the cycle and is a result of accomplishing all the previous steps. Typically, this final stage will be tested by re-administering the same 360 survey, at least 9 months (and usually 12) after the initial instance of the cycle. This will enable individuals to assess whether any visible changes have occurred in the eyes of others, and to internalise others' perceptions in order to enhance self-awareness.

Thus, reputation is the ultimate goal of coaching and development interventions, and effective coaching helps clients curate and upgrade their personal career brand. Although this idea may seem somewhat counterintuitive, because of the common belief that coaching should facilitate changes in a person's 'true self', reputation is a much more tangible and consequential variable, as the most relevant manifestation of personality is always in the eye of the beholder. As the great David Bowie once noted: 'I am only the person the greatest number of people think I am.' What others think of us is much more consequential than what we think of ourselves. Even when others' views of us are inaccurate, they are still critical: we all get hired, promoted and fired on the basis of what others make of us.

In other words, it does not matter so much how you think of yourself; what matters most is how other people see you. And when what you think of yourself is out of touch with what other people think of you, then there's only marginal value to your self-views. Quantitative reviews of scientific studies indicate that other-ratings of personality (reputation) are a better predictor of future performance than are self-ratings (identity).[82] For example, reputation predicts academic achievements and job performance much better than people's self-views do.[83] This evidence is also consistent with biographical evidence on the distorted self-views that many salient historical figures held. Consider the fact that most brutal dictators, including Hitler, Stalin and Idi Amin, had rather positive views on themselves, and even believed they were altruistic moral leaders in the pursuit of a better world.

As the next chapter explains, organisations that ignore employees' weaknesses – or 'developmental opportunities', to use the politically correct HR term – will pay the consequences. Technical brilliance often coexists with 'toxic assets': Dominique Strauss-Kahn, Oscar Pistorius and Bill Clinton are just three examples of people who were extremely talented in their fields yet also careless about their dark side tendencies. The more political and toxic the culture of an organisation, the more this type of individual will thrive, much like bacteria relish polluted environments. Sadly, although these qualities often advance individuals' careers, they do so at the expense of the group's or organisation's welfare.

CHAPTER 6

The dark side
of talent

This chapter examines the dark side of talent, those undesirable or counterproductive tendencies that coexist with
positive qualities, explaining why so many capable and techni-
cally impressive individuals often go off the rails. As the chapter
shows, counterproductive work behaviours, such as acts of
bullying, theft and dishonesty, are frequently predicted by dark
side personality qualities. In particular, the dark triad – narcissism, Machiavellianism and psychopathy – has been extensively
researched and found to be fairly common in normal work settings. Individuals with these (and other problem) characteristics
are especially toxic when they occupy positions of leadership.
This is not unusual, since dark side traits often help individuals
to climb up the hierarchy of an organisation, though as much as

these qualities can be adaptive and make people successful, their success comes at the expense of other employees.

* * *

Although few qualities are more desirable than talent, and the overwhelming majority of discussions on talent focus on its bright side, talent has a dark side, too. In fact, no model of talent is complete if it omits individuals' dysfunctional qualities. These dark side tendencies are ubiquitous, with most individuals displaying at least two or three potential career derailers, and as many as 15 per cent of the population meeting clinical criteria for personality related problems.[1] Furthermore, one may expect pathological manifestations of the dark side to be present in more or less every organisation, including at the top of the management structure.

In this respect, there are two noteworthy points. First, the fact that even the most talented individuals will have some problem characteristics. These dark side features are often the consequence – a side effect – of their actual talents. In other words, virtues and faults tend to coexist in the same people, and certain faults are just undesirable manifestations of virtues, particularly extreme strengths. For example, highly confident people will tend to undermine others and have deluded self-views; very creative people may have poor attention to detail and jump from one idea to the next without being able to focus on anything for too long; and people with extreme social skills may end up manipulating others. Second, the same quality may be a virtue for certain things, but a handicap for others. For instance, risk-taking may be an asset for nascent entrepreneurs but a liability for health-and-safety officers; creativity may be a virtue in advertising copywriters, but a considerable problem in accountants; and extraversion may be a source of talent in salespeople but a tedious distraction in librarians. While these may seem like somewhat trivial and oversimplified examples, it is hard to imagine any talent attribute that is universally useful or free of any negative consequence, particularly when manifested to excess.

At times, the dark side of talent may confer an advantage to the individual, but at the expense of others (e.g., colleagues, subordinates, or the organisation). For example, deception may help dishonest employees advance their careers, and greed may propel selfish individuals to positions of power, but such personal gains come at a high cost for the collective, which would benefit more from the career advancement and leadership of honest, talented and altruistic people. Likewise confidence helps people get promoted, but it is competence that allows them to do their jobs well. In that sense, the individual short-term success conferred by dark side attributes is offset by the less fortunate long-term consequences for the group. This is particularly salient in toxic organisational cultures, which reward dark side characteristics and enable poisonous personalities to thrive. Barclays Bank traders and the LIBOR scandal is a textbook example of this phenomenon.

One of the major practical reasons for evaluating the dark side of talent is the pervasiveness of counterproductive work behaviours (CWBs) in organisations. Unethical and antisocial work behaviours, such as rule-bending, cyber-loafing, bullying and theft, cost the economy billions. To name just a couple of examples, consider the Enron and WorldCom accounting scandals, which during the first year alone amounted to $40 billion[2] – as much as the entire US homeland security budget. Or the 2008 global financial crisis, which was a result of cumulative deception, manipulation and misrepresentation by unethical bankers and their co-opted governments, and cost the world economy $25 trillion.[3]

While the bright side of talent predicts career success and work-related effectiveness, the dark side predicts failure and derailment.[4] As recent reviews have pointed out:

> Optimism, integrity, and self-authenticity may predict health and happiness, but personality traits such as Machiavellianism, narcissism and psychopathy may predict misbehaviour.[5]

Several decades of research indicate that CWBs, defined as intentional attempts to harm employees or organisations, are rather pervasive and problematic.[6]

Much like living in society, working with others requires making sacrifices and suppressing individual interests to conform to certain rules or act in ways that are beneficial to others. Furthermore, working with others involves a considerable amount of deliberate prosocial behaviour and the ability to inhibit selfish and antisocial tendencies. CWBs threaten social harmony at work, as well as jeopardising people's ability to build and maintain relationships. In that sense, CWBs are the exact reverse of good organisational citizenship, though the two may be manifested at the same time. Thus you can show good levels of organisational citizenship and still engage in CWBs; or display neither.

CWBs are so ubiquitous that they are now considered a key component of job performance,[7] not least because of how they impact other employees and the organisation.[8] Acts of aggression, deviance, retaliation and revenge play a critical role in lowering employee morale and productivity.[9] Likewise verbal or physical harassment, bullying, cyber-bullying and theft will harm an organisation's output by demotivating staff and wasting organisational resources. Some have therefore suggested that any behaviour that results in outcomes that are harmful to the organisation may be considered counterproductive.[10] These behaviours are often driven by contextual factors, but they are also a function of personality characteristics, such as the dark side traits discussed in this chapter.

Behaviour is always a function of both the situation and personal qualities, which interact to make certain behaviours more likely than others. For instance, an aggressive person will be more likely to display anger towards a co-worker when they are under stress or pressure. By the same token, cool-headed and diplomatic individuals will require much more provocation and stress to behave in an aggressive manner. Thus personality dictates someone's predisposition to react in more or less antisocial ways to a given situation – it is a person's probability to do X in a particular context. If organisations want to mitigate CWBs they will need to detoxify their culture as well as sift out problem employees. This can be done by attending to people's dark sides. No matter how talented employees are, if they cannot keep their dark sides in check they will, sooner or later, engage in CWBs and harm their co-workers and the organisation.

The negative consequences of the dark side are exacerbated in leaders, because they affect a larger number of people and, through their actions, decisions and values, shape the culture of the organisation. When individual employees behave badly, their behaviour will only affect a small number of people and, if the culture is not too corrupt, those individuals will be punished and expelled from the organisation. However, when leaders behave in an explosive, irrational, aggressive or corrupt manner, their poor reputation will trickle down the organisation and instil a culture of fear, frustration, or repression, which will tend to encourage similar behaviours throughout the wider workforce.

A CLOSER LOOK AT THE DARK SIDE

While there are different ways to conceptualise the dark side of talent, most definitions focus on individual characteristics that have an undesirable, antisocial, or dysfunctional side. These characteristics are dispositional in nature, meaning they comprise fairly stable personality traits. This implies that a person's dark side may trigger recurrent interpersonal issues, as opposed to causing one-off or sporadic problem behaviours. The most comprehensive and authoritative taxonomy of the dark side was put forward by Joyce and Robert Hogan, two leading psychologists who pioneered the use of personality assessments for employment screening.[11] Their model postulates the existence of sub-clinical (milder) versions of personality disorders in the workplace. These dysfunctional dispositions derail employees by harming their ability to build and maintain positive interpersonal relations with others, and they predict how people will respond in situations of stress or low self-monitoring. In fact, dark side tendencies are largely a coping mechanism for individuals who are faced with taxing environmental demands – usually other people.

There are two main circumstances under which the dark side of personality influences behaviours. First, when people are under pressure, because their cognitive resources are depleted and they have less energy to manage impressions and monitor their reputation. Secondly, when people are overly relaxed, which leads them to let their guard down and lessen social inhibitions. This situation sees people 'just being themselves', and is commonly observed when one is surrounded by close friends or relatives. Conversely, the dark side of personality will be less likely to emerge when people are trying to make a good impression, such as during first dates or job interviews. In these instances they will monitor their behaviour carefully, adhere to social protocols and suppress their undesirable and antisocial tendencies. Think about the typical questions we are asked during job interviews. What are your biggest strengths? Why did you apply for this job? Where do you see yourself in five years' time? Such questions are open invitations to present the most favourable and formidable aspects of our character while suppressing the toxic ones. Even when we are asked to describe our biggest defect, the idea is not for us to reveal our true faults, but to come across in a positive light – which explains why the most common answers are: 'I'm a perfectionist' or 'I'm not good at self-promotion'.

It is therefore no wonder that the dark side is hard to spot during interviews and other short-term interactions. There is abundant evidence for the fact that narcissists interview well, and the charisma of psychopaths is often disguised as talent, particularly when interviewers are distracted by candidates' social skills. These toxic individuals 'are not manifestly disagreeable or disruptive, but their valuation of reward and costs, willingness to overlook obligations and reciprocity, and lack of emotional commitment to others likely undermine the binding influence of interpersonal relationships'.[12] Luckily, there are better alternatives than interviews for detecting the dark side. Scientifically valid personality assessments can spot both clinical and subclinical features, even when respondents are trying to hide them. In fact, hundreds of academic studies have highlighted significant correlations between psychometrically assessed dark side tendencies and relevant work-related outcomes, from individual performance and good and bad organisational citizenship, to team and organisational effectiveness.

In addition, new tools have recently emerged to identify dark side characteristics in the wider population (not just job applicants) and naturalistic settings. One such tool is linguistic extraction software – text analytics – which can be used to infer dark side qualities based on the frequency and type of words people use on social media sites, such as Facebook or Twitter.[13] For example, narcissists are much more prone to using self-referential words, such as 'I', 'me' or 'mine'. People with psychopathic tendencies are more likely to swear, post negative comments and insult others – not to mention troll. Obsessional people may be expected to make fewer spelling mistakes, write more and use words such as 'completed' and 'correct'.[14]

Although there are multiple dark side qualities, three particular traits have received more attention than the rest, namely narcissism, psychopathy and Machiavellianism. These traits are usually referred to as the 'dark triad', and individuals who display them have a tendency to be more 'callous, selfish, and malevolent in their interpersonal dealings'.[15] . Likewise individuals with high scores on the dark triad also have an ability to exploit and manipulate people outside work-related domains, such as in personal relationships.[16] The next sections discuss the dark triad in more detail.

Narcissism: entitlement and megalomania at work

No other dark side trait has been discussed and researched as widely as narcissism. There are two main reasons for this. First, narcissism has wide organisational and career implications, ranging from entry-level employees to top leaders. And second, at any level of the organisational hierarchy, and in relation to any outcome (good or bad), the effects of narcissism are rather complex. The main reason for this is that narcissism is associated with both benefits and drawbacks, for the individual and for the organisation, and our fascination with narcissism as a topic of study is manifested by our attraction to narcissists themselves, who are commonly depicted as the main protagonists and heroes in books and movies.

Consider the case of Steve Jobs, one of the most widely discussed leaders of our time. Although Jobs deserves credit for creating one of the most successful companies in modern history, his personality was deplorable. Without attempting a full-blown psychological diagnosis of the man, it is clear that Jobs displayed many undesirable attributes, which cost him dearly at various points in his career. Jobs's personality profile was so dreadful that many psychologists and management experts have referred to Apple as a 'paradox'. How can someone as toxic and dysfunctional create and lead one of the top businesses and admired brands of all time? Many of Jobs's central personality qualities are emblematic of narcissism. In the words of Jef Raskin, who is best known for helping Jobs develop the first Macintosh computer:

> He is a dreadful manager ... I have always liked Steve, but I have found it impossible to work for him ... He acts without thinking and with bad judgment ... He does not give credit where due.[17]

The above passage highlights the maladaptive tendencies of narcissism at work. Impulsive and risky decision-making, a

propensity to belittle others and take credit for their achievements, and an inability to work well with people. In addition,
Jobs was famous for his reality distortion capacity, which
enabled him to see the world through a self-serving and deluded
prism. Freud referred to this characteristic of narcissism as
an ego-syntonic *Weltanschauung* or worldview – a tendency
to interpret things in a way that inflates one's ego, even if it
means being completely detached from reality. Narcissists' self-
centredness, sense of entitlement and arrogance all contribute
to the delusion that they are the centre of the universe and that
the world revolves around them. It is this disproportionate fan-
tasised talent that fuels narcissists' megalomaniac visions, which
are often effective at drawing in followers and captivating fans.
It should, however, be noted that for every narcissist who suc-
ceeds at executing his grandiose vision – e.g., Steve Jobs, Silvio
Berlusconi, even Donald Trump, who has got further than most
people would have thought – there are many more who fail
(think David Brent or Michael Scott in *The Office*).

The case of Donald Trump is particularly interesting
because it highlights the double-edged sword that is narcissism. On the one hand, narcissists display a wide range of
undesirable characteristics, such as arrogance, bluntness and
aggression. On the other hand, their self-confidence may be
accompanied by some charm, which enables them to captivate
audiences and in some cases even fake competence. As *The
Economist* recently noted:

> Trump is quick-witted, charismatic, and, during years as a
> reality television star, has built an outrageous public persona
> around his gargantuan ego. Uncertainty over whether this is
> self-parody or undiluted egomania is part of the act.[18]

Our adoration of narcissists is nothing new. In fact, research into narcissism stretches back to the very beginnings of scientific psychology in the late nineteenth century. The origin of the term is the Greek myth of Narcissus, a handsome hunter who, upon contemplating his own reflection in a pool, fell in love with himself. He remained fixated on his image and lost any interest in life, eventually dying in solitude, or drowning in his own reflection. Freud wrote extensively about narcissism, highlighting both its bright and dark sides.[19] In small amounts, narcissism may encourage prosocial behaviours, driving the desire to gain others' approval, respect and admiration. However, an overdose of narcissism leads to seeing other people merely as an audience and being too self-obsessed to pay attention to them. Freud saw such pathological narcissism as 'auto-eroticism', an antisocial form of self-love whereby individuals' need for self-admiration is too strong to allow them to care about others, unless they are devoted fans of them.

Whether at clinical or sub-clinical levels, the symptoms of narcissism are generally the same: 'a grandiose preoccupation with one's own self-importance; that is, the belief that one is special and more important than others . . . fantasies of unlimited success . . . hypersensitivity to criticism . . . entitlements . . . exploitativeness . . . and lack of empathy'.[20] In a normal world one would expect this profile to be associated with a wide range of negative career outcomes, but in the real world we live in the effects of workplace narcissism are rather more mixed. For instance, meta-analytic studies have found no association between narcissism and job performance,[21] job satisfaction,[22] or organisational citizenship.[23] However, under specific circumstances, narcissists may be expected to excel. For example, sales jobs requiring short-term impression management rather than long-term relationships; challenging tasks that enable individuals to impress an audience and gain status; or assignments that involve persuading others that one is creative. Interestingly, research shows that although narcissists are no more creative than average, they tend to succeed at faking creativity.[24] Furthermore, narcissists are more likely to emerge as leaders, and to become prominent politicians[25] and CEOs,[26] particularly in the US.

That said, narcissism has also been associated with a wide range of negative work outcomes, such as cheating, bullying, lying and white-collar crime.[27] Indeed, meta-analytic studies report a consistent positive association between narcissism and CWBs, so as narcissism scores increase people's tendency to harm others and the organisation also increases.[28] As Otto Kernberg, a prominent psychiatrist and influential thinker in this area, noted: narcissists are 'clearly exploitative and sometimes parasitic. It is as if they feel they have the right to control and possess others and to exploit them without feeling guilt feelings – and, behind a surface which very often is charming and engaging, one senses coldness and ruthlessness.'[29] It appears that the effects of narcissism on others are partly dependent on time. During early interactions, narcissists are likely to come across as confident, charming and entertaining, but as time goes by they are more likely to behave in hostile, cold and aggressive ways.[30]

This behavioural deterioration may be accelerated if narcissists are criticised. Indeed, narcissists react quite violently when they feel challenged or threatened, attacking their critics and belittling them.[31] As reviewers have noted, 'the workplace is full of potential self-esteem threats – poor performance reviews, competition from co-workers, difficulties mastering new technologies, failed projects – and highly narcissistic individuals are hypervigilant to perceived threats'.[32] In general, narcissists go from anger to aggression faster and more intensely than other individuals do. Such antisocial behaviours are often masked, particularly when narcissists engage in seemingly prosocial activities. In fact, narcissists may appear quite altruistic, particularly if this offers them an opportunity to enhance their reputation and acquire higher social status. This may explain the proliferation of self-made billionaires – e.g., Bill Gates, Mark Zuckerberg, Warren Buffett and Carlos Slim – who could all vie for the title of the most generous or philanthropic man in the world much like Rockefeller and Carnegie were competing for the same accolade during their time. Whilst some may be genuinely altruistic, many more couple their generosity with a clear history of being ruthless, mean and pathologically ambitious. Thus competitive philanthropy[33] may be understood as narcissistic altruism (or just narcissism) in disguise.

Psychopathy: social predators at work

Another main component of the dark triad is psychopathy, which is characterised by a

> lack of concern for both other people and social regulatory mechanisms, impulsivity, and a lack of guilt or remorse when their actions harm others. Interpersonally, [psychopaths] are often skilled impression managers, who are glib and charismatic.[34]

In its original conception, psychopathy – like narcissism – was regarded as a clinical trait. However, milder manifestations of this trait are widely represented in the normal population, particularly in the corporate world. In a famous lecture entitled 'The Predators among Us', Robert Hare observed that 'not all psychopaths are in prison – some are in the board room'. To some degree, Ponzi schemes, internet fraud, insider trading, corruption and embezzlement may all be attributed to psychopathic tendencies that are unleashed at work.[35] According to some estimates, as many as 3 million US employees may fit the criteria for fully fledged psychopathy,[36] though the number of individuals at work who display sub-clinical or minor psychopathic tendencies may be expected to be exponentially higher.

Despite the popular interest in workplace psychopathy, academic research on the topic is relatively scarce, and the effects of workplace psychopathy – both negative and positive – are often exaggerated.[37] Although preliminary research indicates that 360-degree assessments can be effectively used to identify workplace psychopaths,[38] they tend to overestimate the number of actual psychopaths at work, producing many false positives.[39] That said, reliable psychological tools can be used to assess both clinical and sub-clinical levels of psychopathy and predict a range of CWBs, even after normal or bright side personality characteristics are taken into account.[40]

Furthermore, studies that jointly examine 360s, psychological assessments and objective performance ratings report that psychopathic individuals are more commonly found in corporate settings than in the overall population, and that they tend to display a mix of good and bad characteristics at work: 'Psychopathy is positively associated with in-house ratings of charisma/presentation style (creativity, good strategic thinking and communication skills) but negatively associated with ratings of responsibility/performance (being a team player, management skills, and overall accomplishments).'[41] Psychopathic individuals are also more likely to gravitate towards entrepreneurial careers, not least because of their lower sensitivity to risk and potential failure.[42]

Laboratory studies evaluating emotional responses to others' emotions show that psychopathic individuals experience positive emotions when they see others suffering, and negative emotions when they don't.[43] Yet psychopathic individuals are often just less emotional than other people, which may confer an advantage on them when it comes to making decisions – emotionality tends to cloud judgement, and the ability to remain cold when making decisions, particularly concerning other people, can no doubt be beneficial.[44]

Psychopathic people are also more likely to be 'careerist', meaning they achieve success via non-performance-based activities.[45] As leaders, they are more likely to be hands-off managers and exercise a laissez-faire leadership style.[46] Unsurprisingly, teams led by more psychopathic individuals tend to be less engaged and more dissatisfied with their jobs.[47] Thus, although the motivations and behaviours associated with psychopathy may propel individuals to the higher echelons of an organisation, the organisation – and society – will pay a high price for it. Despite the potential benefits for the individual, one academic review concluded:

> Psychopathy is in fact a personality disorder characterised by lack of empathy and guilt, shallow affect, manipulation of other people and severe, premeditated and violent antisocial behaviour. Individuals with psychopathy generate substantial societal costs both as a direct financial consequence of their offending behaviour and lack of normal participation in working life, but also in terms of the emotional and psychological costs to their victims.[48]

Leonardo DiCaprio's portrayal of Jordan Belfort in *The Wolf of Wall Street* illustrates the bright and dark side of psychopathy well. A charismatic risk-taker with the ability to charm clients and employees, Belfort lacks any moral remorse and is clearly driven by a desire to break the rules and defy the law, so long as he can increase his own wealth and power. This type of personality is commonly found in successful criminals, from Al Capone to Pablo Escobar and 'El Chapo' Guzmán, who are often known for their ability to make cool-headed and calculated decisions even under extreme pressure. The fact that so many Hollywood movies have depicted successful psychopathic criminals is testimony to our fascination with their personality, which partly explains why they are able to get away with their crimes (at least for some time).

Machiavellianism: the dark side of political skills

Machiavellianism, the third component of the dark triad, has been studied extensively since the 1970s, not just in the context of management and organisational psychology, but also in relation to politics. If you watch *House of Cards*, think of Francis Underwood as the epitome of Machiavellianism: an astute political operator who experiences no guilt for manipulating and deceiving others; a cynical and ethically feeble player, exceedingly focused on his own interests and with very limited empathy for others. Machiavellians are particularly successful in highly political and informal settings, where their manoeuvres are relatively unconstrained by strict processes and bureaucratic barriers.

As the label indicates, the concept of Machiavellianism is inspired by the writings of Niccolò Machiavelli, in particular

The Prince.[49] In this book, which is an essay on the accumulation of political power, Machiavelli provides a succinct but compelling case for the effectiveness of leaders who are socially intelligent but unethical, focused on accomplishing their own personal goals even if it means harming others. Here are some of the key lessons from the book:

Everyone sees what you appear to be, few experience what you really are.

If an injury has to be done to a man it should be so severe that his vengeance need not be feared.

Of mankind we may say in general they are fickle, hypocritical, and greedy of gain.

In addition, there is Machiavelli's most famous lesson – 'the end justifies the means' – which cannot actually be found in any passage of the book, or in any of his other writings. However, the gist of this quote is emblematic of Machiavelli's thinking and captures the essence of the Machiavellian personality well. Being ruthless and inconsiderate, and using any resources you can – no matter how damaging this might be to others – to accomplish what you want. Unsurprisingly, there is a strong overlap between Machiavellianism and psychopathy, in that both are characterised by clear deficits in moral standards and empathy.[50] However, we generally tend to think of Machiavellians as more subtle and socially adept types than psychopaths. In that sense, it has been noted that Machiavellians may function effectively only if their intentions are backed up by social skills – otherwise they will come across as obnoxious and be socially ineffective.[51]

Moreover, given that Machiavellians tend to disrespect the key principles of social exchange – the rules that enable individuals to work together and form high-performing groups, organisations and societies – it can be expected that, sooner or later, most of them will struggle to achieve success in their careers. As academic reviews recently noted:

> Machiavellians' tendency to violate principles of social exchange [weakens] their connection to others ... and their pursuit of success via political machination rather than direct attention to their work may further degrade their performance.[52]

It is therefore not surprising that Machiavellian individuals are more likely to engage in CWBs, especially the type that concerns mistreatment and betrayal of work colleagues. For example, laboratory studies show that Machiavellians have crooked ethical views that lead to moral disengagement and justification of their corrupt and antisocial behaviours, so they are more likely to hurt others and not regret it.[53]

BEYOND THE DARK TRIAD

Narcissism, Machiavellianism and psychopathy are not the only dark side personality traits. The Hogan Dark Side framework outlines 11 career derailers that encapsulate socially undesirable and toxic behavioural tendencies that are manifested under too much or too little external pressure, e.g., under stress, when people's guards are down, or when they are just being themselves.[54] Table 2 overleaf provides a description of these traits, with the negative behavioural implications of high scores and the positive implications of low scores. These 11 derailers can be interpreted as milder – and more adaptive – manifestations of clinical personality disorders.[55]

Table 2: The Hogan Dark Side Personality Model

	Low scores	High scores
Moving Away from People		
Excitability	Cool headed even under pressure, consistent, calm.	Volatile, easily disappointed and lacking a clear sense of direction.
Scepticism	Positive and steady, cooperative and trusting.	Cynical, mistrusting and prone to holding grudges.
Cautiousness	Open, warm, willing to try new things and decisive.	Fearful, avoidant and unassertive.
Reserve	Socially engaging, sympathetic and relationship-oriented.	Distant, isolated, unsocial and seemingly indifferent to others.
Leisureliness	Cooperative, open to feedback and able to express feelings.	Passive-aggressive, irritated and prone to feeling unappreciated.
Moving Against People		
Boldness	Unassuming, self-aware and able to handle criticism.	Entitled, overconfident and hypercompetitive but deluded.

	Low scores	High scores
Mischievousness	Genuine, compliant, reliable and cooperative.	Risky, impulsive and manipulative (often with charm).
Colourfulness	Quiet, self-restrained, task-focused and low-key.	Easily distracted, dramatic and prone to enjoy the spotlight.
Imagination	Practical, open to others' ideas and realistic.	Eccentric, unconventional and lacking in follow-through.
Moving Towards People		
Diligence	Relaxed, forgiving, flexible and able to meet deadlines.	Obsessive, rigid, and prone to procrastinate and micromanage.
Dutifulness	Independent, self-sufficient and tough-minded.	Indecisive, ingratiating, and too eager to please and conform.

The Hogan model provides a comprehensive framework for predicting and explaining problematic behaviours at work. No matter how competent and capable people are, their bright side will be accompanied by a dark side, which contains the seeds of their potential destruction. The 11 derailers described above indicate precisely how people are likely to derail, in what ways they are likely to fail, and why they may struggle to build and maintain relationships. These derailers can be organised according to three major clusters, which correspond to Karen Horney's model of dysfunctional dispositions.[56] The *moving away from people* cluster concerns withdrawal from social interaction, a

disinvestment in relationships. The *moving against people* cluster concerns social intimidation, psychological dominance and
charming manipulation – a constellation that is often referred to
as the 'charisma cluster'. And *moving towards people* concerns
counterproductive conformity, dependence and an unhealthy
eagerness to please and impress others.

As you may have noted, the dark triad is represented in the
Hogan classifications, though under different labels. Boldness
represents narcissism; mischievousness represents psychopathy;
and Machiavellianism is represented by both scepticism and mischievousness, in that Machiavellians are cynical and politically
savvy psychopaths. Although Table 2 highlights only the pros
of low scores and the cons of high scores, there are also pros in
high scores and cons in low scores (more on this below). Finally,
the critical factor in determining whether these toxic assets will
lead to problem behaviours and become career derailers is the
degree to which individuals are self-aware and able to monitor
their behaviours and manage their reputation. Most normal
adults display at least two or three derailers, and it is unusual
to find individuals with none. However, even individuals with
all 11 derailers – and there are some! – may be able to operate
effectively at work, so long as they are able to tame their dark
side and keep their derailers in check.

It is not uncommon – particularly in the corporate world – to
find leaders with many elevated dark side scores who can, nonetheless, demonstrate excellent levels of performance: their teams
are engaged and their organisations profitable. This apparent
disconnect between leaders' dysfunctional potential and their
impressive accomplishments, a sort of overachievement, may be
most visible when one compares their strong 360-degree assessment results with their relatively 'poor' personality scores. Such

leaders are probably good at self-monitoring, avoiding stress or pressure and keeping their guard up in order to inhibit toxic or counterproductive behaviours at work. The Hogan model of dark side traits is the most widely used framework for identifying and mitigating leader derailers, and it is used particularly extensively in the context of coaching and development interventions. But what do we know about the dark side of leadership?

THE DARK SIDE OF LEADERSHIP

A great deal of research on the dark side of talent has been conducted on leaders. In this regard, academics have noted that the dark side encapsulates 'flawed interpersonal strategies that can degrade a leader's capacity to build and maintain high-performing teams'.[57] Furthermore, research indicates that leadership development interventions benefit from focusing on the dark side, in part because dark side traits predict how leaders respond to coaching and change interventions.[58] For example, studies suggest that narcissism consistently impairs leaders' ability to monitor their own performance, resulting in self-evaluations that are overly lenient or favourable. Indeed, even when narcissists are given objective feedback on their behaviour they still interpret events in a way that enables them to maintain a grandiose self-view.[59] Unsurprisingly, narcissistic leaders are also more likely to resist developmental and coaching interventions altogether.

Although narcissistic leaders are often regarded as visionary and inspirational, they tend to make more impulsive and risky decisions, causing their firms to perform in unpredictable and dangerous fashions.[60] Narcissists do excel at communicating bold and ambitious visions, which allows them to draw people in and shape followers' beliefs. These effects are particularly strong on people who are submissive and insecure – so, the opposite of a narcissist. Thus narcissism is most effective when it is manifested within 'toxic triangles', comprising a narcissistic leader, susceptible followers and contaminated environments.[61] Yet, despite their apparent leadership aura, narcissistic leaders are less interested in other people's feelings and less likely to engage in ethical behaviours, and not just when they are in corrupt settings. Studies report that narcissistic leaders are generally rated lower on integrity by others who know them well.[62]

Fortunately, narcissists' delusions of grandeur are rarely matched by others' views of them. Narcissists tend to provide higher self-ratings of leadership competence while actually being rated more poorly by others, and display more antisocial behaviours towards colleagues.[63] In addition, narcissistic leaders are more likely to react defensively to negative feedback, not least because it conflicts with their inflated, albeit superficial, self-concept.[64] There is arguably no better way to spot a narcissist than to question his talents and see how he responds – the more self-obsessed and deluded a leader is, the angrier this will make him. And when CEOs are more narcissistic they tend to pay unreasonably high sums for company acquisitions, presumably a reflection of their egos and sheer overconfidence.[65]

Despite these adverse effects, dark side tendencies are often instrumental in propelling individuals to leadership positions. Indeed, there is no shortage of evidence for the positive effects of undesirable qualities on individual career success. For example, studies have shown that 1 standard deviation decrease in agreeableness – a trait that is negatively related to narcissism, Machiavellianism and psychopathy – is associated with a 2.8 per cent increased probability of being a manager.[66] In other words, the less you care about other people, the more likely you are to be chosen to manage people! This finding is also supported by large-scale meta-analytic studies showing that agreeableness is positively correlated with leader effectiveness, but negatively correlated with leader emergence.[67] Other studies suggest that moderate elevations in dark side trait scores may make leaders more effective than extremely low or extremely high scores. For instance, leaders who are very disagreeable may tyrannise their subordinates; but leaders who are very agreeable may be too nice and conflict averse to confront poor performers and deal with controversial issues.[68]

Studies have also linked dark side personality traits to transformational leadership – a leadership style displayed by individuals who are generally visionary, warm, inspirational and charismatic. Some derailers, such as the colourful trait, which concerns being eccentric and attention-seeking, are positively related to transformational leadership, not least because people who possess them tend to seek and attract others' attention, and form relationships quickly. However, in the long run colourful leaders are less capable of being able to form and maintain effective teams, and their likelihood of derailing is high.[69] Other dark side traits, such as being reserved and cautious, have been negatively linked to transformational leadership. Interestingly, inspirational leaders are also more likely to be mischievous (Hogan's term for psychopathic).[70]

THE BRIGHT SIDE OF THE DARK SIDE

Dark side attributes are almost universally undesirable, but that doesn't mean that they are always disadvantageous. Most dark side qualities can be interpreted as a degree of deviation from otherwise normal traits, which explains their adaptive side. For example, there is a clear Darwinian element to the dark triad, as narcissism, psychopathy and Machiavellianism evolved to facilitate self-serving strategies and manipulation tactics that enhance competition at the expense of collaboration. Although in the long-term altruism, compassion and cooperation favour group survival, in the short-term there are advantages for individuals who can deceive and influence others, and focus more on their own than other people's well-being. In order to live in groups we must have some rules, and for groups to function effectively it is essential that most people play by those rules. That said, in any group a minority of people will benefit from violating the rules and taking shortcuts.

Consider the case of Argentina, the country I was born in. At the individual level, Argentines are fairly smart and educated. However, they are also known for being cheeky and cunning, and a cultural characteristic of Argentines is what's called *viveza criolla* – being streetwise and willing to bend the rules. Although this may normally be considered adaptive on an individual level, the fact that so many people are too astute to follow rules has created perpetual social chaos, and Argentina has been declining more or less steadily since the 1910s. In contrast, people in Singapore may be considered social geeks: they are introverted, studious and so respectful of the rules that they are hyper-conformist and individually unimaginative. Yet, unsurprisingly, these collectivistic tendencies have turned Singapore into one of the most prosperous and admirable nations of the past 50 years. To be clear, Singaporeans may have a dark side, too – being overly cautious, diligent and reserved – however, the absence of dark triad traits seems logically connected to the nation's achievements, as much as the presence of dark side traits is to Argentina's failures. Importing a few Argentines to Singapore would probably not be enough to corrupt the country, though one would expect those crooked imports to thrive there. Evolutionary psychologists refer to this phenomenon as 'negative frequency-dependence selection': the fitness advantage of traits will tend to increase when those traits are less common, even if they are generally negative.[71] Greedy bastards, for instance, will do much better when they are surrounded by honest altruists rather than by other greedy bastards.

Studies evaluating the dark side of managers' personalities report that several derailers are positively associated with career success, including job performance.[72] For example, narcissism plays a key role in propelling individuals to leadership positions. First, by increasing people's motivation for being in charge and occupying positions of power, creating a deep yearning for power.[73] And second, by helping individuals *seem* more leader-like. Not just in the US, where hubris and excessive self-belief are particularly rewarded, but throughout the world lay perceptions of leadership are increasingly narcissistic. For all the talk of humility and altruism as essential ingredients of leadership, the truth is that people are generally perceived as being leadership material when they display confidence, rather than competence, as self-belief, extraversion and charisma are generally perceived as solid indicators of leadership potential. In reality, however, these attributes only help individuals *emerge* as leaders; they have little to do with actual leadership effectiveness. There is no doubt that narcissists are able to create positive impressions on others and come across as leaders even when they lack actual talent for leadership.

Clearly, narcissism helps individuals appear more competent, not least because they spend more time talking about themselves and in self-promotion.[74] This is particularly useful when talent is evaluated via interviews or other situations that involve short-term interpersonal interactions. Being self-deceived or deluded about one's skills and abilities is advantageous because it enables one to fake competence to others: when you are unaware of your faults, it is easier to hide your insecurities from others; and when you think you are really talented, it is easier to fool others into believing that you have some talent. Thus narcissists fake talent in the same way that good salesmen sell bad products – by convincing themselves first that what they have is amazing. Likewise, studies show that although narcissists are no more creative than average, they are generally better at *seeming* creative to others.[75] In short, fooling yourself is an effective strategy for fooling others, and narcissists are good at fooling themselves. Naturally, in a world where people were capable of spotting talent – and distinguishing between confidence and competence – this advantage would disappear. Sadly, though, we are easily conned by people who have conned themselves.

Narcissism has also been found to confer some advantages in relation to entrepreneurship. In particular, narcissistic individuals are more likely to have entrepreneurial intentions, not least because of their unrealistic and overly optimistic hopes of success. Many entrepreneurs are motivated by narcissistic desires – e.g., to be the next Warren Buffett, Bill Gates, or Estée Lauder. On the one hand, this combination of reality distortion and megalomania is problematic because it propels individuals to career choices where the probability of success is less than 1 per cent (and much lower than in traditional employment alternatives, at least in the industrialised world). On the other hand, overconfidence will pay off for a minority of individuals when they do succeed, not to mention the social benefits of having a few individuals achieve *big* levels of success.

For example, a large number of people around the world benefit from the .0001 per cent of Silicon Valley entrepreneurs who accomplish their mega-ambitious entrepreneurial intentions, while those who fail pay the price themselves, implying no cost for the collective. Survey data from the Global Entrepreneurship Monitor (GEM), the most important source of data for global start-up and self-employment activity, indicate that self-perceived talent is a major driver of entrepreneurial intentions.[76] Thus, if you feel that you can be the next Elon Musk or Jeff Bezos you will be more likely to take the risk of launching a business, even though such delusions of grandeur will most likely lead to failure. What is ironic is that this hubristic overconfidence that characterises the entrepreneurial mind-set occasionally ends up benefitting others. So, what begins as a narcissistic dream may create progress and innovation to others.

Narcissism is not the only dark side trait that is often rewarded in work settings. Machiavellian people have a wider repertoire of social skills, and are capable of manipulating and influencing others by pretending to agree with them and hiding their true intentions. Hence they have been referred to as social chameleons.[77] This enables Machiavellians to form powerful social networks and gain power and respect while they pursue their own agendas. Machiavellianism is also associated with higher levels of cynicism and distrust, and this is particularly useful during negotiations or when dealing with individuals who are themselves Machiavellian.[78] For instance, HR and talent management professionals with certain Machiavellian tendencies are more likely to be immune to the claims of snake-oil salesmen and consultants who attempt to sell them bogus services. Conversely people with very low Machiavellian scores may believe everything they hear and pay a high price for their prosocial naivety. Furthermore, more than any other dark side trait, Machiavellianism also confers the advantage of hiding the undesirable qualities associated with that trait, whereas other dark side attributes tend to be more visible and explicit.

There is also a bright side to psychopathy. Research has shown that psychopathic individuals may benefit from their low empathy levels: when you don't care about others, you are able to make more ruthless decisions and prioritise business interests over people issues.[79] As scholars have noted:

> individuals who are psychopathic in their personal orientation prosper in business and corporate settings, particularly if their work requires a rational, emotionless behavioural style; a consistent focus on achievement even if that achievement comes at the cost of harm to others; a willingness to take risks; and the social skills of the charismatic.[80]

Studies have also examined the prevalence of dark side personality traits across different occupational families.[81] The results suggest that some derailers, such as diligence, are much more common than others, such as dutifulness or imagination, and that there are clearly some job-related derailers – traits that are much more likely to be manifested in certain careers than in others. For example, high scores on excitable, cautious and dutiful are much more likely to be seen in the legal sector, whereas high scores on colourful and low scores on imaginative are more commonly seen in retail.

Following the same logic, one may also conceive of situations where lacking dark side qualities is disadvantageous. Consider the case of a person with high leadership aspirations but very low narcissism scores; or someone with very low Machiavellianism scores who is tasked with managing a highly political and corrupt organisation. Thus there are multiple career implications for all dark side attributes, both positive and negative. The critical point is to become aware of these implications, and to avoid focusing only on one's strengths: 'Nothing might spell our doom faster than failing to appreciate our limitations.'[82]

CHAPTER 7

The future of talent

This chapter discusses emerging trends in talent identification, speculating about how technology may reshape talent management practices in years to come. Although the growing complexity of workplace experiences has been grossly exaggerated, generational changes in personality and the widespread penetration of technology in every aspect of life are likely to reshape the talent landscape. Most notably, a majority of millennial employees will cause overall levels of narcissism and self-entitlement at work to rise, which will make self-awareness – especially awareness of one's limitations – more important (and rare) than ever. At the same time, two other competencies – curiosity and entrepreneurship – will be pivotal to enable employees to be autonomous learners and value-generators at work. Thus individuals who are modest and self-critical, capable of exploiting opportunities that drive innovation, and possess a hungry mind will be in increasing demand. A final change discussed in this chapter concerns the transition to the talent-on-demand economy, where organisations are able to exploit technology to attract key people on a project basis, and most individuals are assessed without going through a formal selection process.

* * *

What might the future of talent bring? When trying to answer this question, there are three key factors to consider; these factors are likely to reshape the landscape of talent in the next few years. First, the millennial mind-set. In particular, the alarming scientific evidence for the skyrocketing levels of narcissism among generation Y, and what that implies for organisations. How can we manage employees when they are increasingly self-centred and entitled? And, more importantly – since they will, sooner or later, be in charge – how will they manage and lead others? Second, the growing importance of three critical work competencies, namely self-awareness (to help people make better career decisions and develop their talents), curiosity (to navigate the sea of information we live in, never ceasing to be learning animals, and to handle the challenges of a global and complex world), and entrepreneurship (to turn stagnant ideas into innovative products and services, and to exploit opportunities in the face of crisis). The third key factor is the rise of the reputation economy, where each member of the workforce is worth only as much as their reputation – the collective and public impression we have of their talent and capabilities. Imagine a world in which everybody's identity is made up not only of legal documents, but some sort of portable talent passport, comprising his past career achievements as well as a future-oriented career potential score. These metrics could be curated by independent talent judges (whether human or otherwise) and owned by employees: it would be the talent equivalent of an eBay seller rating or an Uber driver rating, and not necessarily limited to specific jobs. Such changes will require new technologies for identifying talent and potential, but if integrated properly they will shake up the talent identification industry by closing the gap between supply and demand and by increasing people's career fit and productivity, to everybody's benefit. In other words, we can expect these changes to make the employment market more efficient.

THE COMPLEXITY DELUSION

Niels Bohr, the celebrated quantum physicist, once noted that 'it's very difficult to make predictions – especially about the future'. In reality, making predictions is easy, but getting them right is not. It is therefore true, as Abraham Lincoln observed, that 'the best way to predict the future is to invent it'. With this in mind I shall approach this chapter not so much with the goal of forecasting what the future of talent may be but by making the case for what it *should* be. Around 40 per cent of this chapter is about forecasting, and 60 per cent about prescribing, though it will not be so easy to determine which part is which, not least because predictions and prescriptions originate from the same phenomena: past and present talent management practices.

When speculating about the future of work, it is quite common to overemphasise the impact of technology and globalisation to point out that the world has never been so complex and unpredictable. Consultants and thought gurus love to talk about a world that is 'VUCA' (volatile, uncertain, complex and ambiguous), but there is not much hard evidence for the idea that, in the experience of employees, jobs are systematically more VUCA today than they were in the 1950s, the 1850s, or 500 BC. Of course, today's technologies are much more sophisticated than yesterday's, but as technology advances the complexity of experience and the experience of complexity tend to decline. For example, email is technologically more complex than traditional post, but it is a lot easier for humans to communicate via email than by post. Along the same lines, mobile dating apps are technologically more complex than nightclubs and bars, yet it is arguably simpler, less ambiguous and more prescriptive to approach someone via Tinder than in person in a bar. The odds of success are not just bigger, they can also be quantified more accurately.

It should also be noted that, though the average person from the eighteenth century would struggle to adapt to a modern work environment, it would be equally difficult for our contemporaries to adapt to the demands of the eighteenth century: more physical strain, more reliance on knowledge (consider how ignorant you feel today when you cannot access Google or Wikipedia), and no attention to meaning or purpose. In contrast, the average professional working in an industrialised market today expects to be spoiled with a career rather than a job, and may refuse to work for employers who don't attend to their work–life balance needs, or who fail to provide them with a meaningful sense of purpose.

Although we have a natural tendency to forget the past and treat the present as completely unprecedented, everything we say about technology today has been said thousands of times before, even in times of far less technological development. In other words, we have a tendency to see our present circumstances as totally new even though they aren't. Unfortunately, our failure to examine the past makes it hard to understand the present, and harder still to predict the future: if you don't know how you got here, you surely won't know where you are going to end up next.

Perhaps the thought that we are living in a unique, sophisticated and challenging era makes us feel better about ourselves – it provides certain narcissistic reassurance. There is even a specific cognitive bias, called the Travis syndrome, to describe our tendency to overrate the significance of the present vis-à-vis the past.

According to the United Nations, there are around 240 million migrant workers in the world today. These are people who are working outside their country of birth, either legally or illegally. Although this figure may seem large, it is a small fraction (less than a tenth) of the 4 billion workers who inhabit the world today. For all the talk of globalisation as a recent phenomenon, it has a very long history, with big movements of people being quite common in ancient Greece, Mesopotamia, Egypt and Rome, not to mention Genghis Khan's expansion of the Mongol empire into Asia and Europe eight centuries ago. Not only did these places attract larger proportions of migrants than today's megalopolises, they were also less hospitable to them. Moreover, the globalised cities of the past were almost certainly more VUCA than today's megalopolises – e.g., New York, London, Hong Kong – as people had to travel much longer to reach them, with less knowledge of what to expect, and lower prospects of success, particularly if we take into consideration that survival rates were significantly lower. Likewise, today the career prospects of Syrian refugees are more VUCA than those of Ivy League graduates, but less VUCA than those in equivalent circumstances two or three centuries ago, particularly if they are educated.

Thus, as technological advances have gained in complexity,

they have in fact made most areas of life simpler and more predictable, much like trains and cars have made travel more convenient, and less complex, than when we relied on horses. We can now access information about products, services and people before we interact with them in the physical world. Experience is now imagined before it is real. Moreover, the distributed knowledge of the world can be retrieved in just a few seconds' browsing the internet. And the amount of data available to track and predict individual and collective human behaviours is truly unprecedented. All these systems are no doubt complex compared to the technologies of decades ago, which is why they have simplified our adaptation to the world.

Ray Kurzweil, the restless polymath who is Google's chief of engineering, regards technology as the final stage in human evolution. In his view, we have reached the limits of biological evolution, so we can only evolve further by merging, and becoming one, with technology.[1] Just like our ancestors enhanced their adaptation to the world – and evolved – by manipulating fire, using combat and hunting tools and inventing the wheel, digital technologies have enabled us to become even smarter than other species, and outperform fellow humans with no access to those technologies (e.g., fast wi-fi, the internet, computers and smart-phones). But the key reason for this is that technology makes life simpler for us, so we can accomplish the same tasks by exerting less effort, or achieve greater results if we exert the same effort. In short, technological innovations are making us smarter – or at least faster – so long as we can rely on technology. The world would be more VUCA only if we suddenly had to stop relying on technology. When systems are down and computers say no, it is only then that we experience the limits of our human capabilities and the VUCA aspects of our world become apparent.

THE MILLENNIAL MIND

Although our adaptation to the world is increasingly mediated by technology, the essence of work is still about interacting with people rather than machines, even if such interactions are facilitated by machines. It therefore makes sense to evaluate changes, not just in technology, but also in people. This issue is often addressed by examining generational changes in talent. More specifically, how will the next generation of employees and employers impact the world of work? How will they interact? How should they be managed? How can we engage them? How will they manage and lead?

In the next decade, millennials will represent the majority of the workforce in virtually all parts of the world. This is already true for large multinationals, where the proportion of millennials will increase to around 75 per cent in the next 10 years. It is therefore unsurprising that discussions about millennials are now ubiquitous. Unfortunately, however, such discussions are rarely supported by data, with most arguments being based on intuitive observations about people in their 20s or 30s, as opposed to systematic and representative comparisons between actual generations (e.g., how 20-year-olds today differ from 20-year-olds in the 1990s, 1970s, or 1950s).

Generational changes are smaller than people think. People just don't change that much from one generation to the next, or even within the scope of several generations. If you think that human evolution has taken place over 2 million years, you will realise that a 100-year timeframe is pretty insignificant. This is also consistent with the idea that, from a broad psychological perspective, our needs and behaviours have always been and meant the same, even if they are now expressed through Snapchat or LinkedIn rather than primitive hunter–gatherer rituals. Our desire to get along, get ahead and find meaning has always dictated the grammar of social interactions, no matter how those particular interactions are manifested.

With this in mind, it is astonishing that in the past century psychological studies have documented significant increases in attitudes and values related to narcissism, as well as psychological measures of narcissism. The bulk of this scientific research has been conducted by Jean Twenge,[2] a social psychologist and the author of *Generation Me*, a magnificent book on the subject. These increases in egocentric and entitled attitudes and behaviours are particularly noticeable in millennials, the most narcissistic generation to date. For example, representative studies on American college students estimate that up to 15 per cent of students in their 20s now meet the criteria for narcissistic personality disorder or display pronounced narcissistic traits.[3] Although robust historical data are harder to obtain, the figure was probably under 5 per cent just a couple of decades ago. Consider the fact that in the 1950s only 12 per cent of students described themselves as 'an important person'; by the 1980s the figure had increased to 80 per cent. Furthermore, Twenge's data highlight an even steeper increase in narcissism between the early 1980s and the mid-2000s, particularly in women, who traditionally have been less narcissistic than men. This explains why some leading psychiatrists have made the case for reconceptualising narcissism as a normal trait rather than a psychiatric disorder.[4] It is not sufficiently rare now to be considered a clinical or abnormal personality trait.

Although America is more narcissistic than other countries – after all, it is the nation that gave us Hollywood, Facebook, Paris Hilton, Kanye West and Kim Kardashian – increases in entitlement and egotistical traits have been reported for a wide range of countries. For example, large-scale studies in China have found generational increases in narcissism for millennials, and that such increases are particularly pronounced in wealthier, more educated and urban families. Of course, this may also be the product of China's one-child policy (introduced around 1980) as only children are more likely to be spoiled and self-centred. By the same token, individualistic countries are generally more narcissistic than collectivistic societies.[5] Still, it is a fairly universal feature of millennials to be more entitled, less interested in others, and more spoiled than previous generations.[6]

Importantly, these effects are found even when studies are able to control for the influence of age on generational or cohort effects. In other words, it is not only true that college students or youngsters are more narcissistic than adults, but also that millennials (of all ages) are generally more narcissistic than previous generations were at the same age.[7] The key question, therefore, is not whether millennials are more narcissistic, but what implications this has, in particular for work-related practices and talent management. In other words, what does it mean that the dominant generation of our time sees itself as extraordinary and destined for greatness?

To answer this question, it is useful to return to Freud's idea that a universal challenge for humans is to manage the tension between our selfish desire to get ahead and our prosocial desire to get along.[8] In Freud's view, this tension is often too challenging for people to solve by themselves, which is why people need leadership. That is, Freud argued that the fundamental role of a leader is to squash people's individualistic and self-centred tendencies, so that they can shift from getting ahead to getting along, and understand that they will achieve what they want only if they are first able to cooperate with others. What this means is that leaders are largely responsible for inhibiting the narcissistic drives of their followers or subordinates, so that they can be more collaborative and cooperative and able to work in teams. Clearly, achieving this goal will be much harder if individuals are naturally more narcissistic. A leader in charge of egotistical people, who are mostly in it for themselves and so focused on their own presumed greatness that they are incapable of appreciating others, will face a much bigger challenge than a leader who is responsible for individuals who are more selfless and other-oriented. Thus generational increases in narcissism will harm our ability to work in teams, and since every significant accomplishment of civilisation is the result of coordinated team effort, the prospect of a more narcissistic and individualistic society is indeed rather bleak.

That said, three critical competencies may mitigate the adverse effect that narcissism will have on the workplace, namely:

1. *Self-awareness*, which is the capacity to translate reputation (how others see us) into identity (how we see ourselves).

2. *Curiosity*, which is the capacity to transform information into knowledge.

3. *Entrepreneurship*, which is the capacity to turn creativity into innovation. When manifested inside large or traditional organisations it is called intrapreneurship.

Self-awareness: an antidote to narcissistic hubris

Self-awareness, defined as the ability to understand how others see you, has always mattered, in particular for leaders. But in a world where self-delusion and overconfidence are the norm, those capable of understanding their limitations will have a particular advantage. The only way individuals can improve in their jobs is by understanding how they affect others, and since leaders' behaviour affects a large number of people, self-awareness is pivotal in leaders.[9] The more self-obsessed people are, the less likely they are to respond positively to feedback, because being too self-focused distracts you from paying attention to your actual performance.[10]

Since managers, millennials and males are more likely to be narcissistic, and more prone to over-estimating their intelligence, creativity and leadership potential,[11] interventions aimed at developing talent must help recipients better understand their limitations. There is therefore no better antidote to narcissistic hubris than a reality check, and self-awareness can provide it. Studies indicate that leaders who are more self-aware – those whose self-views are closely aligned to other people's views on them, such as in 360 assessments – tend to be more effective.[12] Furthermore, leaders who are more self-critical are seen as more self-aware by their peers and subordinates.[13] And when leaders lack self-awareness, their dark side tendencies become more toxic and destructive, not least because they are unable to recognise and inhibit them.[14]

The situation is no different when it comes to entry-level employees, as meta-analytic studies show that self-ratings of performance are only weakly related to supervisors' ratings, not least because employees are too lenient in their self-evaluations of performance.[15] To make matters worse, such delusions of grandeur are often deceptive, leading to public manifestations of confidence that are frequently interpreted as competence. Conversely, when people are self-critical and aware of their limitations, they are less likely to fake competence, either deliberately or inadvertently. It follows that self-awareness is beneficial not just for the individual, but also for the group. The more self-aware employees are, the more likely they will be to perceive gaps between their actual and desired competence levels, and in closing these gaps they develop actual, rather than self-perceived, talents, which is advantageous to the organisation. It is, of course, possible that self-awareness does not translate into development and talent gains. For instance, in harshly self-critical employees, awareness of their limitations may be self-defeating and cause them to give up. Yet it is hard to conceive of any effective developmental intervention that is not rooted in self-awareness. To be clear, self-awareness may not be sufficient, but it is nonetheless necessary, for upgrading one's talent. A recent survey of global executive coaching practices found that self-awareness is the most sought-after competency (ahead of people skills, empathy and listening skills) in CEO coaching programmes.[16]

Curiosity: the importance of a hungry mind

Curious individuals have hungry minds. They are thirsty for knowledge and feel a strong urge to close the gap between what they know and what they don't.[17] This requires being aware of one's limitations and knowledge gaps, or what psychologists refer to as 'meta-cognition' (knowing what you know). When curious individuals feel that they don't know something, they feel uncomfortable, which motivates them to learn and acquire more knowledge. Thus, curiosity involves the ability to identify knowledge gaps and translate information into knowledge in order to close those knowledge gaps. In addition, curious people are more likely to expose themselves to novel information or knowledge that challenges their own beliefs. That is, they are more open to new ideas and capable of questioning their own beliefs.[18] This makes curiosity a self-perpetuating quality: on the one hand, it drives people to know more; on the other hand, it also motivates people to distrust what they know, propelling them to know even more. It is therefore clear that curiosity is a strong driver of expertise and a key predictor of what employees are likely to learn on and off the job. Eric Schmidt notes that a major pillar in Google's recruitment strategy is to hire 'learning animals', while recruiters for accounting giant EY observe that 'to be a standout, candidates need to demonstrate technical knowledge in their discipline, but also a passion for asking the kind of insightful questions that have the power to unlock deeper insights and innovation for our clients'.[19]

From an evolutionary perspective, curiosity is linked to superior adaptation, because it increases an individual's desire to explore new environments, which enables curious individuals to find resources before their peers do. Its neurological basis is associated with the experience of arousal in the presence of novelty, and pleasure (relief) when novelty becomes familiar.[20] The idea that 'curiosity kills the cat' is inconsistent with the reproductive and survival benefits conferred by curiosity. For example, the American black bear has survived most of its evolutionary rivals by being more curious than them.[21]

The origins of human curiosity are perceptual, and the preference for novel stimuli is already expressed in some individuals during infancy. Some babies attend to novel stimuli, such as unfamiliar objects or strangers, for longer, and their psychological connection with such novelties is experienced as positive affect. These early infant preferences predispose humans towards childhood and adult curiosity,[22] which explains why curious individuals are also more likely to be sensation-seekers, enjoy high-adrenalin experiences and have higher boredom susceptibility.[23] Accordingly, brain imaging studies demonstrate that curious individuals experience a sort of mental high in anticipation of knowledge. Their brains are more excited and restless until they can find the answer to unanswered questions.[24] In other words, curious people are addicted to learning.

Although psychologists have long argued that curiosity plays a pivotal role in the development of children's intellect,[25] society and education often inhibit our curiosity. Indeed, adult intellectual development is largely conservative, for its goal is to preserve what we already know and take things for granted. In that sense, a curious adult is a child who has survived.

All this is particularly salient in modern, real-world settings, which require learning, adaptation and performance in the presence of complex and intellectually demanding problems. For instance, studies have shown that curiosity does not just improve students' academic performance,[26] it also helps employees adapt to novel and changeable work environments, mostly by promoting information-seeking behaviours.[27] Furthermore, a recent investigation demonstrated that curiosity predicts higher levels of job performance even when individuals' personality and intelligence are taken into account; this indicates that curiosity has unique and novel paths to career success, not explained by other, traditional, assessments.[28]

When organisations hire curious individuals, they acquire employees who are dispositionally inclined to seek out challenging activities, as well as more interested in absorbing knowledge. This disposition is not only a key determinant of learning and expertise, it is also linked to higher levels of engagement and subjective well-being, for curious people are more intrinsically motivated and able to find meaning in complex and challenging work roles.[29]

However, despite the benefits of curiosity, the quest for knowledge also comes at a price, namely slower decision-making. Indeed, the ability to find quick solutions to a problem is a short-term advantage that compromises long-term learning, so there is a natural tension between thinking fast – thinking without thinking – and deep inquisitiveness.[30] In a world characterised by information overload, ignoring information may be as adaptive as paying attention to it. In that sense, the capacity to translate information into *valuable* knowledge may require the ability to suppress one's appetite for empty and meaningless (but also addictive) information.

Today, we are constantly bombarded by captivating ads and stories, but that type of content is not intellectually nutritious for our hungry mind. While it is tempting to spend our evenings and weekends reading the *Daily Mail* online or watching the Kardashians – i.e., popular culture and trash TV have higher sensory appeal than Goethe and Dostoyevsky – this type of information is to curiosity what refined sugar and fast food are to our diet. Our evolutionary ancestors did not live in a world of food oversupply, and they were physically active all day. Their survival was facilitated by an instinctual tendency to maximise calorific intake and minimise calorific output. Although we have inherited this predisposition from them, it is no longer adaptive when the presence of food is abundant and our physical mobility is limited. But self-control and willpower can defy our instincts in order to protect our health. By the same token, curiosity can defy our natural tendency to attend to and consume novel, sensational information by focusing our learning efforts on more nutritious content. Distraction is the fast food of the mind. Superior animals spend more time on exploration than entertainment and relaxation.[31] Curious societies will outperform the rest, and cognitively complex jobs will be less likely to be automated.

Entrepreneurship: the engine of organisational growth

Although most people think of entrepreneurship as an occupational category or job status (concerning people who start or own a business), a more effective way to conceptualise entrepreneurship is as a set of behaviours that, even if displayed within someone else's organisation (rather than the business one founded), is the catalyst of growth and innovation. As experts have noted: 'a better way to think of entrepreneurship is in terms of an activity or a set of related activities that contribute to growth and innovation. Thus an entrepreneur is simply someone who engages in these activities, regardless of whether they have or not started their own business.'[32]

In the future, more and more organisations will be interested in acquiring entrepreneurial talent. They will need people who can generate creative ideas and, more importantly, turn those ideas into actual innovations. Such individuals are sometimes described as 'intrapreneurs', for intrapreneurship is the corporate or organisational manifestation of entrepreneurship.[33] This interest is based on three major reasons.

First, an understanding that innovation is critical to their long-term success and survival. This idea is captured in well-known management sayings, such as 'innovate or die', or 'disrupt or be disrupted'.[34] In other words, it is not possible for businesses to stay static for a long time – they either go forward or go under. Therefore innovation is a critical engine of growth and organisational effectiveness. Companies need to keep finding ways of doing things better, to come up with new ideas, and better services and products, as well as more effective internal processes.

Second, a realisation that, though innovation leads to growth, growth inhibits innovation. In other words, as companies become bigger and more successful, they also become victims of their own success, shifting focus from disruption, risk and experimentation to maintenance, conservation and bureaucracy. This is true even for some of the organisations commonly hailed as the most innovative companies in the world. Consider the fact that Microsoft, Amazon, Google, Facebook and Apple acquired hundreds of start-ups in the past decade alone – because they are now too busy managing their own success to innovate. Their major strategy is to innovate via acquisitions, not only by acquiring innovative and creative products and ideas (and eliminating potential competitors), but also by incorporating new entrepreneurial talent. Unfortunately, most founders fail to fit into the culture of the acquiring company, so they usually leave shortly after the acquisition.

The third reason is an understanding that the key jobs of the future may be hard to predict. Indeed, it is already hard to determine objectively what the critical positions of growth and productivity are in any large firm today, but predicting what may happen in five or ten years is even harder. Likewise, innovation is, by definition, unpredictable. To be new and useful, ideas, products and services must be hard, if not impossible, to forecast, and all innovation requires many tries and a high degree of experimentation to work – trial and error, rejection and repetition. That said, one can bet on some individuals to be the key drivers of innovation in the future. In other words, it is hard to know what shape creativity will take in the future, but some individuals stand a much higher probability of being responsible for it than others. Through our own research[35] we identified four key characteristics that highly entrepreneurial individuals display:

- *Creativity*: the capacity to generate ideas that are both novel and useful. Contrary to popular belief, creative ideas are not the product of random or serendipitous moments, such as an apple falling on Newton's head while he was taking a nap. Instead, creative people have lots of ideas all the time, and while most ideas may not be very original or useful, quantity does lead to quality.[36] Although creativity depends on a wide range of factors, it is largely enhanced when individuals have higher levels of intelligence and expertise. Furthermore, creative individuals are generally more open to new experiences, which makes them more dissatisfied with the status quo. That's why they tend to suppress fewer unusual ideas, even when they may seem ridiculous or inappropriate. It is this combination of domain-specific knowledge, non-conformity, eccentricity and ability that provides the ideal context for creative ideas to be generated more frequently.[37]

- *Opportunism*: the tendency to spot gaps in the market and interpret events as opportunities. It is not about being in the right place at the right time, but being more receptive and sensitive to possibilities. Typically, opportunism requires a good degree of expertise in a given field, as well as the capacity to see problems from a slightly different perspective. In fact, people who see opportunities often suffer from a certain degree of reality distortion or optimistic bias, so they are more likely to focus on potential rewards and ignore potential threats. This perception of the world generates enthusiasm and excitement, though rarely for long as new opportunities will keep emerging and competing with older ones. In that sense opportunistic individuals are prone to display a pro-change bias – the belief that new is always better than old and should therefore replace it.[38]

- *Proactivity*: the tendency to follow through and get ideas implemented and executed. Persistence, coordination, organisation and drive are needed to get any creative idea executed, and the main problem organisations face today isn't a shortage of ideas, but a lack of mechanisms – including people and teams – to turn those ideas into actual innovations (e.g., products, services and solutions). Thus proactive individuals follow through, find ways to navigate the bureaucratic and risk-averse processes that resist innovation in big corporations, and make things happen.

- *Vision*: the ability to understand the big picture, find a long-term strategy or mission and sell it to others. This is the critical difference between an ephemeral innovation and long-lasting success. To understand why something matters, and be able to explain that to others in order to enlist their efforts and support in an entrepreneurial venture, leaders need vision. Ultimately, most visions are associated with a strong desire to change the status quo and improve the world – the desire to cause positive change and progress.

Crucially, this set of competencies is found not only in traditional entrepreneurs but also among intrapreneurs, so the attributes that help individuals transform creative ideas into actual innovations are the same whether they have started their own business or are employed by other people, even in large and traditional organisations. In the future, entrepreneurial people will be an attractive talent commodity for all organisations, not just ambitious and innovative start-ups. They will be better able to adapt to change and to turn creative ideas into innovative products and services. This will make them a key driver of growth and progress. Moreover, when entrepreneurial people recognise and exploit opportunities, they close the gap between demand and supply, making markets more efficient (e.g., Uber, Airbnb and OpenTable). If organisations can attract, identify and engage entrepreneurial employees, and turn them into intrapreneurs, they will be more likely to innovate and grow. If they don't, they will probably stagnate and die.

Entrepreneurialism will also be a key requirement for succeeding in non-traditional careers, such as self-employment or the so-called sharing or gig economy. When the rules of the game are informal, and the major determinant of success is the ability to exploit opportunities and sell those opportunities to others, as well as being able to sell one's own time and talent, one has to behave in entrepreneurial ways. Thus when deciding whom to engage with in a business or commercial transaction, one of the key talent differentiators is people's capacity to contribute new ideas and create value.

FUTURE TALENT IDENTIFICATION TOOLS

Another feasible prediction is that in future the vast majority of people who represent the workforce (potential and actual) will have a public profile that provides information on their talent, employability and career success. To the extent that even more people will be spending even more time online, and through ever more devices, we can expect novel talent signals (indicators) to emerge in the future, and such signals could be integrated to produce a robust and informative reputation score that represents every person's talent or potential. To use a simple analogy, consider the case of Uber drivers. Every Uber driver has a score, which is the average rating provided by all his customers after each ride. That score is dynamic, because it is updated with every customer rating. However, once drivers have been rated by a large number of passengers – say 50 or 100 – their ratings don't change much, and we can assume that a driver's rating is a fairly stable and reliable measure of his talent. Hence it should predict the service quality he will offer to prospective customers. Now imagine that every working adult in the world has a similar number, derived not just from other people's ratings of them (e.g., customers, 360-appraisals, referees, LinkedIn endorsements), but also from objective measures of their past job performance, psychometric test scores, career achievements and even consumer preferences (for example, their Netflix movie choices or Spotify playlist could be used to estimate their fit with a specific organisational culture, and their TripAdvisor reviews could be used to infer their personality). Although we are not quite there yet, the individual pieces of the puzzle are already available – and the motivation is certainly there to complete it – for matching people to the right jobs and organisations, which would be advantageous to everyone – recruiters, employers and employees.

Despite the wide repertoire of scientifically valid talent identification tools, the past decade has generated an unprecedented level of innovation and new developments in this area. Many of these new tools evaluate qualities that are directly related to talent. Even if the application of these tools may not have focused on HR or talent management yet, the potential for doing so is unquestionable. Most of these methods have emerged as the result of the digital revolution and ubiquity of the smartphone. As marketers have repeatedly pointed out, there are now more iPhones being sold per day than people being born, and this gap keeps widening – sales of iPhones continue to go up, and fertility rates continue to go down. It is tempting to speculate about the potential causal connection between the two (the more time we spend on our iPhones, the less time we invest on physical interaction with others).

Table 3: A Comparison between Traditional and New Talent Identification Tools

Attributes assessed	Traditional tools	New tools
Personality traits, attitudes, values	Self-reports	Web scraping and social media analytics
Past performance, current performance	Biodata Supervisory ratings	Internal big data and predictive analytics

Attributes assessed	Traditional tools	New tools
Intelligence, job-related knowledge, personality traits	IQ tests Situational judgement tests	Gamification
Expertise, social skills, motivation, intelligence	Interviews	Digital interviews Voice profiling
Experience, past performance, technical skills and qualifications	CVs and résumés References	Professional social networks (LinkedIn)
Performance, competencies, reputation	360-degree assessments	Crowdsourced reputation/ peer-ratings

We are therefore spending much of our time online and, unlike in the analogue world, the digital world records all of our behaviours, producing unprecedented quantities of data. In 2013, IBM famously estimated that 90 per cent of all the digital data ever recorded has been produced in the last two years.[39] Moreover, 80 per cent of all the pictures ever taken have been taken in the past 12 months (the majority probably selfies). As *The Economist* pointed out, the collective time people have spent watching 'Gangnam Style' on YouTube would have been sufficient to build 20 Empire State Buildings.[40] All these behaviours leave online traces, which marketers refer to as our 'online footprint' or 'digital reputation'. Many of the advances around new talent signals consist of looking at these digital breadcrumbs or behavioural traces online.

Consider LinkedIn, which is the most explicit attempt to automate the talent identification industry (and has recently been acquired by Microsoft). On the one hand, LinkedIn is really just the modern version of the CV and the phone directory combined. It is used very widely in recruitment, but most talent inferences are still made by human judges relying on their intuition. On the other hand, some of its features, such as the endorsements section, have been quantified and standardised so they lend themselves to more systematic and objective analyses. The problem is that most endorsements are not very informative. The number one reason to endorse someone is to get them to endorse us back; the second most common reason is that they have already endorsed us, so we want to return the favour. The more exciting advancements in this area consist of computer-generated algorithms that attempt to translate this and other digital footprints into simple reputational metrics.

Web scraping and social media analytics

Imagine taking someone's Twitter, Facebook or LinkedIn profile and translating it into a talent score, or any other information that can be used to quantify that person's suitability, potential or fit for a given role. This approach, known as social media analytics, has been validated by several scientific studies that have provided compelling evidence for its potential as a talent identification tool. In particular, Michal Kosinski and his Cambridge colleagues have shown that you can tell a great deal about a person's psychological profile by mining their Facebook Likes – the Facebook groups or pages users choose to endorse. This makes sense given that Facebook Likes are the virtual equivalent of identity claims, in that they are used to communicate information about values, attitudes and preferences, all of which relate to wider dispositions, like personality.

Some of these associations are quite intuitive. For example, people with higher IQs tend to Like science, *The Godfather* and Mozart, while people with lower IQs tend to Like Harley Davidsons or Sephora products. Other associations would have been harder to guess. For example, one of the critical markers of having a high IQ was Liking curly fries! Because of the improbability of this finding, it was covered widely in the popular media, leading to a systematic increase in the Liking of curly fries (at least on Facebook, rather than in the real world). Unfortunately, that didn't lead to a systematic increase in actual IQ scores, and as soon as many people with lower IQ scores started Liking curly fries, that activity ceased to be a sign of a high intelligence. This is a useful reminder of how machine algorithms work: they are dynamic rather than static, and can therefore adjust and auto-correct as more and better data are generated.

Facebook Likes can also be used to infer personality characteristics, such as curiosity and openness to new experiences. For example, open and curious people Like intellectual and philosophical authors, such as Plato and Oscar Wilde, whereas people with low curiosity and openness scores Like NASCAR stock car races, Oklahoma State University and 'I don't read', a Facebook group for people who hate books and are proud to report it.

Overall, half of the variability in scientifically measured personality and intelligence scores can be predicted by a person's Likes (assuming they have enough Likes in their profile, though one would guess that the scarcity of Likes is also indicative of certain personality characteristics). Given how quick and widely applicable the implementation of social media analytics is compared to traditional psychometric tests, their relative accuracy is quite remarkable. For a start, these machine algorithms are significantly more accurate than humans at estimating people's personality scores.[41] If you are interested in trying this out, you can visit applymagicsauce.com and see what your Facebook Likes say about your personality.

Social media analytics can also be used to mine unstructured data, such as free text. Using different linguistic processing tools, we can see the degree to which certain words are indicative of different personality attributes, and look out for the particular words that talented (and untalented) individuals use. Scientists have analysed the most frequent words used in blogs as a function of bloggers' personalities.[42] For example, neurotics say things like 'awful', 'horrible' and 'depressing'. Extraverts talk about 'bars', 'drinks' and 'Miami'. Agreeable people talk about 'hugs', 'mornings' and 'togetherness'. Disagreeable people talk about porn and swear. Conscientious people talk mostly about 'completing' things – it's the obsessional nature of being conscientious! And curious people talk about 'poetry', 'art' and 'narrative' – a word that should always help you when you are trying to impress people. Although the individual correlations between specific words and personality are generally low, they can be quite predictive when combined together – imagine that each word plays the role of an individual question in a psychometric test.

But has this approach been implemented in practice, or used to design any potential talent identification tool, or is this all just academic research? Although the answer is closer to the latter, there are already tools for translating open text into personality trait predictions, including IBM Watson's Personality Insights engine.[43] This free and publicly available engine requires one simply to copy–paste a chunk of text into a screen to obtain a detailed report on the writer's personality. A similar technology has been used to develop apps that translate email content into personality attributes. Most notably, Crystalknows.com uses machine-learning algorithms to infer the profiles of email senders, and even provides suggestions on how to draft emails that are well suited to the recipient's personality. For instance, if someone is very impatient and impulsive, you will be advised to keep your emails short and get straight to the point; if someone is very diligent or conscientious, you will be advised to check your email for typos and provide detailed information about things, etc. In the future, organisations may employ similar tools to scrape employees' emails and try to evaluate their talent or potential for a given role. Although this would probably cause some privacy or anonymity concerns, if the outcome is fairer and leads to better decisions and a more objective way to evaluate talent, employees may be persuaded of the benefits. Needless to say, this methodology is already used in programmatic marketing, which crunches search and email data from free email providers (e.g., Gmail, Yahoo!, or Hotmail) to serve target ads to the user.

Internal big data and predictive talent analytics

Another technological development in talent identification concerns internal big data, the data organisations capture in-house in order to identify critical markers of talent from existing organisational performance metrics. Imagine companies using quantified self apps, such as Fitbit or the Apple watch, in order to monitor employee engagement or productivity levels. Or to create algorithms that monitor the content and context of email traffic: whom employees email and what they say. This methodology is based on a very old scientific principle, which is that past behaviour is a good predictor of future behaviour. Accordingly, if you track what people do at work, you should be able to infer what they are likely to do in the future. Predictions are particularly useful when they can connect individual and group-level variables. For example, big data may be used to link real-time individual sales performance with customer service feedback or organisational revenues; or to look at the relationship between employee engagement and aggregate productivity levels. In this way, organisations may be able to identify high potential employees who may be flying under the radar and might go unnoticed, particularly if subjective performance evaluations are being used.

The most successful attempts to use internal big data productively have been found in professional sports. The 2011 film *Moneyball* depicts the true story of baseball manager Billy Beane, who defied all odds by turning round a small and unpromising team and winning a record 20 consecutive games, despite spending little money on players. Beane's killer weapon was hiring a data scientist to analyse vast amounts of data on player performance to avoid making any intuitive transfer- and team-selection decisions. By the same token, many well-known sports teams are basing their insights and management decisions on internal big data, linking thousands of player behaviours to individual and team performance indicators to predict not just future performance, but also injuries and conduct problems. For example, the top Italian football club AC Milan are reported to have 60,000 data points for each player.[44] Although humans are unable to draw inferences from such large volume datasets, computer algorithms can be used to identify the critical triggers of success and failure, enhancing a manager's ability to build high-performing teams.

Likewise, internal big data can highlight the hidden dynamics that drive positive organisational outcomes. For example, logistics and transport companies can inspect on-board computer data from delivery trucks to monitor drivers' safety behaviours. Rapidly delivered and instantly analysed data are not used just to improve individual and organisational effectiveness, but also to provide employees with objective real-time feedback on their performance. For example, dashboard or phone apps may present employees with an hourly scorecard of their key performance metrics (e.g., error rate, revenues, call completion rate, or customer conversion figures).[45]

A common approach for collecting in-house big data is the use of sociometric badges. These are sensors that track employees' movements at work, in particular the quantity and duration of interactions with others. This technique was pioneered by MIT researchers and can be used to map the dynamics of organisational life. For example, data can reveal the connections between different employees, the breadth and density of their networks, where people go for advice or gossip, and how ideas and information spread within an organisation. As a result, managers may be able to evaluate the effectiveness of informal teams, and identify individuals who are central nodes in the network. These people presumably have stronger connections with colleagues and therefore are more useful to the organisation. You can think of smartwatches or smartphones as the sociometric badges of the digital age, so most people are in effect tracked during their working hours and beyond. Just like these devices are counting how many steps you take every day, different apps could be deployed to map your networks and relationships, and not just at work.

Another emerging methodology within organisational big data concerns open source feedback ratings. The most popular example of this is Glassdoor, a TripAdvisor for workplaces. The site enables employees to rate their jobs, work experience and organisations, as well as their managers and leaders. These ratings are available to anyone, though in anonymised form, enabling employers and potential employees to get a sense of the organisational culture, including the pros and cons of different workplaces. These crowdsourced data can highlight important links between employees' work experiences and organisational effectiveness. Furthermore, there is probably no easier and quicker way to evaluate the overall performance of leaders than to compare these ratings across different time periods or with those of rival organisations. Some large companies, such as Amazon, have pioneered similar methods but internally. More specifically, Amazon encourages every employee and manager to leave feedback on their interactions with other employees or managers using an anonymised feedback aggregator, which operates just like product reviewer feedback. Although this process may take feedback to an extreme – and be rather time consuming – it provides a clear vehicle for collecting real-time and ongoing data on people's work performance, representing an alternative to the outdated annual performance review.

Digital interviewing and voice profiling

Another area of innovation in talent identification tools concerns digital interviewing and voice profiling. This methodology demonstrates considerable potential for upstaging the traditional job interview, which is still the most common approach for evaluating job fit and talent. While it is hard to estimate how many interviews are conducted every year, it is also unfeasible to think of any job offer that isn't preceded by some form of interview. Thus the market is already huge. Can technology make interviews cheaper, faster, more efficient or accurate?

The answer, at least to some of these questions, is yes. The jury is still out on accuracy, but there is no doubt that new technologies have sterilised and standardised the interview process, making it more cost-effective and cheaper. For instance, digital interview providers, such as HireVue, who mine around 80 million data points from a 20-minute video interview, and link that data to performance or valid personality variables to infer relevant talent signals from the interview, are eliminating the intervention of a human judge or reliance on human intuition to gauge people's potential. Since structured interviews provide a robust methodology for inferring talent-relevant personality traits,[46] one would expect machine-learning algorithms to pick up relevant signals of talent during video-recorded interviews. As Norbert Wiener, the father of cybernetics and one of the pioneers of artificial intelligence, noted: 'if we can do anything in a clear and intelligible way, we can do it by machine'.[47] Furthermore, it is obviously possible to combine both machine and human inferences on an interviewee's potential, and these independent predictions may have additive effects on the prediction of future outcomes.

Another alternative, based on a similar methodology, is voice profiling. Companies can translate certain properties of the voice – ignoring the actual content of the message – into markers of personality, ability and future performance. Although the idea that each voice is unique makes intuitive sense, some voice profiling tools, such as Jobaline, are based on a rather unconventional premise: instead of trying to decode a candidate's personality, intelligence, or mood state, they aim to predict 'the emotion that that voice is going to generate on the listener'.[48] In other words, the algorithm functions as a mechanical judge in a voice-based beauty contest. Desirable voices are invited to the next round, where they are judged by humans, while undesirable voices are eliminated from the contest. Although this may sound unfair, it should be noted that the algorithm merely predicts the decisions that human judges would make. In other words, algorithms are just mirroring – and anticipating – the decisions that humans would make, albeit often unconsciously. Too often we are quick to criticise computers for being prejudiced when they are only replicating human prejudice, which we happily ignore!

Customer service companies can mine real-time email and phone conversations to assess the quality and efficiency of transactions. Advances in voice-profiling software can even enable companies to detect the level and type of affect displayed by customer service agents and elicited in their clients, irrespective of the content of the conversation.

Although voice profiling represents a promising start in harnessing technology to spot great potential employees – it is just a start, with many questions still to be answered. Until we are able to understand precisely how a person's voice may contribute to organisational effectiveness, and whether it does so better than alternative attributes that a candidate can control, we should regard voice profiling only as an interesting experiment.

Gamified profiling tools

A final area of innovation in talent identification is gamification, which concerns making boring things more fun or game-like by incorporating some of the features of video games in other areas, such as psychological assessments and personnel selection.[49] In this context, gamification attempts to enhance user experience by either shortening or 'fun-gineering' profiling tools, which in the talent identification industry have traditionally involved extrinsically motivated candidates. The majority of people who are evaluated for staffing purposes are interested only in the outcome – getting the job – so most employers don't care about whether they find the experience enjoyable. However, if talent identification tools could be made more interesting or appealing to the applicant pool, organisations might be able to profile potential candidates before they even apply for jobs. The pre-hiring market represents the main area of application for gamified assessments. According to Markets and Markets, by 2020 the gamification industry will be worth $11 billion.[50]

In what is probably the first mass-market example of gamification, Nintendo's Brain Training successfully gamified some of the typical questions found in IQ tests. Although the alleged benefits of brain training – e.g., improved cognitive performance, IQ score gains and enhanced attention – are strongly contested, the game became an instant hit among Japanese commuters, and enjoyed worldwide success with the release of the Nintendo DS console. The advent of smartphones gave birth to a more recent attempt to gamify IQ tests, namely the Lumosity app. This app – see lumosity.com – offers a wide range of game-like brain teasers for the business-to-consumer market. Like Nintendo's Brain Training, the focus of Lumosity is on intellectual development rather than identification, but since players who excel on its games can be expected to have a high IQ, one may expect them to publish their scores online so that recruiters and employers can access them. Another firm, Pymetrics, has gamified neuropsychological tests that assess basic cognitive, emotional and interpersonal skills. By applying machine-learning algorithms to a person's performance on the games, Pymetrics creates a personalised career profile, which is then made available to companies and recruiters. Pymetrics has assessed over 100,000 job candidates, and has a growing number of client organisations, including Fidelity and Anheuser-Busch.

Other attempts to gamify talent identification tools have focused on specific job domains, such IT. For instance, HackerRank hosts a range of games that can be used to evaluate the programming skills of software engineers. Some games require candidates to write code, which is subsequently scored by the site's algorithms. This enables potential employers to rank candidates on the basis of their expertise without having to administer any additional tests. Another provider of gamified assessment for talent identification is HR Avatar, which puts candidates through interactive job simulations that evaluate personality characteristics associated with sales and customer service jobs. Like most gamified personality assessments, HR Avatar's simulations are essentially situational judgement tests. Candidates are presented with different scenarios requiring a choice between a limited number of decisions, and each decision is associated with a different personality profile. For example, one such scenario may require the candidate to play the role of a hotel manager and respond to complaints by needy customers. Attending to such complaints may indicate higher levels of agreeableness, which may indicate higher customer orientation and potential for the job.

More sophisticated versions of gamified assessments have included interactive movies shot from a point-of-view perspective. For example, the game Insanely Driven, which I created for Reckitt Benckiser, a global consumer goods company, immerses candidates in scenarios that require decisions to be made under pressure, and finding a compromise between getting ahead and getting along.[51] Candidates' choices reflect not only aspects of their personalities, but also their values, enabling the company to assess corporate fit. In what is probably the most comprehensive public version of a scientifically robust gamified assessment, Red

Bull's Wingfinder game (www.wingfinder.com) enables participants to identify their best career-related aptitudes by completing
picture-based personality tests and quick logical-reasoning
quizzes. The test evaluates the RAW components of talent and
provides participants with a free report on their job potential
and vocational strengths.

A PROMISE, YES – A REVOLUTION, NOT YET

Although it would be premature to evaluate the accuracy and
utility of new talent identification tools here – academic research
is only just beginning to do so – it is feasible to speculate about
the value of these methods for advancing and improving the talent
identification industry. After all, many of these new methodologies are offered by start-ups and new players in the field who
are trying to disrupt the industry. The key question, for now, is
whether these tools are effectively tapping into relevant talent
signals, and, if so, whether these signals are new, or whether they
merely represent new ways to capture traditional signals, such as
the RAW ingredients of talent described in Chapter 3.

There are already too many new tools to keep track of, but
most fall into the four categories discussed above, namely
web scraping (including social media analytics), gamification,
internal/in-house big data (also known as predictive talent
analytics) and digital interviewing (voice and video profiling).
While we await scientific evidence on the accuracy of these tools
(in particular, peer-reviewed evidence that they can predict job
performance as well as or better than established tools), it is
important to note that accuracy is not the only thing organisations care about. As a matter of fact, many companies and

talent management consultants don't seem to care about accuracy, which explains why the Myers–Briggs test is the most widely used assessment tool in the world.

Moreover, even when talent management practitioners claim to value accuracy, they are often unable to evaluate it effectively, particularly if it involves consulting validity studies from scientific publications, most of which are hard to find and written in an inaccessible language. The type of validity that most HR and talent management managers care about is face validity – i.e., whether the results or a profile *seem* accurate from an intuitive point of view. In other words, do the people who are designated as talented by the assessment seem talented, according to common sense? And as you have probably guessed, common sense is neither common nor accurate. Perhaps this explains why there is often a big gap between the tools that real-world practitioners treasure and those that scientists recommend.

It is also noteworthy that even when a tool is accurate there are other factors to consider, such as costs. Often, organisations end up opting for talent identification tools that are less accurate but cheaper. This is unfortunate as the return on investment from finding more suitable candidates clearly offsets the higher price of more accurate tools. Another factor that is often considered is user experience, or how engaging the tools are from a candidate's or test-taker's perspective. This is where many of the gamified assessment tools are strong competitors, even when their accuracy is elusive or yet to be demonstrated. Organisations are increasingly opting for tools that are shorter, more enjoyable and less cumbersome to the candidate. It should be noted that there are some advantages to this approach, even if it sacrifices some accuracy: if more engaging tools can attract a bigger number of candidates to the assessment process, decreases in accuracy may be compensated by increases in suitable candidates. For example, if your candidate pool consists of 10,000 people and the accuracy of your tool is 60 per cent, you should still be able to find more suitable candidates than if the accuracy of your tool is 75 per cent but you only have 50 people to choose from. Thus there is a natural tension between accuracy and user experience: things that are more fun tend to be less accurate, but they attract more candidates; and things that are more accurate end up requiring a greater level of investment and focus from the test-taker, so they are generally less popular. To improve the user experience while also improving, or at least maintaining, accuracy will generally end up increasing costs.

Finally, legal constraints, anonymity concerns and ethical guidelines must be considered when evaluating the potential pros and cons of traditional and novel talent identification tools. Some tools may be fairly accurate, cheap and have good user experience, particularly if candidates don't need to do anything and they have already been profiled, such as in the case of Facebook-based algorithms. But how ethical, legal and intrusive are these approaches? There has always been a tension between scientific discoveries and unethical applications, in any field of science. Right now, ethical boundaries seem to be setting the limits to what new technologies can achieve: there is a clear gap between what we could and should know, and technology keeps widening it.

There is no doubt that new profiling tools represent a big promise: the fundamental promise of evaluating a much bigger proportion of the workforce. The current market for commercial assessment tools is growing, but it is still a fraction of what it could be. There are roughly 40 million assessments completed each year for HR or talent purposes (this includes not only talent identification, but also development). Yet there are 4 billion working people in the world. Therefore, 99 per cent of the potential talent pool is untapped. Most of the people in that group will undergo some sort of vetting process, notably a job interview. However, the mechanisms by which their talents are judged and decisions about their future careers are made are rather informal and amateurish. As a result, too many people end up in the wrong job or career, which leads to underperformance, disengagement, alienation and massive productivity loss for their economies. In a world where almost half of the population has online access, and smartphone sales continue to grow, bringing connectivity to more and more remote places, the potential value of digital talent tools should not be underestimated. But before this potential can turn into actual progress and reality, it is important that the accuracy of these new tools is refined, and that any ethical and cost-related issues are addressed. If or when that happens, organisations anywhere will have much wider access to talent, much like social media has enabled people to have wider access to people or the internet has enabled much quicker and wider access to information, though this does not make people automatically wiser.

Many of the new methods and novel talent signals discussed in this chapter are already here, and they are probably here to stay. To the average HR practitioner they may seem quite futuristic, but everything that is now mainstream was once regarded as exotic and unlikely. To paraphrase William Gibson – who coined the term 'cyberspace' in 1982 – 'the future is already here, just not evenly distributed'. Thus what may sound like science fiction today could be only a small step further than what will become common tomorrow.

To draw a parallel from the world of retail and commerce,

consider the fact that in most places many of the features of the physical environment have already been digitised and quantified. Whenever we visit a new destination, we can just evaluate the reputations of shops, restaurants or bars by looking up their ratings on our phones. All we need is to be online. Perhaps in the future the same will apply to people. You may be walking down Oxford Street or the Champs-Elysées or Fifth Avenue and pick up reputational signals from the people around you, accessing their musical preferences, work history, or current thoughts and emotions – assuming of course that they are OK to share them, though most people already do this online, even with strangers. In mobile dating, where technology and innovation are far more advanced than in HR and talent tools, apps have already been developed that enable wearable technology to access somebody's past dating history, including ratings and reviews from previous dates, while interacting with the person in the physical world. You could see the same technology being used for job interviews, networking events, or random social encounters with strangers.

Ultimately, if these technologies advance and can be leveraged, we will move to a world where most people will have been profiled already, so they won't need to complete additional talent identification assessments. This would mean an Uber- or Tinder-like talent market, where you can just pull out your phone to request talent on demand. But a key requirement for this is that we have reliable measures to make accurate evaluations about every individual in the talent pool: independent, non-gameable reputational scores that can give employers relative certainty that the person they are about to hire will be able to perform the job in the future. In other words, an accurate signal of talent. In low-level jobs, this has happened already. Companies such as Fiverr,

Upwork and Amazon Mechanical Turk are in effect a sort of eBay for jobs and the on-demand jobs market. But the question remains whether the same methodology and tools can be successfully implemented for highly qualified positions or leadership roles; that is, at the high end of the talent spectrum. Will hiring a good leader be as easy as buying a book on Amazon?

CHAPTER 8

Final thoughts

This chapter provides some concluding remarks. The big take-home message of this book is that although we are living in the age of talent, there is much progress to be made in our talent management interventions. As the chapter notes, one of the problems with talent is that people habitually overestimate how much they know about it. This delusion is problematic, to say the least. In addition, people are also prone to overrate their own talents in most areas of achievement. Ultimately, what organisations need to achieve is obvious: to spot, attract and retain talent before their competitors do, just like Barcelona Football Club did with Lionel Messi, the Argentine star. In the end what matters most is not organisations' ability to make employees happy, but their facility to enable them to perform to a level that surpasses their expectations and makes them achieve great things.

* * *

Popular interest in talent is a double-edged sword. On the one hand, it is reassuring that so many individuals, including HR professionals and organisational decision-makers, seem to appreciate the value of talent, particularly in the world of business. For example, many large organisations estimate that their best employees are at least 50 per cent more valuable, in terms of output, than their average employees.[1] On the other hand, this has enabled too many amateurish and nonsensical opinions to flourish. Everybody, it seems, has a talent philosophy these days. Yet few people seem to know much about talent, and if they were aware of the science of talent they would be less compelled to reinvent it, to play it by ear, or to come up with their own philosophy.

Accordingly, recent reviews have observed that 'talent can mean whatever a business leader or writer wants it to mean'[2] (echoing Lewis Carroll's Humpty Dumpty, who explains: 'When *I* use a word, it means just what I choose it to mean – neither more nor less'). For example, a survey of talent models used in 13 global organisations, including Boeing, Chase Manhattan, Dell, Eli Lilly, Hewlett Packard, Southwest Airlines and Sun Microsystems, showed that none of these companies used the same definition of talent.[3]

Perhaps because talent is about people, and most people, in particular HR professionals and managers, spend a great deal of time interacting with people, it is tempting to fall into the trap of thinking that one is an expert on talent matters. This is not dissimilar to laypeople's belief that they are experts in psychology – after all, psychology is about human behaviour, which they can all observe on a regular basis. Yet, there is a science to human behaviour and a science to talent, just like there is a science to astrophysics or Egyptology. And although the average person in the world may know more about people than astrophysics or Egyptology, their knowledge is still intuitive and not accurate enough to replace evidence-based insights.

Unfortunately, the talent management industry is full of char-latans. And the less aware they are of their ignorance, the more they seem to succeed at persuading others of their expertise. There are, alas, no quality control mechanisms or barriers to entry for anyone willing to give advice on talent. In that regard, Jeffrey Pfeffer recently noted that the leadership development industry resembles the days of pre-scientific medicine, when a wide range of practitioners (e.g., spiritual healers, shamans, homeopaths) operated freely in an unregulated environment and in the absence of any established paradigm. The same observation can be extended to the entire talent management field. For every academic or scientifically credible author there appear to be hundreds of self-proclaimed experts, gurus and thought-leaders. The problem is not only that their advice is counterproductive, but that it also seems intuitively right to most potential clients and the general public. In response, aca-demics react as they do in other fields of expertise: by making their science more complex, abstract and incomprehensible to the average practitioner.

To overcome the conceptual chaos and intellectual confusion that characterises the field, it is essential to take a step back and attempt to understand the most fundamental question about talent – what is it? In this book I have provided four simple definitions for the term. These are meant to be straightforward guides that can easily be applied to make an initial inference about a person's talent and lead subsequent attempts to measure it. We can translate these guides into four critical talent questions that can be asked when we are interested in determining whether individuals possess talent or not:

1. *Are the individuals part of the 'vital few' who contribute a disproportionate amount to the organisation?* This question refers to the Pareto rule, and even if the answer is yes, it is also important to establish whether these same individuals would be among the vital few in your competitor's workforce, particularly the firms that are outperforming yours.

2. *If not, would they be part of that group if they performed to their best?* This question comprises both the maximum performance and performance minus effort definitions of talent. If a person's average output is not a reflection of their potential, or if they seem to underperform, they may still be considered talent if the only missing piece to make them part of the vital few is motivation.

3. *If not, are they in the right place?* In other words, would they perform better in a different role or context, one that would be a better fit for their natural personality? This question refers to the personality in the right place rule – few people are talented in every area, and talent is always the product of the fit between a person's disposition and the requirements of the task.

4. *Finally, are these individuals aware of how talented they are?* Or do they over- or underestimate their talents? Since talent also involves the ability to judge one's own ability, we may expect people's talents to increase if their self-awareness increases.

FINDING MESSI

To illustrate how these four principles may be used to evaluate someone's talent, consider the case of Lionel Messi, widely regarded as the best football player of modern times, if not all time. Although Messi's teammates – Neymar, Iniesta, Suárez – are some of the best footballers in the world, he is consistently the key contributor to Barcelona's goals, assists and results, and single-handedly accounts for around 50 per cent of these critical stats. In addition, he has broken every single historical record at the club, leading many experts to describe the Barcelona of the past few years – perhaps the best team of all time – as 'Messidependent'. As for the best Messi can do, he is the only player in history to have won the best player of the world award five times, holds records for most goals and assists scored in one season in the Champions League (the world's most prestigious club tournament) and in 'El Clásico' matches (against Real Madrid), and has scored many of the best goals ever. Thus his maximum performance is unrivalled, and given how consistently he displays his best there is hardly any difference between his maximum and typical performances. Furthermore, Messi's brilliance is displayed with effortless elegance – he makes things look easy and his talents stand out even when he doesn't appear to try very hard. Yet, Messi's accomplishments with Argentina, his national team, pale in comparison. While Messi has won an astonishing 25 titles with Barcelona, he has failed to win a single professional trophy with Argentina, which has led him to resign from the national team (to focus on his Barcelona career). Clearly, Messi's style, personality and skills are a much better fit with Barcelona than Argentina, which is why his performance and talents are so clearly manifested with the former but not the latter team.

Like Barcelona Football Club, whose scouts enrolled Messi in their youth academy at the age of 13, when he was clearly very green, most organisations hope to spot talent before their competitors do. But it is important to remember that early manifestations of talent are still undeveloped potential, even in the most brilliant and talented of individuals. Although it is often assumed that talented people are good at things without being taught,[4] even when talented individuals display a clear predisposition for greatness in their field, and their talents are expressed early on, their full potential must still be developed. Thus coaching, training and other enriching environmental experiences are important catalysts of talent. Based on the findings discussed in this book, it is possible to reach four major conclusions about the development of talent in organisations:

1. *People may change, but don't expect miracles*: Although human beings tend to look for categorical answers, psychological questions are rarely that simple. The question of whether people change does not have a simple answer. Clearly, people can change – behaviour is largely the product of conscious decisions and deliberate choices, particularly in high-stake settings. At the same time, most people behave in fairly consistent ways throughout their adult lives, and these consistent patterns of behaviour can be predicted once you have sufficient information on the person's past behaviour. Most notably, a person's personality, intelligence and values – which are the major markers of dispositional individual differences and key determinants of talent – are remarkably stable from early

adulthood onwards. Major changes in these attributes are possible, but improbable, particularly when they involve going against the direction of inherent predispositions (e.g., an uncreative person becoming creative, an introverted person becoming extraverted, a dim person becoming smart). And in the unlikely event that they occur, it is usually as the result of extreme environmental pressures, such as coaching.

2. *People won't grow unless you help them*: Most people will only develop if they get help. The main reason is that they have a natural tendency to lack self-awareness. So, unless you help them, they will probably be unaware of what and how they need to change. Coaching interventions vary widely, but to produce effective change they always provide accurate feedback on the coachee's performance and potential, which increases their self-awareness. It is possible to enhance a person's self-awareness without causing any subsequent change; but it is not possible to create positive changes unless the person first becomes self-aware. Thus self-awareness is necessary, but not sufficient, for effective changes to take place. In addition, creating change is easier than maintaining it. The key challenge of developmental interventions is therefore to produce durable improvements in a person's behaviours. If this is accomplished, their workplace reputation will improve, making them more effective. However, personal effectiveness does not always translate into benefits for the organisation, so it is important to set change goals that align with the organisation's agenda.

3. *Change interventions tend to help those who need it the least*: One of the key determinants of coaching effectiveness is whether the coachee is actually interested in changing. Developmental interventions on individuals who are insufficiently motivated to change will tend to be less successful. Sadly, of course, it is those individuals who would benefit from coaching the most. Indeed, people who do not care about their impact on others, who are deluded about their own abilities or in denial about their toxic habits and faults would be the perfect customers for any coaching intervention, in that they have a lot of room for improvement and should therefore profit the most. However, those same individuals are generally sceptical about coaching and resistant to most change interventions, rendering even the best coaches ineffective. As the saying goes, 'You can lead a horse to water, but you can't make it drink.' Conversely, individuals who keenly sign up for training, learning and development programmes, and respond enthusiastically to coaching initiatives, are probably more self-aware, open to feedback and interpersonally skilled to begin with. They are the best coachees, because they need the least amount of coaching to improve.

4. *Coachability is a key ingredient of talent*: Although talent is partly developed, some people are more likely to seek and benefit from development than others. In other words, some people have more talent for developing their talents, because they are more coachable. They are more likely to pay attention to their mistakes and learn from them; they are more receptive to negative feedback; they

are less likely to blame others for their own wrongdoings. Above all, they are not overconfident or complacent, but are eager to keep growing and developing. Thus coachability is the quality by which talent self-replicates, so it can be considered a key component of talent itself. This is why in talent, as in many other domains, the rich get richer and the poor get poorer.

It is also noteworthy that some of the key functions of coaching may take place even in the absence of formal coaching interventions. Most notably, formal and informal mentoring can tackle some of the issues addressed by coaching, though in mentoring the focus tends to be more diverse and less performance-based. In addition, mentors are typically more experienced members of the organisation helping out more junior colleagues; the sessions are less structured than in coaching and the duration tends to be long-term.

MOST PEOPLE ARE LESS TALENTED THAN THEY THINK

'Truth is like poetry.
And most people hate poetry'.

THE BIG SHORT

As seen in Chapter 2, there are four major ways to define talent: according to the 80/20 rule; according to the maximum performance rule; as performance minus effort; or as personality in the right place. Yet even when people agree with these precepts, that doesn't mean that they will be better able to quantify their own talents. The main obstacle impeding this is the so-called self-enhancement or illusory superiority bias. That is, the fact that most people are overly optimistic when judging their talents. In other words, people are generally less talented than they think.

Most people are average but think they are outliers. The mere thought of being average is generally more insulting to them than the idea of being special, even in a bad way. People would rather be abnormal than average, mostly because of the narcissistic benefits of feeling unique. This is particularly true in Western/individualistic societies, and less true in Eastern/collectivistic societies, but the reality is that most places in the world have already been infested by American individualism (consumerism). Kim Kardashian is as big in China as she is in America, and it won't take long for the next icon of trash culture to emerge from China and be exported to America.

This is why people are so keen on the notion that everybody is talented in their own way, an idea that represents the essence of the strengths approach to talent. Needless to say, this idea contradicts any credible data on talent. It is akin to the idea that everybody deserves a gold medal, and is little more than pseudo-intellectual populism. Since robust data suggest that a few individuals make a disproportionately high contribution to their job and organisation, that when different individuals do their best – because they are motivated – their performance still differs quite widely, and that some people achieve more by trying less and some people achieve less by trying more, it is irrational to deny that some people are more talented than others.

And yet, several psychological studies show that most people consider themselves better than average in virtually every domain of competence. For example, most people think that their memory[5] and health[6] are better than average, and that their romantic relationships are better than average.[7] Most managers think that they are better leaders and businesspeople than average,[8] and most athletes think they are better than their peers.[9] In some domains of talent, the better-than-average bias is rather extreme. As many as 90 per cent of drivers think they are better than average.[10] Around 90 per cent of high school students rate their social skills as better than average, and virtually all university professors think their teaching skills are better than average.[11]

In our own research, we have highlighted the pervasive inaccuracy of self-estimates of ability, particularly when it comes to talent and intelligence. Our studies differ from the better-than-average studies in that they also include an objective measure of people's ability, thus enabling us to quantify how accurate self-estimates actually are. The methodology is simple but robust. First, participants complete a scientifically valid test of talent (e.g., creativity, mathematics or verbal intelligence); next, they are shown a normal distribution of scores, including the average and standard deviation for the population; then, they are asked to estimate their own score vis-à-vis the norm. For instance, if the task is to work out what their verbal IQ is, they are told that the average is 100 points, and that 66 per cent of the population scores between 85 and 115. Given the detailed instructions, and the fact that individuals have just completed a test about the abilities they are asked to estimate, one would expect a high correlation between a person's self-estimate and their actual test score. However, the typical correlation between these two variables is around .20,[12] which indicates that there is a mere 4 per cent overlap between how smart people are and how smart they think they are. Thus if you imagine a Venn diagram illustrating the overlap between self-perceived and actual talent, the two circles would barely touch. Meta-analyses indicate that self-perceived job performance correlates very weakly with supervisors' ratings of job performance, mostly because employees' rate their own performance too positively, particularly when they perform poorly.[13] This is especially true in Western cultures, where people are less self-critical and less modest about their skills and achievements, and where bragging is often rewarded.

Even when people are told about the better-than-average bias, most individuals believe that this bias does not apply to them, something psychologists have labelled blind-spot bias[14] – the belief that you are not as biased as others in your self-evaluations of talents. And if you think that this ubiquitous optimism is a healthy habit, think again. Overconfident employees are less likely to develop self-awareness and accept negative feedback. Overconfident leaders are less likely to respond positively to coaching and development interventions. And people in general will find it harder to accept the success of their peers when they are themselves deluded about their own talent and contribution to the organisation. It is for this reason that the relationship between pay and pay satisfaction is notoriously weak. Even in the presence of clear performance criteria, most people think that they deserve to earn more than their peers, not least because they perceive their own talents and motivation to exceed those of their peers.[15]

Yet, a great deal of modern talent management practices foster and reinforce people's unrealistic self-estimates of ability. For example, several large corporations, such as Wayfair Inc. and the Boston Consulting Group, are thinking of eliminating negative feedback from their performance evaluations, so that employees would receive either positive feedback or no feedback at all.[16]

Likewise, in much of the HR world (particularly in the US), the term 'weaknesses' has become so politically incorrect that it has been replaced with 'opportunities'.

This feel-good approach to talent management is not only killing the little self-awareness most employees have, it also suggests that every employee matters as much as every other. Assuming that every employee has potential, and therefore deserves to be developed, reduces the return on investment from talent management interventions, not least because organisational performance will increase much more when the performance of the key players improves than when the weakest players do better. Moreover, what people need is honest feedback on their potential, rather than confirmation of their talent delusion. When employees are made aware of their limitations, they have a chance to close the gap between their actual and ideal selves, and improve. When they are told that they are more talented than they actually are, they risk making overly ambitious decisions and trying to punch above their weight. As Charles Bukowski put it in his novel *Women*:

> But then if you lied to a man about his talent just because he was sitting across from you, that was the most unforgivable lie of them all, because that was telling him to go on, to continue, which was the worst way for a man without real talent to waste his life, finally. But many people did just that, friends and relatives mostly.[17]

One of the major problems with talent is that in order to persuade others that you have it, it is often enough just to persuade yourself. From an evolutionary psychology perspective, this is one of the few apparent benefits of overconfidence. Although thinking that you are better than you actually are will usually get you in trouble (because you underestimate threats and danger, as well as your competence deficits, which decreases your motivation to work hard to get better), it can also help you hide your insecurities from others. In other words, if you are unaware of your weaknesses you will probably not convey many insecurities to others, and others may be misled into thinking that you are competent – for you seem confident in your abilities. Thus an accidental benefit of being overconfident about your talents is that others may be fooled into agreeing with you about how talented you are. But make no mistake; although this can help individuals to fake competence in the short term, it comes at the long-term detriment of the group or collective. An organisation, or society, that worships those who worship themselves, even when they lack talent, is a deluded and fraudulent society.

Famous quotes, such as that usually attributed to Henry Ford – 'Whether you believe you can do a thing or not, you are right' – or Virgil's 'They can because it's thought they can' highlight our unfortunate adherence to the principle that confidence breeds competence. As the weak relationship between self-estimated and actual ability and the better-than-average bias show, the majority of people who think they are able are actually not able, and whether you think you can do it or not, you are probably wrong (particularly when you think you can). Pick any two individuals at random and the one who is most satisfied with his own talents will probably be deemed more talented by others. In a world where people were able to evaluate talent correctly, not just in others but also in themselves, this wouldn't happen. In our world, however, Bertrand Russell's seminal observation holds true: 'The whole problem with the world is that fools and fanatics are always so certain of themselves.'

HAPPINESS IS OVERRATED

Conversations about talent often end up shifting from productivity and career success to personal well-being and happiness. The main premise underlying this is that organisations and managers should focus on making their employees happy, and that employees should prioritise happiness over any other career goals. However, the idea that organisations are ultimately interested in making their employees happy is hardly realistic. What employers care about, even in the case of non-profit organisations, is productivity, performance and organisational effectiveness. It is only because employee engagement enhances these variables that they are interested in boosting it; not for the sake of making people happy. Unlike engagement, happiness does not translate into higher levels of performance or productivity. In fact, nothing of value would ever be created unless people were somewhat unhappy and therefore motivated to change the status quo. Civilisation, with all of its artistic, social and scientific masterpieces, is the product of dissatisfied people who medicated their unhappiness with extraordinary accomplishments. Conversely, happy individuals are generally too content and complacent to create – they have no imbalance to address, and are not sufficiently annoyed by the status quo to attempt to change it.

Clearly, there has been a very favourable evolution in the nature of work over the past 100 years. With the advent of Fordism and F. W. Taylor's system of scientific management, employees became dehumanised and regarded as industrial extensions of a mechanical system, or individual components of the same machine. Although this era saw the emergence of management psychology as a scientific discipline, its focus was to boost productivity at the expense of employee well-being. Discussions of purpose and meaning were completely unthinkable at the time, and the reality of successful workers resembled the Marxist notion of alienation – but that was the norm. With the emergence of HR as a regulatory employee protection body in the 1950s, the average experience of employees began to improve, but the relationship between employers and employees was still merely transactional and extrinsic from a motivational perspective. This turned HR into a bureaucratic procurement entity and employees into instrumental salary-men, or *Homo economici*: rational and pragmatic minds focused on the pursuit of extrinsic rewards and the avoidance of losses. From the late 1960s onwards, with the rise of humanist and positive psychology, HR began to focus on employee well-being, creating a significant shift in how people regard work. We are now living in the aftermath of this era, the age of the spiritual workaholic.

Throughout the industrialised world, most people are no longer content with jobs – they want careers. Where there was once Taylorisation, we now have the gamification of work. Employees want consumer-like experiences and HR has been co-opted by PR and marketing departments to promote organisational cultures as a sort of Club Med. The most attractive places to work boast sushi chefs, table tennis, laundry service and unlimited vacations as some of their perks, and on top of that they promise employees meteoric career progressions and the ability to 'change the world'. But to think that every worker in the world can potentially be engaged, or assume that there are enough fulfilling jobs in the world for everyone, is absurd. It is, alas, only the top 1 per cent who can legitimately aspire to such interesting and hedonistic vocational adventures, while the rest must cope with unexciting and mundane jobs. This reality is in stark contrast with popular claims that everybody can find meaning at work, and that career crafting is a realistic option for most. Furthermore, in developed economies a substantial proportion of the workforce has been led to believe that they deserve to be happy at work – if their jobs can't make them happy, they ought to switch or quit, for they are being deprived of a universal right.

This nonsensical view of work as a vehicle for self-actualisation or spiritual fulfilment is creating a great deal of pressure on the average employee to find the perfect job. It has raised career aspirations beyond what is feasibly achievable, and may arguably backfire: although challenging goals motivate, unrealistic goals are defeating. There is no point in aspiring to be the next Elon Musk or Steve Jobs if the chances of success are less than .0000000001 per cent and, on top of that, such aspirations lead you to reject available – and objectively better – job opportunities. Moreover, as hundreds of social psychological studies have shown, it is not possible to force people to be happy, and trying to be happy often generates the opposite result. As Alan Watts noted: 'When you try to stay on the surface of the water, you sink; but when you try to sink, you float.' Likewise, the more energy you devote to being happy, the less happy you will be. Like engagement, happiness may or may not emerge as the product of work, but it is the nature of your work that will drive or diminish happiness. In other words, happiness is a collateral symptom. Clearly, it is possible to do great work and be unhappy; and it is equally possible to be happy without doing any great work.

Ludwig Wittgenstein, one of the greatest philosophers of all time, noted: 'I don't know why we are here, but I'm pretty sure that it is not in order to enjoy ourselves.' In light of the common optimism that characterises 99 per cent of the current writings on employee engagement and well-being, Wittgenstein's observation seems almost heretical. Yet two important points underlie this seemingly cynical and pessimistic remark about the meaning of life. First, there is no objective indication that in the past 100 years human beings have experienced any significant increases in job or life satisfaction. And if you think there are any subjective indicators for this, they are probably just manifestations of deluded wishful thinking. The French movie *La Haine* provides a powerful metaphor to illustrate this phenomenon. It is the story of a man who is falling from a 50-storey tower block but keeps repeating to himself *'Jusqu' ici tout va bien'* (So far so good). It is not the fall, but the landing, that hurts. A more poetic, and no doubt positive, depiction of this phenomenon can be found in Oscar Wilde's masterful quote about optimism: 'We are all in the gutter, but some of us are looking at the stars.'

Secondly, even if we were somehow empowered to make employees happy, there are no clear reasons for wanting to do so. The benefits of happiness are mostly confined to the individual rather than the collective. Moreover, people's happiness is often disconnected with objective indicators of well-being or achievement – there's a reason why the academic term for happiness is *subjective* well-being. And it is feasible to think of happy work environments where employees are having way too much fun to be productive. Too much getting along can inhibit getting ahead, and there's a tension between happiness and productivity. Organisations and societies benefit most from high-performing employees, and a certain degree of dissatisfaction and unhappiness may be a bigger catalyst of productivity than happiness is. Really, we don't need any Chief Happiness Officers.

THE AGE OF TALENT

We are living in a talent-obsessed era. As organisational psychologists have noted,

> there is increasing agreement that the unique competitive advantage organisations have today lies in their people, their human resource management practices and systems, and their cultures ... We are now in the era of human capital; to be successful, organisations need to unleash the talents of their people.[18]

Indeed, the war for talent, which formally started 20 years ago, is in full swing and arguably the only two wars that are discussed more frequently are the war on drugs and the war on terror. And like those wars, the only rational or data-driven conclusion one may reach about the war for talent is that we are losing it: the war for talent has become the war on talent.

As this book has argued, some of the major problems we face are due to a misunderstanding of what talent actually is, and a general tendency to overrate our ability to manage talent – a talent delusion. Although the word 'talent' has become a common term in the world of work, inundating popular media blogs as well as business publications around the globe, *The Economist* notes that 'companies do not even know how to define *talent*, let alone how to manage it'.[19] Unsurprisingly, in every domain of talent, there is generally a mismatch between employees' views of their own talent and how talented their organisations think they are.[20] In fact, even when talent is narrowly defined, such as in the case of intellectual ability, there is only a weak relationship between people's perceived and actual talent. Why would we expect people to make the right career choices if they don't know what their skills are? How can leaders and decision-makers nurture and develop talent if they are unable to spot it, let alone understand it, in the first place?

These incongruent talent perceptions cause problems for both parties: for employees, it leads to unrealistic expectations and a sense of entitlement; for organisations, it leads to promoting and hiring the wrong people at the expense of overlooked, better alternatives. As a result, the discrepancy between talent and success is wider than it should be.[21] In a rational world, talent and success would overlap substantially. In the real world, however, individual success has less to do with talent because too many people advance their careers without helping their organisation to advance.

Talent management is the most salient topic facing HR professionals today,[22] and it's been noted that most, if not all, HR practitioners are at least partly engaged in talent management functions today.[23] So much so that some regard talent management as merely a new term for the critical and strategic functions of HR, which have been recently rebranded as people or talent analytics. Yet, despite the central importance of talent management in the real world of business, there is a huge scientific-practitioner gap in talent management.[24]

Unfortunately, HR practitioners are generally lukewarm about academic research on their subject.[25] What's worse, they emulate other professionals – and laypeople in general – in thinking that their intuition and experience are enough to make insightful and accurate observations about people. This is one of the main problems with psychology: although most people are interested in it, they also believe they are experts in it. Compared to other scientific fields of knowledge, such as quantum physics or organic chemistry, psychology feels rather intuitive. After all, it is about people and most of us spend a great deal of time interacting with people – therefore, we must all be experts. However, there is a science to understanding and predicting human behaviour, and intuitive judgements about psychology are as subjective, and wrong, as intuitive judgements about quantum physics and organic chemistry. Perhaps more problematically, the wider appeal of talent as a topic of public interest, and a key theme in self-management and career development conversations, has added a great deal of noise to the literature in this field. Indeed, the leadership development and talent management industries have largely been corrupted by wishy-washy advice from self-proclaimed experts and unqualified gurus. Thinking around talent has been hijacked by the self-help movement, and the result is a proliferation of populist and toxic advice, ungrounded in science yet highly effective at misleading HR practitioners and decision-makers in their talent-related activities.

As a result, and as indicated by the pervasive disengagement levels among employees, the ubiquity of passive job-seeking, the appeal of self-employment and the rise of entrepreneurship porn, almost 20 years after the concept of the war for talent was first introduced we have made no visible progress on winning this war. To make matters worse, a substantial amount of money and resources have been devoted to this war and, much like in the wars on drugs or terror, without results.

Still, not all is lost. If we can use what we know about talent while ignoring ill-founded advice, we shall see light at the end of the tunnel. And while the application of evidence-based principles will help, it is perhaps even more important to abolish counterproductive practices. Thus, realising that the seemingly intuitive and commonsensical approaches that have always been in place may, in fact, be wrong and destructive is the single most important thing HR practitioners can do to improve. As Mark Twain wrote, 'It ain't what you don't know that gets you into trouble. It's what you know for sure that just ain't so.'

REFERENCES

PREFACE

1. Schofield, TM. On my way to being a scientist. *Nature* 2013;497(7448):277–8, doi:10.1038/nj7448-277a.

CHAPTER I

1. Chambers E, Foulon, M, Handfield-Jones, H, Hankin, S and Michael III, E. The war for talent. *McKinsey Q.* 1998;3:44–57, doi:10.4018/jskd.2010070103.
2. http://www.economist.com/news/britain/21601032-new-student-loans-system-proving-more-expensive-expected-fees-fi-fo-fum?zid=316&ah=2f6fb672faf113fdd3b11cd1b1bf8a77.
3. http://www.economist.com/node/21534792?zid=316&ah=2f6fb-672faf113fdd3b11cd1b1 bf8a77.
4. http://www.wsj.com/articles/total-u-s-auto-lending-surpasses-1-trillion-for-first-time-1439478198.
5. http://www.trainingindustry.com/blog/blog-entries/how-big-is-the-training-market.aspx.
6. Kaiser, RB and Curphy, G. Leadership – a development: The failure of an industry and the opportunity for consulting psychologists. *Consult. Psychol. J. Pract. Res.* 2013;65(4):294–302, doi:10.1037/a0035460.

7. Cappelli, P and Keller, J. Talent management: Conceptual approaches and practical challenges. *Annu. Rev. Organ. Psychol. Organ. Behav.* 2014;1(1):305–31, doi:10.1146/annurev-orgpsych-031413-091314.

8. Tansley, C. What do we mean by the term 'talent' in talent management? *Ind. Commer. Train.* 2011;43(5):266–74, doi:10.1108/00197851111145853.

9. Ibid.

10. Florida, R. The economic geography of talent. *Ann. Assoc. Am. Geogr.* 2002;92(4):743–55, doi:10.1111/1467-8306.00314.

11. Ng, TWH and Feldman, DC. How broadly does education contribute to job performance? *Pers. Psychol.* 2009;62:89–134.

12. Scullion, H, Collings, DG and Caligiuri, P. Global talent management. *J. World Bus.* 2010;45(2):105–8, doi:10.1016/j.jwb.2009.09.011.

13. https://hbr.org/2013/05/talent-management-boards-give/.

14. Harter, JK, Schmidt, FL and Hayes TL. Business-unit-level relationship between employee satisfaction, employee engagement, and business outcomes: A meta-analysis. *J. Appl. Psychol.* 2002;87(2):268–279, doi:10.1037/0021-9010.87.2.268.

15. Davenport, TH, Harris, J, and Shapiro, J. Competing on talent analytics. *Harv. Bus. Rev.* 2010;88:52–8, doi:Article.

16. Pfeffer, J. *Leadership BS: Fixing Workplaces and Careers One Truth at a Time.* New York: Harper Business (2015).

17. http://qz.com/375353/half-of-us-workers-have-left-a-job-because-they-hated-their-boss/

18. Jones, JR and Harter, JK. Race effects on the employee engagement– turnover intention relationship. *J. Leadersh. and Organ. Stud.* 2005;11:78–88, doi:10.1177/107179190501100208.

19. Wahyu Ariani, D. The relationship between employee engagement, organizational citizenship behavior, and counterproductive work behavior. *Int. J. Bus. Adm.* 2013;4:46–57, doi:10.5430/ijba.v4n2p46.

20. Appelbaum, SH, Iaconi, GD and Matousek, A. Positive and negative deviant workplace behaviors: Causes, impacts, and solutions. *Corp. Gov.* 2007;7(5):586–98, doi:10.1108/14720700710827176.

21. https://hbr.org/2014/05/managing-the-immoral-employee/.

22. O'Connell, M and Kung, M-C. The cost of employee turnover. *Ind. Manag.* 2007;49(1):14–19.

23. https://www.americanprogress.org/
issues/labor/report/2012/11/16/44464/
there-are-significant-business-costs-to-replacing-employees/.

24. Cappelli, P and Keller, J. Talent management: Conceptual
approaches and practical challenges. *Annu. Rev. Organ.
Psychol. Organ. Behav.* 2014;1(1):305–31, doi:10.1146/
annurev-orgpsych-031413-091314.

25. Incidentally, in the same time period marriages have become more
ephemeral, too.

26. Hogan, R and Chamorro-Premuzic, T. Personality and career
success. *APA Handb. Personal. Soc. Psychol. Vol. 4. Personal.
Process. Individ. Differ.* 2015;4:619–38, doi:10.1037/14343-028.

27. Ashford, SJ, Lee, C and Bobko, P. Content, cause, and consequences of job insecurity: A theory-based measure and substantive
test. *Acad. Manag. J.* 1989;32(4):803–29, doi:10.2307/256569.

28. http://careerbuildercommunications.com/candidatebehaviour/.

29. http://www.economist.com/news/business/21612191-social-
network-has-already-shaken-up-way-professionals-are-hired-its-
ambitions-go-far.

30. Scullion, H, Collings, DG and Caligiuri, P. Global talent
management. *J. World Bus.* 2010;45(2):105–8, doi:10.1016/j.
jwb.2009.09.011.

31. Bidwell, M. Paying more to get less: The effects of external hiring
versus internal mobility. *Adm. Sci. Q.* 2011;56(3):369–407,
doi:10.1177/0001839211433562.

32. Ng, TWH and Feldman, DC. Organizational tenure and
job performance. *J. Manage.* 2010;36(5):1220–50,
doi:10.1177/0149206309359809.

33. Cappelli, P and Hamori, M. Understanding executive job search.
Organ. Sci. 2014;25(5):1511–29, doi:10.1287/orsc.2013.0871.

34. https://www.bluesteps.com/blog/
record-breaking-executive-search-industry.

35. Although this quote is difficult to attribute, it would be incorrect
to pretend it's mine (and it is attributed more to Warren Buffett
than to anyone else).

36. Cappelli, P and Keller, J. Talent management: Conceptual
approaches and practical challenges. *Annu. Rev. Organ.
Psychol. Organ. Behav.* 2014;1(1):305–31, doi:10.1146/
annurev-orgpsych-031413-091314.

37. Kwon, K and Rupp, DE. High-performer turnover and firm performance: The moderating role of human capital investment and firm reputation. *J. Organ. Behav.* 2013;34:129–50, doi:10.1002/job.

38. Lidsky, D. It's not just who you know. *Fast Co.* 2007;(115):56.

39. Boswell, WR, Zimmerman, RD and Swider, BW. Employee job search: Toward an understanding of search context and search objectives. *J. Manage.* 2012;38(1):129–63, doi:10.1177/0149206311421829.

40. Bates, T. Self-employment entry across industry groups. *J. Bus. Ventur.* 1995;10(2):143–56, doi:10.1016/0883-9026(94)00018-P.

41. http://www.economicmodeling.com/2014/02/06/americas-self-employment-landscape/.

42. Oyelere, RU and Belton, W. Coming to America: Does having a developed home country matter for self-employment in the United States? *Am. Econ. Rev.* 2012;102(3):538–42, doi:10.1257/aer.102.3.538.

43. Blanchflower, DG. Self-employment in OECD countries. *Labour Econ.* 2000;7(5):471–505, doi:10.1016/S0927-5371(00)00011-7.

44. Thurik, AR, Carree, MA, van Stel, A and Audretsch, DB. Does self-employment reduce unemployment? *J. Bus. Ventur.* 2008;23(6):673–86, doi:10.1016/j.jbusvent.2008.01.007.

45. Bender, KA and Roche, K. Educational mismatch and self-employment. *Econ. Educ. Rev.* 2013;34:85–95, doi:10.1016/j.econedurev.2013.01.010.

46. http://www.economist.com/news/britain/21676792-why-more-britons-are-working-themselves-uber-conundrum.

47. http://www.economist.com/news/economic-and-financial-indicators/21660991-self-employment.

48. http://www.theatlantic.com/business/archive/2011/09/the-freelance-surge-is-the-industrial-revolution-of-our-time/244229/.

49. http://www.economist.com/blogs/freeexchange/2015/10/gig-economy?zid=297&ah=3ae0fe266c7447d8a0c7ade5547d62ca.

50. Startienė, G, Remeikienė, R and Dumčiuvienė, D. Concept of self-employment. *Econ. Manag.* 2010;15:262–75.

51. Griffeth, RW. A meta-analysis of antecedents and correlates of employee turnover: Update, Moderator tests, and research implications for the next millennium. *J. Manage.* 2000;26(3):463–88, doi:10.1177/014920630002600305.

52. http://www.economist.com/blogs/buttonwood/2013/07/work-and-growth?zid=297&ah=3ae0fe266c7447d8a0c7ade5547d62ca.

53. Zwan, P van der, Hessels, J and Rietveld, CA. The pleasures and pains of self-employment: A panel data analysis of satisfaction with life, work, and leisure. 2015. Tinbergen Discussion Paper, 15-099/VII.

54. Blanchflower, DG. Self-employment in OECD countries. *Labour Econ.* 2000;7(5):471–505, doi:10.1016/S0927-5371(00)00011-7.

55. Blanchflower, DG. Self-employment: More may not be better. *Swedish Econ. Policy Rev.* 2004;11:15–74, doi:http://www.nber.org/papers/w10286.pdf.

56. http://www.forbes.com/sites/scotthartley/2012/03/25/conspicuous_creation/.

57. http://www.forbes.com/sites/dinagachman/2013/01/10/are-entrepreneurs-the-rock-stars-of-today/.

58. http://www.entrepreneur.com/article/245574.

59. https://hbr.org/2014/01/the-dangerous-rise-of-entrepreneurship-porn.

60. Frese, M and Gielnik, MM. The psychology of entrepreneurship. *Annu. Rev. Organ. Psychol. Organ. Behav.* 2014;1(1):413–38, doi:10.1146/annurev-orgpsych-031413-091326.

61. Thurik, AR, Carree, MA, van Stel, A and Audretsch, DB. Does self-employment reduce unemployment? *J. Bus. Ventur.* 2008;23(6):673–86, doi:10.1016/j.jbusvent.2008.01.007.

62. Frese, M and Gielnik, MM. The psychology of entrepreneurship. *Annu. Rev. Organ. Psychol. Organ. Behav.* 2014;1(1):413–38, doi:10.1146/annurev-orgpsych-031413-091326.

63. Shane, SA. *The Illusions of Entrepreneurship.* New Haven, CT: Yale UP (2008).

64. Kuratko, DF. The emergence of entrepreneurship education: Development, trends, and challenges. *Entrep. Theory Pract.* 2005;29(5):577–98, doi:10.1111/j.1540-6520.2005.00099.x.

65. http://www.forbes.com/sites/jasonnazar/2013/09/09/16-surprising-statistics-about-small-businesses/#2af0e44a3078.

66. Cromie, S and Hayes, J. Business ownership as a means of overcoming job dissatisfaction. *Pers. Rev.* 1991;20(1):19–24, doi:10.1108/00483489110006853.

67. *The Economist, Managing Talent: Recruiting, Retaining and Getting the Most from Talented People*, eds. M Devine and M

Syrett. London: Profile Books (2006), p.45.

68. https://hbr.org/2012/10/the-danger-of-celebritizing-en.

69. Frese, M and Gielnik, MM. The psychology of entrepreneurship. *Annu. Rev. Organ. Psychol. Organ. Behav.* 2014;1(1):413–38, doi:10.1146/annurev-orgpsych-031413-091326.

70. http://www.huffingtonpost.com/2012/01/20/global-entrepreneurship-is-on-the-rise_n_1216921.html.

71. Twenge, JM. A review of the empirical evidence on generational differences in work attitudes. *J. Bus. Psychol.* 2010;25(2):201–10, doi:10.1007/s10869-010-9165-6.

72. Twenge, JM, Miller, JD and Campbell, WK. The narcissism epidemic: Commentary on modernity and narcissistic personality disorder. *Personal. Disord. Theory, Res. Treat.* 2014;5(2):227–29, doi:10.1037/per0000008.

CHAPTER 2

1. http://99u.com/articles/20490/talent-is-persistence-what-it-takes-to-be-an-independent-creative.

2. http://www.self-esteem-enhances-life.com/talents-T3.html.

3. http://www.gallup.com/businessjournal/412/exactly-what-talent-anyway.aspx.

4. McDaniel, MA. Gerrymandering in personnel selection: A review of practice. *Hum. Resour. Manag. Rev.* 2009;19(3):263–70, doi:10.1016/j.hrmr.2009.03.004.

5. Borkenau, P, Mauer, N, Riemann, R, Spinath, FM and Angleitner, A. Thin slices of behavior as cues of personality and intelligence. *J. Pers. Soc. Psychol.* 2004;86(4):599–614, doi:10.1037/0022-3514.86.4.599.

6. Rule, NO and Ambady, N. Face and fortune: Inferences of personality from managing partners' faces predict their law firms' financial success. *Leadersh. Q.* 2011;22(4):690–96, doi:10.1016/j.leaqua.2011.05.009.

7. http://pubsonline.informs.org/doi/abs/10.1287/orsc.1090.0481?journalCode=orsc.

8. Lipovetsky, S. Pareto 80/20 law: Derivation via random partitioning. *Int. J. Math. Educ. Sci. Technol.* 2009;40(2):271–7, doi:10.1080/00207390802213609.

9. Andriani, P and McKelvey, B. Managing in a Pareto world calls

for new thinking. *Management* 2011;14(2):90–118.

10. Grosfeld-Nir, A, Ronen, B and Kozlovsky, N. The Pareto managerial principle: When does it apply? *Int. J. Prod. Res.* 2007;45(10):2317–25, doi:10.1080/00207540600818203.

11. http://www.economist.com/node/9988840.

12. http://www.economist.com/node/17848429.

13. Cappelli, P and Keller, J. Talent management: Conceptual approaches and practical challenges. *Annu. Rev. Organ. Psychol. Organ. Behav.* 2014;1(1):305–31, doi:10.1146/annurev-orgpsych-031413-091314.

14. http://www.economist.com/node/17848429.

15. Sackett, PR. Revisiting the origins of the typical–maximum performance distinction. *Hum. Perform.* 2007;20(3):179–85, doi:10.1080/08959280701332968.

16. Cronbach, LJ and Meehl, PE. Construct validity in psychological tests. *Psychol. Bull.* 1955;52:281–302, doi:10.1037/h0040957.

17. DuBois, CL, Sackett, PR, Zedeck, S and Fogli, L. Further exploration of typical and maximum performance criteria: Definitional issues, prediction, and White–Black differences. *J. Appl. Psychol.* 1993;78(2):205–11, doi:10.1037/0021-9010.78.2.205.

18. Klehe, U-C and Anderson, N. Working hard and working smart: Motivation and ability during typical and maximum performance. *J. Appl. Psychol.* 2007;92(4):978–92, doi:10.1037/0021-9010.92.4.978.

19. Ones, DS and Viswesvaran, C. A research note on the incremental validity of job knowledge and integrity tests for predicting maximal performance. *Hum. Perform.* 2007;20(3):293–303, doi:10.1080/08959280701333461.

20. Klehe, U-C and Anderson, N. Working hard and working smart: Motivation and ability during typical and maximum performance. *J. Appl. Psychol.* 2007;92(4):978–92, doi:10.1037/0021-9010.92.4.978.

21. Ployhart, RE, Lim, B-C and Chan, K-Y. Exploring relations between typical and maximum performance ratings and the five factor model of personality. *Pers. Psychol.* 2001;54:809–43, doi:10.1111/j.1744-6570.2001.tb00233.x.

22. Karau, S and Williams, KD. Interpersonal relations and group social loafing: A meta-analytic review and theoretical integration. *J. Pers. Soc. Psychol.* 1993;65(4):681–706,

doi:10.1037/0022-3514.65.4.681.

23. Klehe, U-C and Latham, G. What would you do—really or ideally? Constructs underlying the behavior description interview and the situational interview in predicting typical versus maximum performance. *Hum. Perform.* 2006;19(4):357–82, doi:10.1207/s15327043hup1904_3.

24. Chamorro-Premuzic, T, Ahmetoglu, G and Furnham, A. Little more than personality: Dispositional determinants of test anxiety (the big five, core self-evaluations, and self-assessed intelligence). *Learn. Individ. Differ.* 2008;18(2):258–63, doi:10.1016/j.lindif.2007.09.002.

25. Beus, JM and Whitman, DS. The relationship between typical and maximum performance: A meta-analytic examination. *Hum. Perform.* 2012;25(5):355–76, doi:10.1080/08959285.2012.721831.

26. Sackett, PR, Zedeck, S and Fogli, L. Relations between measures of typical and maximum job performance. *J. Appl. Psychol.* 1988;73(3):482–6, doi:10.1037/0021-9010.73.3.482.

27. Sackett, PR. Revisiting the origins of the typical–maximum performance distinction. *Hum. Perform.* 2007;20(3):179–85, doi:10.1080/08959280701332968.

28. Ployhart, RE, Lim, B-C and Chan K-Y. Exploring relations between typical and maximum performance ratings and the five factor model of personality. *Pers. Psychol.* 2001;54:809–43, doi:10.1111/j.1744-6570.2001.tb00233.x.

29. Klehe, U-C and Anderson, N. Working hard and working smart: Motivation and ability during typical and maximum performance. *J. Appl. Psychol.* 2007;92(4):978–92, doi:10.1037/0021-9010.92.4.978.

30. Saatchi, C. *Question*. London: Phaidon Press (2010), p.29.

31. Ackerman, PL. Nonsense, common sense, and science of expert performance: Talent and individual differences. *Intelligence* 2014;45(1):6–17, doi:10.1016/j.intell.2013.04.009.

32. Ruthsatz, J, Ruthsatz, K and Stephens, KR. Putting practice into perspective: Child prodigies as evidence of innate talent. *Intelligence* 2014;45(1):60–65, doi:10.1016/j.intell.2013.08.003.

33. Roberts, BW. Back to the future: Personality and assessment and personality development. *J. Res. Pers.* 2009;43(2):137–45, doi:10.1016/j.jrp.2008.12.015.

34. Almlund, M, Duckworth, AL, Heckman, J and Kautz, T. *Personality Psychology and Economics*. 2011. NBER Working Paper No. 16822, doi:10.1016/B978-0-444-53444-6.00001-8.

35. Hogan, J and Holland, B. Using theory to evaluate personality and job-performance relations: A socioanalytic perspective. *J. Appl. Psychol.* 2003;88(1):100–12, doi:10.1037/0021-9010.88.1.100.

36. http://www.theguardian.com/technology/2014/feb/20/facebook-turned-down-whatsapp-co-founder-brian-acton-job-2009.

37. http://www.businessinsider.com/successful-people-who-failed-at-first-2015-7.

38. Ibid.

39. Davenport, TH, Harris, J and Shapiro, J. Competing on talent analytics. *Harv. Bus. Rev.* 2010;88:52–8, doi:Article.

40. Kristof-Brown, A and Guay, RP, Person–environment fit. In: *APA Handbook of Industrial and Organizational Psychology, Vol. 3: Maintaining, Expanding, and Contracting the Organization*. 2011:3–50, doi:10.1037/12171-001.

41. Oh, I-S, Guay, RP, Kim, K, et al. Fit happens globally: A meta-analytic comparison of the relationships of person–environment fit dimensions with work attitudes and performance across East Asia, Europe, and North America. *Pers. Psychol.* 2014;67(1):99–152, doi:10.1111/peps.12026.

42. Wanous, JP, Poland, TD, Premack, SL and Davis, KS. The effects of met expectations on newcomer attitudes and behaviors: A review and meta-analysis. *J. Appl. Psychol.* 1992;77(3):288–97, doi:10.1037/0021-9010.77.3.288.

43. Hogan, J and Holland, B. Using theory to evaluate personality and job-performance relations: A socioanalytic perspective. *J. Appl. Psychol.* 2003;88(1):100–112, doi:10.1037/0021-9010.88.1.100.

44. Almlund, M, Duckworth, AL, Heckman, J and Kautz, T. *Personality Psychology and Economics*. 2011. NBER Working Paper No. 16822, doi:10.1016/B978-0-444-53444-6.00001-8.

CHAPTER 3

1. Beus, JM and Whitman, DS. The relationship between typical and maximum performance: A meta-analytic examination. *Hum. Perform.* 2012;25(5):355–76, doi:10.1080/08959285.2012.721831.

2. Campbell, JP and Wiernik, BM. The modeling and assessment of work performance. *Annu. Rev. Organ. Pyschol. Organ. Behav.* 2015;2:47–74, doi:10.1146/annurev-orgpsych-032414-111427.

3. Kuncel, NR, Ones, DS and Sackett, PR. Individual differences as predictors of work, educational, and broad life outcomes. *Pers. Individ. Dif.* 2010;49(4):331–6, doi:10.1016/j.paid.2010.03.042.

4. Viswesvaran, C, Ones, DS and Schmidt, FL. Comparative analysis of the reliability of job performance ratings. *J. Appl. Psychol.* 1996;81(5):557–74, doi:10.1037/0021-9010.81.5.557.

5. Campbell, JP and Wiernik, BM. The modeling and assessment of work performance. *Annu. Rev. Organ. Pyschol. Organ. Behav.* 2015;2:47–74, doi:10.1146/annurev-orgpsych-032414-111427.

6. Ryan, AM and Ployhart, RE. A century of selection. *Annu. Rev. Psychol.* 2014;65:693–717, doi:10.1146/annurev-psych -010213-115134.

7. Sturman, MC, Cheramie, R and Cashen, LH. The impact of job complexity and performance measurement on the temporal consistency, stability, and test–retest reliability of employee job performance ratings. *J. Appl. Psychol.* 2005;90(2):269–83, doi:10.1037/0021-9010.90.2.269.

8. Silzer, ROB and Church, AH. The pearls and perils of identifying potential. *Ind. Organ. Psychol.* 2009;2:377–412, doi:10.1111/j.1754-9434.2009.01163.x.

9. Ryan, AM and Ployhart, RE. A century of selection. *Annu. Rev. Psychol.* 2014;65:693–717, doi:10.1146/annurev-psych -010213-115134.

10. Armstrong, PI, Day, SX, McVay, JP and Rounds, J. Holland's RIASEC model as an integrative framework for individual differences. *J. Couns. Psychol.* 2008;55(1):1–18, doi:10.1037/0022-0167.55.1.1.

11. Fruyt, F and Mervielde, I. RIASEC types and big five traits as predictors of employment status and nature of employment. *Pers. Psychol.* 1999;52(3):701–27, doi:10.1111/j.1744-6570.1999.tb00177.x.

12. Hogan, R, Chamorro-Premuzic, T and Kaiser, RB. Employability and career success: Bridging the gap between theory and reality. *Ind. Organ. Psychol.* 2013;6(1):3–16, doi:10.1111/iops.12001.

13. Campbell, JP and Wiernik, BM. The modeling and assessment of work performance. *Annu. Rev. Organ. Pyschol. Organ. Behav.*

2015;2:47–74, doi:10.1146/annurev-orgpsych-032414-111427.

14. Schmidt, FL. The role of general cognitive ability and job performance: Why there cannot be a debate. *Hum. Perform.* 2002;15(1-2):187–210, doi:10.1080/08959285.2002.9668091.

15. Earp, BD and Trafimow, D. Replication, falsification, and the crisis of confidence in social psychology. *Front. Psychol.* 2015;6:621, doi:10.3389/fpsyg.2015.00621.

16. Lyons, BD, Hoffman, BJ and Michel, JW. Not much more than G? An examination of the impact of intelligence on NFL performance. *Hum. Perform.* 2009;22(3):225–45, doi:10.1080/08959280902970401.

17. Judge, T and Kammeyer-Mueller, JD. On the value of aiming high: The causes and consequences of ambition. *J. Appl. Psychol.* 2012;97(4):758–75, doi:10.1037/a0028084.

18. Simonton, DK. Talent and its development: An emergenic and epigenetic model. *Psych. Rev.* 1999;106:435–57, doi:10.1037/0033-295X. 103.3.435.

19. Bell, ST, Villado, AJ, Lukasik, MA, Belau, L and Briggs, AL. Getting specific about demographic diversity variable and team performance relationships: A meta-analysis. *J. Manage.* 2011;37(3):709–43, doi:10.1177/0149206310365001.

20. Meyer, GJ, Finn, SE, Eyde, LD et al. Psychological testing and psychological assessment. A review of evidence and issues. *Am. Psychol.* 2001;56:128–65, doi:10.1037/0003-066X.56.2.128.

21. Levashina, J, Hartwell, CJ, Morgeson, FP and Campion, MA. The structured employment interview: Narrative and quantitative review of the research literature. *Pers. Psychol.* 2014;67(1):241–93, doi:10.1111/peps.12052.

22. Schmidt, FL and Hunter, JE. The validity and utility of selection methods in personnel psychology: Practical and theoretical implications of 85 years of research findings. *Psychol. Bull.* 1998;124(2):262–74, doi:10.1037/0033-2909.124.2.262.

23. Stewart, GL, Dustin, SL, Barrick, MR and Darnold, TC. Exploring the handshake in employment interviews. *J. Appl. Psychol.* 2008;93(5):1139–46, doi:10.1037/0021-9010.93.5.1139.

24. Roth, PL and Huffcutt, AI. A meta-analysis of interviews and cognitive ability: Back to the future? *J. Pers. Psychol.* 2013;12(4):157–69, doi:10.1027/1866-5888/a000091.

25. Huffcutt, AI, van Iddekinge, CH and Roth, PL. Understanding

applicant behavior in employment interviews: A theoretical model of interviewee performance. *Hum. Resour. Manag. Rev.* 2011;21(4):353–67, doi:10.1016/j.hrmr.2011.05.003.

26. Hamdani, MR, Valcea, S and Buckley, MR. The relentless pursuit of construct validity in the design of employment interviews. *Hum. Resour. Manag. Rev.* 2014;24(2):160–76, doi:10.1016/j.hrmr.2013.07.002.

27. Ibid.

28. Thornton, GC and Gibbons, AM. Validity of assessment centers for personnel selection. *Hum. Resour. Manag. Rev.* 2009;19(3):169–87, doi:10.1016/j.hrmr.2009.02.002.

29. Schmidt, FL and Hunter, JE. The validity and utility of selection methods in personnel psychology: Practical and theoretical implications of 85 years of research findings. *Psychol. Bull.* 1998;124(2):262–74, doi:10.1037/0033-2909.124.2.262.

30. Schmitt, N. Personality and cognitive ability as predictors of effective performance at work. *Annu. Rev. Organ. Psychol. Organ. Behav.* 2013;1(1):45–65, doi:10.1146/annurev-orgpsych-031413-091255.

31. Kuncel, NR, Ones, DS and Sackett, PR. Individual differences as predictors of work, educational, and broad life outcomes. *Pers. Individ. Dif.* 2010;49(4):331–6, doi:10.1016/j.paid.2010.03.042.

32. Schmitt, N. Personality and cognitive ability as predictors of effective performance at work. *Annu. Rev. Organ. Psychol. Organ. Behav.* 2013;1(1):45–65. doi:10.1146/annurev-orgpsych-031413-091255.

33. Salgado, JF, Anderson, N, Moscoso, S, Bertua, C and de Fruyt, F. International validity generalization of GMA and cognitive abilities: A European Community meta-analysis. *Pers. Psychol.* 2003;56(3):573–605, doi:10.1111/j.1744-6570.2003.tb00751.x.

34. Kuncel, NR, Ones, DS and Sackett, PR. Individual differences as predictors of work, educational, and broad life outcomes. *Pers. Individ. Dif.* 2010;49(4):331–6, doi:10.1016/j.paid.2010.03.042.

35. Schmidt, FL and Hunter, JE. The validity and utility of selection methods in personnel psychology: Practical and theoretical implications of 85 years of research findings. *Psychol. Bull.* 1998;124(2):262–74, doi:10.1037/0033-2909.124.2.262.

36. Gladwell, M. *Outliers.* New York: Little, Brown (2008), doi:10.3200/SRCH.20.2.48-57.

37. Kuncel, NR, Ones, DS and Sackett, PR. Individual differences as predictors of work, educational, and broad life outcomes. *Pers. Individ. Dif.* 2010;49(4):331–6, doi:10.1016/j.paid.2010.03.042.

38. Devine, DJ and Philips, JL. Do smarter teams do better? A meta-analysis of cognitive ability and team performance. *Small Gr. Res.* 2001;32(5):507–32, doi:10.1177/104649640103200501.

39. Mead, AD and Drasgow, F. Equivalence of computerized and paper-and-pencil cognitive ability tests: A meta-analysis. *Psychol. Bull.* 1993;114(3):449–58, doi:10.1037/0033-2909.114.3.449.

40. Hunter, JE and Hunter, RF. Validity and utility of alternative predictors of job performance. *Psychol. Bull.* 1984;96(1):72–98, doi:10.1037/0033-2909.96.1.72.

41. Chamorro-Premuzic, T and Arteche, A. Intellectual competence and academic performance: Preliminary validation of a model. *Intelligence* 2008;36(6):564–73, doi:10.1016/j.intell.2008.01.001.

42. Elliot, AJ, Maier, MA, Moller, AC, Friedman, R and Meinhardt, J. Color and psychological functioning: The effect of red on performance attainment. *J. Exp. Psychol. Gen.* 2007;136(1):154–68, doi:10.1037/0096-3445.136.1.154.

43. Hausknecht, JP, Halpert, JA, Di Paolo, NT and Moriarty Gerrard, MO. Retesting in selection: A meta-analysis of coaching and practice effects for tests of cognitive ability. *J. Appl. Psychol.* 2007;92(2):373–85, doi:10.1037/0021-9010.92.2.373.

44. Kuncel, NR, Ones, DS and Sackett, PR. Individual differences as predictors of work, educational, and broad life outcomes. *Pers. Individ. Dif.* 2010;49(4):331–6, doi:10.1016/j.paid.2010.03.042.

45. von Stumm, S and Plomin, R. Intelligence, socioeconomic status and the growth of intelligence from infancy through adolescence. *Intelligence* 2015;48:30–36, doi:10.1016/j.intell.2014.10.002.

46. Hyde, JS and Linn, MC. Gender differences in verbal ability: A meta-analysis. *Psychol. Bull.* 1988;104(1):53–69, doi:10.1037/0033-2909.104.1.53.

47. Kuncel, NR, Ones, DS and Sackett, PR. Individual differences as predictors of work, educational, and broad life outcomes. *Pers. Individ. Dif.* 2010;49(4):331–6, doi:10.1016/j.paid.2010.03.042.

48. Hogan, J and Holland, B. Using theory to evaluate personality and job-performance relations: A socioanalytic perspective. *J. Appl. Psychol.* 2003;88(1):100–112, doi:10.1037/0021-9010.88.1.100.

49. Judge, TA, Bono, JE, Ilies, R and Gerhardt, MW. Personality and

leadership: A qualitative and quantitative review. *J. Appl. Psychol.* 2002;87(4):765–80, doi:10.1037//0021-9010.87.4.765.

50. Freund, PA and Kasten, N. How smart do you think you are? A meta-analysis on the validity of self-estimates of cognitive ability. *Psychol. Bull.* 2012;138(2):296–321, doi:10.1037/a0026556.

51. Sedikides, C and Gregg, AP. Self-enhancement: Food for thought. *Perspect. Psychol. Sci.* 2008;3(2):102–16, doi:10.1111/j.1745-6916.2008.00068.x.

52. Allen, TJ, Sherman, JW, Conrey, FR and Stroessner, SJ. Stereotype strength and attentional bias: Preference for confirming versus disconfirming information depends on processing capacity. *J. Exp. Soc. Psychol.* 2009;45(5):1081–7, doi:10.1016/j.jesp.2009.06.002.

53. Morgeson, FP, Campion, MA, Dipboye, RL, Hollenbeck, JR, Murphy, K and Schmitt, N. Reconsidering the use of personality tests in personnel selection contexts. *Pers. Psychol.* 2007;60(3):683–729, doi:10.1111/j.1744-6570.2007.00089.x.

54. Uziel, L. Rethinking social desirability scales: From impression management to interpersonally oriented self-control. *Perspect. Psychol. Sci.* 2010;5(3):243–62, doi:10.1177/1745691610369465.

55. Schlenker, B. Interpersonal processes involving impression regulation and management. *Annu. Rev. Psychol.* 1992;43:133–68, doi:10.1146/annurev.psych.43.1.133.

56. Kleinmann, M. Selling oneself: Construct and criterion-related validity of impression management in structured interviews. *Hum. Perform.* 2011;24(1):29–46, doi:10.1080/08959285.2010.530634.

57. Levashina, J, Hartwell, CJ, Morgeson, FP and Campion, MA. The structured employment interview: Narrative and quantitative review of the research literature. *Pers. Psychol.* 2014;67(1):241–93, doi:10.1111/peps.12052.

58. Hogan, J, Barrett, P and Hogan, R. Personality measurement, faking, and employment selection. *J. Appl. Psychol.* 2007;92(5):1270–85, doi:10.1037/0021-9010.92.5.1270.

59. Hausdorf, PA and Leblanc, MM. Cognitive ability testing and employment selection: Does test content relate to adverse impact? *Appl. HRM Res.* 2003;7(2):41–8.

60. Schmidt, FL and Hunter, JE. The validity and utility of selection methods in personnel psychology: Practical and theoretical implications of 85 years of research findings. *Psychol. Bull.*

1998;124(2):262–74, doi:10.1037/0033-2909.124.2.262.

61. Breaugh, JA. The use of biodata for employee selection: Past research and future directions. *Hum. Resour. Manag. Rev.* 2009;19(3):219–31, doi:10.1016/j.hrmr.2009.02.003.

62. Cole, M, Field, H and Stafford, J. Validity of resumé reviewers' inferences concerning applicant personality based on resumé evaluation. *Int. J. Sel. Assess.* 2005;13(4):321–4, doi:10.1111/j.1468-2389.2005.00329.x.

63. Ng, TWH and Feldman, DC. How broadly does education contribute to job performance? *Pers. Psychol.* 2009;62:89–134.

64. Becker, GS. Investment in human capital: A theoretical analysis. *J. Polit. Econ.* 1962;70(5):9, doi:10.1086/258724.

65. Borman, WC. 360° ratings: An analysis of assumptions and a research agenda for evaluating their validity. *Hum. Resour. Manag. Rev.* 1997;7(3):299–315, doi:10.1016/S1053-4822(97)90010-3.

66. Day, DV, Fleenor, JW, Atwater, LE, Sturm, RE and McKee, RA. Advances in leader and leadership development: A review of 25 years of research and theory. *Leadersh. Q.* 2014;25(1):63–82, doi:10.1016/j.leaqua.2013.11.004.

67. Reissig, S. 360-degree feedback. *Manager* 2011;Summer:30–31, doi:10.2139/ssrn.2288194.

68. DeNisi, AS and Kluger, AN. Feedback effectiveness: Can 360-degree appraisals be improved? *Acad. Manag. Exec.* 2000;14(1):129–39, doi:10.5465/AME.2000.2909845.

69. Borman, WC. 360° ratings: An analysis of assumptions and a research agenda for evaluating their validity. *Hum. Resour. Manag. Rev.* 1997;7(3):299–315, doi:10.1016/S1053-4822(97)90010-3.

70. Day, DV, Fleenor, JW, Atwater, LE, Sturm, RE and McKee, RA. Advances in leader and leadership development: A review of 25 years of research and theory. *Leadersh. Q.* 2014;25(1):63–82, doi:10.1016/j.leaqua.2013.11.004.

71. Christian, MS, Edwards, BD and Bradley, JC. Situational judgment tests: Constructs assessed and a meta-analysis of their criterion-related validities. *Pers. Psychol.* 2010;63(1):83–117, doi:10.1111/j.1744-6570.2009.01163.x.

72. Chamorro-Premuzic, T. Ace the assessment. *Harv. Bus. Rev.* 2015;93(7):118–21.

CHAPTER 4

1. Kahn, WA. Psychological conditions of personal engagement and disengagement at work. *Acad. Manag. J.* 1990;33(4):692–724, doi:10.2307/256287.
2. Van Iddekinge, CH, Roth, PL, Putka, DJ and Lanivich, SE. Are you interested? A meta-analysis of relations between vocational interests and employee performance and turnover. *J. Appl. Psychol.* 2011;96(6):1167–94, doi:10.1037/a0024343.
3. Petty, MM, McGee, GW and Cavender, JW. A meta-analysis of the relationships between individual job satisfaction and individual performance. *Acad. Manag. Rev.* 1984;9(4):712–21, doi:10.5465/AMR.1984.4277608.
4. Rich, BL, Lepine, JA and Crawford, ER. Job engagement: Antecedents and effects on job performance. *Acad. Manag. J.* 2010;53(3):617–35, doi:10.5465/AMJ.2010.51468988.
5. O'Boyle, EH, Forsyth, DR, Banks, GC and McDaniel, MA. A meta-analysis of the dark triad and work behavior: A social exchange perspective. *J. Appl. Psychol.* 2012;97(3):557–79. doi:10.1037/a0025679.
6. Christian, MS, Garza, AS and Slaughter, JE. Work engagement: A quantitative review and test of its relations with task and contextual performance. 2011;68(3):89–136. doi/10.1111/j.1744-6570.2010 .01203.x/abstract
7. Ng, TWH, Sorensen, KL and Yim, FHK. Does the job satisfaction–job performance relationship vary across cultures? *J. Cross. Cult. Psychol.* 2009;40(5):761–96, doi:10.1177/0022022109339208.
8. Hogan, R and Chamorro-Premuzic, T. Personality and career success. In: *APA Handbook of Personality and Social Psychology, Vol. 4: Personality Processes and Individual Differences.* Washington, DC: APA (2015), pp.619–38, doi:10.1037/14343-028.
9. Hogan, R and Blickle, G. Socioanalytic theory. In: *Handbook of Personality at Work*, eds. N Christiansen and R Tett. New York: Routledge (2013), pp.53–70.
10. Freud, S. On narcissism: An introduction [1914]. In: *Standard Edition of the Complete Psychological Works of Sigmund Freud,* Vol. XIV. London: Hogarth Press (1957), pp.73–102.
11. Hogan, R and Chamorro-Premuzic, T. Personality and the laws of history. *Wiley-Blackwell Handb. Individ. Differ.*

2013;(2007):491–511, doi:10.1002/9781444343120.ch18.

12. Stone, B. *The Everything Store: Jeff Bezos and the Age of Amazon*. New York: Little, Brown (2013), doi:10.1007/s13398-014-0173-7.2.

13. Finkle, TA. Richard Branson and Virgin, Inc. *J. Int. Acad. Case Stud*. 2011;17(5):109–22.

14. Isaacson, W. The real leadership lessons of Steve Jobs. *Harv. Bus. Rev*. 2012;90(4).

15. Schneider, B, Ehrhart, MG and Macey, WH. Organizational climate and culture. *Annu. Rev. Psychol*. 2013;64:361–88, doi:10.1146/annurev-psych-113011-143809.

16. Parsons, F. *Choosing a Vocation*. Boston, MA: Houghton Mifflin (1909).

17. Schein, EH. Coming to a new awareness of organizational culture. *Sloan Manage. Rev*. 1984;25(2):3.

18. Schein, EH. *Organizational Culture and Leadership*. San Francisco: John Wiley & Sons (2010), doi:10.1016/j.sbspro.2011.12.156.

19. Van Iddekinge, CH, Roth, PL, Raymark, PH and Odle-Dusseau, HN. The criterion-related validity of integrity tests: An updated meta-analysis. *J. Appl. Psychol*. 2012;97(3):499–530, doi:10.1037/a0021196.

20. Schneider, B, Ehrhart, MG and Macey, WH. Organizational climate and culture. *Annu. Rev. Psychol*. 2013;64:361–88, doi:10.1146/annurev-psych-113011-143809.

21. Hogan, R, Kaiser, RB and Chamorro-Premuzic, T. An evolutionary view of organizational culture. *Oxford Handb. Organ. Clim. Cult*. 2013:1–27.

22. Hogan, R and Chamorro-Premuzic, T. Personality and the laws of history. *Wiley-Blackwell Handb. Individ. Differ*. 2013;(2007):491–511, doi:10.1002/9781444343120.ch18.

23. Kahn, WA. Psychological conditions of personal engagement and disengagement at work. *Acad. Manag. J*. 1990;33(4):692–724, doi:10.2307/256287.

24. Dreyfus, HL and Wrathall, MA. *A Companion to Heidegger*. Oxford: Blackwell Publishing (2007), doi:10.1002/9780470996492.

25. Csikszentmihalyi, M. The flow experience and its significance for human psychology. In: *Optimal Experience: Psychological Studies of Flow in Consciousness*, eds. M Csikszentmihalyi and IS Csikszentmihalyi. Cambridge: Cambridge UP (1988), pp.15–35,

doi:10.1017/CBO9780511621956.002.

26. Xanthopoulou, D, Bakker, AB, Demerouti, E and Schaufeli, WB. Reciprocal relationships between job resources, personal resources, and work engagement. *J. Vocat. Behav.* 2009;74(3):235–44, doi:10.1016/j.jvb.2008.11.003.

27. Akhtar, R, Boustani, L, Tsivrikos, D and Chamorro-Premuzic, T. The engageable personality: Personality and trait EI as predictors of work engagement. *Pers. Individ. Dif.* 2015;73:44–9, doi:10.1016/j.paid.2014.08.040.

28. Inceoglu, I and Warr, P. Personality and job engagement. *J. Pers. Psychol.* 2011;10(4):177–81, doi:10.1027/1866-5888/a000045.

29. Kaiser, RB. The accountability crisis: An overlooked cause of disengagement. Presented in the Dark Side of Engagement Symposium at the 30th Annual Conference of the Society for Industrial–Organizational Psychology (R. Hogan, Chair), April 2015, Philadelphia, PA.

CHAPTER 5

1. Olson, JM, Vernon, PA, Harris, J and Jang, KL. The heritability of attitudes: A study of twins. *J. Pers. Soc. Psychol.* 2001;80(6):845–60, doi:10.1037/0022-3514.80.6.845.

2. Ackerman, PL. Nonsense, common sense, and science of expert performance: Talent and individual differences. *Intelligence* 2014;45(1):6–17, doi:10.1016/j.intell.2013.04.009.

3. Cahan, S and Cohen, N. Age versus schooling effects on intelligence development. *Child Dev.* 1989;60(5):1239–49, doi:10.2307/1130797.

4. Deary, IJ, Yang, J, Davies, G et al. Genetic contributions to stability and change in intelligence from childhood to old age. *Nature* 2012;482(7384):212–15, doi:10.1038/nature10781.

5. Canivez, GL and Watkins, MW. Long-term stability of the Wechsler Intelligence Scale for Children – Third Edition. *Psychol. Assess.* 1998;10(3):285–91, doi:10.1037/1040-3590.10.3.285.

6. Sameroff, AJ, Seifer, R, Baldwin, A and Baldwin, C. Stability of intelligence from preschool to adolescence: The influence of social and family risk factors. *Child Dev.* 1993;64(1):80–97, doi:10.1111/j.1467-8624.1993.tb02896.x.

7. Salthouse, TA. When does age-related cognitive decline

begin? *Neurobiol. Aging* 2009;30(4):507–14, doi:10.1016/j. neurobiolaging.2008.09.023.

8. Hausknecht, JP, Halpert, JA, Di Paolo, NT and Moriarty Gerrard, MO. Retesting in selection: A meta-analysis of coaching and practice effects for tests of cognitive ability. *J. Appl. Psychol.* 2007;92(2):373–85, doi:10.1037/0021-9010.92.2.373.

9. http://money.cnn.com/2016/01/05/technology/ lumosity-brain-train-app-ftc-settlement/

10. Ackerman, PL and Rolfhus, EL. The locus of adult intelligence: Knowledge, abilities, and nonability traits. *Psychol. Aging* 1999;14(2):314–30, doi:10.1037/0882-7974.14.2.314.

11. Ackerman, PL, Beier, ME and Boyle, MO. Working memory and intelligence: The same or different constructs? *Psychol. Bull.* 2005;131(1):30–60, doi:10.1037/0033-2909.131.1.30.

12. Hudson, NW and Roberts, BW. Goals to change personality traits: Concurrent links between personality traits, daily behavior, and goals to change oneself. *J. Res. Pers.* 2014;53:68–83, doi:10.1016/j.jrp.2014.08.008.

13. Guttman, L. Review of *Quiet: The power of introverts in a world that can't stop talking. J. Am. Acad. Child Adolesc. Psychiatry* 2014;53(6):705–7, doi:10.1016/j.jaac.2014.04.007.

14. Srivastava, S, John, OP, Gosling, SD and Potter, J. Development of personality in early and middle adulthood: Set like plaster or persistent change? *J. Pers. Soc. Psychol.* 2003;84(5):1041–53, doi:10.1037/0022-3514.84.5.1041.

15. Roberts, BW, Walton, KE and Viechtbauer, W. Patterns of mean-level change in personality traits across the life course: A meta-analysis of longitudinal studies. *Psychol. Bull.* 2006;132(1):1–25, doi:10.1037/0033-2909.132.1.1.

16. Allemand, M, Zimprich, D and Hendriks, AAJ. Age differences in five personality domains across the life span. *Dev. Psychol.* 2008;44(3):758–70, doi:10.1037/0012-1649.44.3.758.

17. Roberts, BW and Del Vecchio, WF. The rank-order consistency of personality traits from childhood to old age: A quantitative review of longitudinal studies. *Psychol. Bull.* 2000;126(1):3–25, doi:10.1037/0033-2909.126.1.3.

18. Brickman, P, Coates, D and Janoff-Bulman, R. Lottery winners and accident victims: Is happiness relative? *J. Pers. Soc. Psychol.* 1978;36(8):917–27, doi:10.1037/0022-3514.36.8.917.

19. Diener, E, Suh, EM, Lucas, RE and Smith, HL. Subjective well-being: Three decades of progress. *Psychol. Bull.* 1999;125:276–302, doi:10.1037/0033-2909.125.2.276.

20. Kern, ML, Friedman, HS, Martin, LR, Reynolds, CA and Luong, G. Conscientiousness, career success, and longevity: A lifespan analysis. *Ann. Behav. Med.* 2009;37(2):154–63, doi:10.1007/s12160-009-9095-6.

21. Soldz, S and Vaillant, GE. The big five personality traits and the life course: A 45-year longitudinal study. *J. Res. Pers.* 1999;33(2):208–32, doi:10.1006/jrpe.1999.2243.

22. Caspi, A, Moffitt, TE, Newman, DL and Silva, PA. Behavioral observations at age 3 years predict adult psychiatric disorders: Longitudinal evidence from a birth cohort. *Arch. Gen. Psychiatry* 1996;53(11):1033–9, doi:10.1001/archpsyc.1996.01830110071009.

23. Friedman, HS, Kern, ML and Reynolds, CA. Personality and health, subjective well-being, and longevity. *J. Pers.* 2010;78(1):179–216, doi:10.1111/j.1467-6494.2009.00613.x.

24. DeNeve, KM and Cooper, H. The happy personality: A meta-analysis of 137 personality traits and subjective well-being. *Psychol. Bull.* 1998;124(2):197–229, doi:10.1037/0033-2909.124.2.197.

25. Weiss, A, Bates, TC and Luciano, M. Happiness is a personal(ity) thing: The genetics of personality and well-being in a representative sample: Research report. *Psychol. Sci.* 2008;19(3):205–10, doi:10.1111/j.1467-9280.2008.02068.x.

26. Diener, E and Oishi, S. Money and happiness: Income and subjective well-being across nations. In: *Culture and Subjective Well-Being*, eds. E Diener and EM Suh. Cambridge, MA: MIT Press, pp.185–218, doi:10.1.1.208.4409.

27. Ariely, D. *Predictably Irrational.* New York: HarperCollins (2008), p.294, doi:10.2501/S1470785309200992.

28. Hudson, NW and Fraley, RC. Volitional personality trait change: Can people choose to change their personality traits? *J. Pers. Soc. Psychol.* 2015;108(4):1–18, doi:10.1037/pspp0000021.

29. Dickens, WT and Flynn, JR. Heritability estimates versus large environmental effects: The IQ paradox resolved. *Psychol. Rev.* 2001;108(2):346–69, doi:10.1037/0033-295X.108.2.346.

30. Hall, DT, Otazo, KL and Hollenbeck, GP. Behind closed doors: What really happens in executive coaching. *Organ. Dyn.*

1999;27(3):39–53, doi:10.1016/S0090-2616(99)90020-7.

31. Sherman, SA. The Wild West of executive coaching. *Harv. Bus. Rev.* 2004;82(11):82–90.

32. Theeboom, T, Beersma, B and van Vianen, AEM. Does coaching work? A meta-analysis on the effects of coaching on individual level outcomes in an organizational context. *J. Posit. Psychol.* 2014;9(1):1–18, doi:10.1080/17439760.2013.837499.

33. Grant, AM. The impact of life coaching on goal attainment, metacognition and mental health. *Soc. Behav. Personal. Int. J.* 2003;31(3):253–63, doi:10.2224/sbp.2003.31.3.253.

34. Ely, K, Boyce, LA, Nelson, JK, Zaccaro, SJ, Hernez-Broome, G and Whyman, W. Evaluating leadership coaching: A review and integrated framework. *Leadersh. Q.* 2010;21(4):585–99, doi:10.1016/j.leaqua.2010.06.003.

35. Peterson, DB. Measuring change: A psychometric approach to evaluating individual coaching outcomes. Presented at the annual conference of the Society for Industrial and Organizational Psychology, April 1993, San Francsico, CA.

36. Theeboom, T, Beersma, B and van Vianen AEM. Does coaching work? A meta-analysis on the effects of coaching on individual level outcomes in an organizational context. *J. Posit. Psychol.* 2014;9(1):1–18, doi:10.1080/17439760.2013.837499.

37. Luthans, F and Peterson, SJ. 360-degree feedback with systematic coaching: Empirical analysis suggests a winning combination. *Hum. Resour. Manage.* 2003;42(3):243–56, doi:10.1002/hrm.10083.

38. Richardson, KM and Rothstein, HR. Effects of occupational stress management intervention programs: A meta-analysis. *J. Occup. Health Psychol.* 2008;13(1):69–93, doi:10.1037/1076-8998.13.1.69.

39. Kotsou, I, Nelis, D, Grégoire, J and Mikolajczak, M. Emotional plasticity: Conditions and effects of improving emotional competence in adulthood. *J. Appl. Psychol.* 2011;96(4):827–39, doi:10.1037/a0023047.

40. Andrews, G and Harvey, R. Does psychotherapy benefit neurotic patients? A reanalysis of Smith, Glass, and Miller data. *Arch. Gen. Psychiatry* 1981;38(11):1203–8.

41. Aguinis, H, Culpepper, SA and Pierce, CA, Differential prediction generalization in college admissions testing. *J. Edu. Psychol.*

2016;108(7):1045–59.

42. Butler, A, Chapman, J, Forman, E and Beck, A. The empirical status of cognitive-behavioral therapy: A review of meta-analyses. *Clin. Psychol. Rev.* 2006;26(1):17–31, doi:10.1016/j.cpr.2005.07.003.

43. Bond, FW, Hayes, SC, Baer, RA et al. Preliminary psychometric properties of the Acceptance and Action Questionnaire-II: A revised measure of psychological inflexibility and experiential avoidance. *Behav. Ther.* 2011;42(4):676–88, doi:10.1016/j.beth.2011.03.007.

44. Baumeister, RF, Campbell, JD, Krueger, JI and Vohs, KD. Does high self-esteem cause better performance, interpersonal success, happiness, or healthier lifestyles? *Psychol. Sci. Public Interes.* 2003;4(1):1–44, doi:10.1111/1529-1006.01431.

45. De Haan, E, Culpin, V and Curd, J. Executive coaching in practice: What determines helpfulness for clients of coaching? *Pers. Rev.* 2011;40(1):24–44, doi:10.1108/00483481111095500.

46. Gaddis, BH and Foster, JL. Meta-analysis of dark side personality characteristics and critical work behaviors among leaders across the globe: Findings and implications for leadership development and executive coaching. *Appl. Psychol.* 2013;64(1):25–54, doi:10.1111/apps.12017.

47. Elliott, R, Bohart, AC, Watson, JC and Greenberg, LS. Empathy. *Psychotherapy (Chic.)* 2011;48(1):43–9, doi:10.1037/a0022187.

48. Anseel, F, Beatty, AS, Shen, W, Lievens, F and Sackett, PR. How are we doing after 30 years? A meta-analytic review of the antecedents and outcomes of feedback-seeking behavior. *J. Manag.* 2015;41:318–48, doi:10.1177/0149206313484521.

49. Theeboom, T, Beersma, B and van Vianen, AEM. Does coaching work? A meta-analysis on the effects of coaching on individual level outcomes in an organizational context. *J. Posit. Psychol.* 2014;9(1):1–18, doi:10.1080/17439760.2013.837499.

50. http://www.ibisworld.com/industry/default.aspx?indid=1533.

51. Joo, B-K. Executive coaching: A conceptual framework from an integrative review of practice and research. *Hum. Resour. Dev. Rev.* 2005;4(4):462–88, doi:10.1177/1534484305280866.

52. McCauley, CD and Hezlett, SA. Individual development in the workplace. In: *APA Handbook of Industrial, Work and Organizational Psychology, Vol. 1: Personnel Psychology.* Washington, DC: APA (2001), pp.313–35.

53. Bozer, G, Sarros, C and Santora, J. Academic background and credibility in executive coaching effectiveness. *Pers. Rev.* 2014;43(6):881–97, doi:10.1108/PR-10-2013-0171.

54. Witherspoon, R. Double-loop coaching for leadership development. *J. Appl. Behav. Sci.* 2014;50(3):261–83, doi:10.1177/0021886313510032.

55. Bozer, G, Sarros, C and Santora, J. Academic background and credibility in executive coaching effectiveness. *Pers. Rev.* 2014;43(6):881–97, doi:10.1108/PR-10-2013-0171.

56. Joo, B-K. Executive coaching: A conceptual framework from an integrative review of practice and research. *Hum. Resour. Dev. Rev.* 2005;4(4):462–88, doi:10.1177/1534484305280866.

57. Ibid.

58. Collins, DB and Ui, EFH. The effectiveness of managerial leadership development programs: A meta-anaysis of studies from 1982 to 2001. *Hum. Resour. Dev. Q.* 2004;15(2):217–48, doi:10.1002/hrdq.1099.

59. Arthur Jr, W, Bennett Jr, W, Edens, PS and Bell, ST. Effectiveness of training in organizations: A meta-analysis of design and evaluation features. *J. Appl. Psychol.* 2003;88(2):234–45, doi:10.1037/0021-9010.88.2.234.

60. Day, DV, Fleenor, JW, Atwater, LE, Sturm, RE and McKee, RA. Advances in leader and leadership development: A review of 25 years of research and theory. *Leadersh. Q.* 2014;25(1):63–82, doi:10.1016/j.leaqua.2013.11.004.

61. de Kets, MFR. Leadership group coaching in action: The Zen of creating high performance teams. *Acad. Manag. Perspect.* 2005;19(1):61–76, doi:10.5465/AME.2005.15841953.

62. Kluger, AN and DeNisi, A. The effects of feedback interventions on performance: A historical review, a meta-analysis, and a preliminary feedback intervention theory. *Psychol. Bull.* 1996;119(2):254–84, doi:10.1037/0033-2909.119.2.254.

63. Wood, AM, Linley, PA, Maltby, J, Kashdan, TB and Hurling, R. Using personal and psychological strengths leads to increases in well-being over time: A longitudinal study and the development of the strengths use questionnaire. *Pers. Individ. Dif.* 2011;50(1):15–19, doi:10.1016/j.paid.2010.08.004.

64. Felin, T and Hesterly, WS. The knowledge-based view, nested heterogeneity, and new value creation: Philosophical considerations on

the locus of knowledge. *Acad. Manag. Rev.* 2007;32(1):195–218, doi:10.5465/AMR.2007.23464020.

65. Grant, AM and Schwartz, B. Too much of a good thing: The challenge and opportunity of the inverted U. *Perspect. Psychol. Sci.* 2011;6(1):61–76, doi:10.1177/1745691610393523.

66. Pfeffer, J. *Leadership BS: Fixing Workplaces and Careers One Truth at a Time.* New York: Harper Business (2015).

67. Andersen, SM and Chen, S. The relational self: An interpersonal social-cognitive theory. *Psychol. Rev.* 2002;109(4):619–45, doi:10.1037/0033-295X.109.4.619.

68. Atwater, LE and Yammarino, FJ. Does self–other agreement on leadership perceptions moderate the validity of leadership and performance predictions? *Pers. Psychol.* 1992;45(1):141–64, doi:10.1111/j.1744-6570.1992.tb00848.x.

69. Freund, PA and Kasten, N. How smart do you think you are? A meta-analysis on the validity of self-estimates of cognitive ability. *Psychol. Bull.* 2012;138(2):296–321, doi:10.1037/a0026556.

70. Heidemeier, H and Moser, K. Self–other agreement in job perfor-mance ratings: A meta-analytic test of a process model. *J. Appl. Psychol.* 2009;94(2):353–70, doi:10.1037/0021-9010.94.2.353.

71. Harms, PD and Crede, M. Emotional intelligence and transfor-mational and transactional leadership: A meta-analysis. *J. Leadersh. Organ. Stud.* 2010;17(1):5–17, doi:10.1177/1548051809350894.

72. Kampa-Kokesch, S and Anderson, MZ. Executive coaching: A comprehensive review of the literature. *Consult. Psychol. J. Pract. Res.* 2001;53(4):205–28, doi:10.1037//1061-4087.53.4.205.

73. Seifert, CF and Yukl, GA. Effects of repeated multi-source feed-back on the influence behavior and effectiveness of managers: A field experiment. *Leadersh. Q.* 2010;21(5):856–66, doi:10.1016/j.leaqua.2010.07.012.

74. Kluger, AN and DeNisi, A. The effects of feedback interven-tions on performance: A historical review, a meta-analysis, and a preliminary feedback intervention theory. *Psychol. Bull.* 1996;119(2):254–84, doi:10.1037/0033-2909.119.2.254.

75. Anseel, F, Beatty, AS, Shen, W, Lievens, F and Sackett, PR. How are we doing after 30 years? A meta-analytic review of the ante-cedents and outcomes of feedback-seeking behavior. *J. Manag.* 2015;41:318–48. doi:10.1177/0149206313484521.

76. Smither, JW, London, M, Flautt, R, Vargas, Y and Kucine, I. Can

working with an executive coach improve multisource feedback ratings over time? A quasi-experimental field study. *Pers. Psychol.* 2003;56:23–44, doi:10.1111/j.1744-6570.2003.tb00142.x.

77. Day, DV, Fleenor, JW, Atwater, LE, Sturm, RE and McKee RA. Advances in leader and leadership development: A review of 25 years of research and theory. *Leadersh. Q.* 2014;25(1):63–82, doi:10.1016/j.leaqua.2013.11.004.

78. Warech, MA, Smither, JW, Reilly, RR, Millsap, RE and Reilly, SP. Self-monitoring and 360-degree ratings. *Leadersh. Q.* 1998;9(4):449–73, doi:10.1016/S1048-9843(98)90011-X.

79. Luthans, F and Peterson, SJ. 360-degree feedback with systematic coaching: Empirical analysis suggests a winning combination. *Hum. Resour. Manage.* 2003;42(3):243–56, doi:10.1002/hrm.10083.

80. Witherspoon, R and White, RP. Executive coaching: A continuum of roles. *Consult. Psychol. J. Pract. Res.* 1996;48(2):124–33, doi:10.1037//1061-4087.48.2.124.

81. Polivy, J and Herman, CP. The false-hope syndrome: Unfulfilled expectations of self-change. *Curr. Dir. Psychol. Sci.* 2000;9(4):128–31, doi:10.1111/1467-8721.00076.

82. Oh, I-S, Wang, G and Mount, MK. Validity of observer ratings of the five-factor model of personality traits: A meta-analysis. *J. Appl. Psychol.* 2011;96(4):762–73, doi:10.1037/a0021832.

83. Connelly, BS and Ones, DS. Another perspective on personality: Meta-analytic integration of observers' accuracy and predictive validity. *Psychol. Bull.* 2010;136(6):1092–122, doi:10.1037/a0021212.

CHAPTER 6

1. Wille, B and de Fruyt, F. Fifty shades of personality: Integrating five-factor model bright and dark sides of personality at work. *Ind. Organ. Psychol.* 2014;7(1):121–6, doi:10.1111/iops.12119.

2. Mazar, N and Ariely, D. Dishonesty in everyday life and its policy implications. *J. Pub. Pol. Market.* 2006;25(1):117–26, doi:10.1509/jppm.25.1.117.

3. http://www.nytimes.com/2014/01/22/business/economy/the-cost-of-the-financial-crisis-is-still-being-tallied.html.

4. Dalal, DK and Nolan, KP. Using dark side personality traits to

identify potential failure. *Ind. Organ. Psychol.* 2009;2(2009):434–6, doi:10.1111/j.1754-9434.2009.01169.x.

5. O'Boyle, EH, Forsyth, DR, Banks, GC and McDaniel, MA. A meta-analysis of the dark triad and work behavior: A social exchange perspective. *J. Appl. Psychol.* 2012;97(3):557–79, doi:10.1037/a0025679.

6. Spector, PE and Fox, S. The stressor-emotion model of counterproductive work behavior. In *Counterproductive Work Behavior. Investigations of Actors and Targets.* Washingon, DC: APA (2005), pp.151–74, doi:10.1037/10893-007.

7. Ng, TWH and Feldman, DC. How broadly does education contribute to job performance? *Pers. Psychol.* 2009;62:89–134, doi:10.1111/j.1744-6570.2008.01130.x.

8. Campbell, JP and Wiernik, BM. The modeling and assessment of work performance. *Annu. Rev. Organ. Pyschol. Organ. Behav.* 2015;2:47–74, doi:10.1146/annurev-orgpsych-032414-111427.

9. Spector, PE. The relationship of personality to counterproductive work behavior (CWB): An integration of perspectives. *Hum. Resour. Manag. Rev.* 2010;21(4):342–52, doi:10.1016/j.hrmr.2010.10.002.

10. Sackett, PR and DeVore, CJ. Counterproductive behaviors at work. In: *APA Handbook of Industrial, Work and Organizational Psychology, Vol. 1: Personnel Psychology.* Washington, DC: APA (2001), pp.145–64, doi:10.4135/9781848608320.n9.

11. Hogan, R and Hogan, J. Assessing leadership : A view from the dark side. *Int. J. Sel. Assess.* 2001;9(1/2):40–51, doi:10.1111/1468-2389.00162.

12. O'Boyle, EH, Forsyth, DR, Banks, GC and McDaniel, MA. A meta-analysis of the dark triad and work behavior: A social exchange perspective. *J. Appl. Psychol.* 2012;97(3):557–79, doi:10.1037/a0025679.

13. Panek, ET, Nardis, Y and Konrath, S. Mirror or megaphone? How relationships between narcissism and social networking site use differ on Facebook and Twitter. *Comput. Human Behav.* 2013;29(5):2004–12, doi:http://dx.doi.org/10.1016/j.chb.2013.04.012.

14. Yarkoni, T. Personality in 100,000 words: A large-scale analysis of personality and word use among bloggers. *J. Res. Pers.* 2010;44(3):363–73, doi:10.1016/j.jrp.2010.04.001.

15. Paulhus, D and Williams, K. The dark triad of personality: Narcissism, Machiavellianism, and psychopathy. *J. Res. Pers.* 2002;36:556–63, doi: 10.1016/S0092-6566(02)00505-6

16. Jonason, PK and Kavanagh, P. The dark side of love: Love styles and the Dark Triad. *Pers. Individ. Dif.* 2010;49(6):606–10, doi:10.1016/j.paid.2010.05.030.

17. Isaacson, W. *Steve Jobs.* New York: Simon & Schuster (2011), p.112.

18. http://www.economist.com/news/briefing/21689539-primary-contest-about-get-serious-it-has-rarely-been-so-ugly-uncertain-or.

19. Jonason, PK and Kavanagh, P. The dark side of love: Love styles and the dark triad. *Pers. Individ. Dif.* 2010;49(6):606–10, doi:10.1016/j.paid.2010.05.030.

20. Grijalva, E and Harms, P. Narcissism: An integrative synthesis and dominance complementarity model. *Acad. Manag. Perspect.* 2013;28(2):1–56, doi:10.5465/amp.2012.0048.

21. O'Boyle, EH, Forsyth, DR, Banks, GC and McDaniel, MA. A meta-analysis of the dark triad and work behavior: A social exchange perspective. *J. Appl. Psychol.* 2012;97(3):557–79, doi:10.1037/a0025679.

22. Bruk-Lee, V, Khoury, HA, Nixon, AE, Goh, A and Spector, PE. Replicating and extending past personality/job satisfaction meta-analyses. *Hum. Perform.* 2009;22(2):156–89, doi:10.1080/08959280902743709.

23. Judge, TA, LePine, JA and Rich, BL. Loving yourself abundantly: Relationship of the narcissistic personality to self- and other perceptions of workplace deviance, leadership, and task and contextual performance. *J. Appl. Psychol.* 2006;91(4):762–76, doi:10.1037/0021-9010.91.4.762.

24. Grijalva, E and Harms, P. Narcissism: An integrative synthesis and dominance complementarity model. *Acad. Manag. Perspect.* 2013;28(2):1–56, doi:10.5465/amp.2012.0048.

25. Brunell, AB, Gentry, WA, Campbell, WK, Hoffman, BJ, Kuhnert, KW and Demarree, KG. Leader emergence: The case of the narcissistic leader. *Pers. Soc. Psychol. Bull.* 2008;34(12):1663–76, doi:10.1177/0146167208324101.

26. Chatterjee, A and Hambrick, DC. Executive officers and their effects on company strategy and performance. *Adm. Sci. Q.* 2007;52:351–86.

27. Campbell, WK, Hoffman, BJ, Campbell, SM and Marchisio, G. Narcissism in organizational contexts. *Hum. Resour. Manag. Rev.* 2010;21(4):268–84, doi:10.1016/j.hrmr.2010.10 .007.

28. O'Boyle, EH, Forsyth, DR, Banks, GC and McDaniel MA. A meta-analysis of the dark triad and work behavior: A social exchange perspective. *J. Appl. Psychol.* 2012;97(3):557–79, doi:10.1037/a0025679.

29. Grijalva, E and Harms, P. Narcissism: An integrative synthesis and dominance complementarity model. *Acad. Manag. Perspect.* 2013;28(2):1–56, doi:10.5465/amp.2012.0048.

30. Paulhus, D. Interpersonal and intrapsychic adaptiveness of trait self-enhancement: A mixed blessing? *J. Pers. Soc. Psychol.* 1998;74(5):1197–208, doi:10.1037/0022-3514.74.5.1197.

31. Bushman, BJ and Baumeister, RF. Threatened egotism, narcissism, self-esteem, and direct and displaced aggression: Does self-love or self-hate lead to violence? *J. Pers. Soc. Psychol.* 1998;75(1):219–29, doi:10.1037/0022-3514.75.1.219.

32. Grijalva, E and Harms, P. Narcissism: An integrative synthesis and dominance complementarity model. *Acad. Manag. Perspect.* 2013;28(2):1–56, doi:10.5465/amp.2012.0048.

33. https://www.washingtonpost.com/news/morning-mix/ wp/2015/12/02/mark-zuckerberg-bill-gates-warren-buffett-and- triumph-of-competitive-philanthropy/

34. O'Boyle, EH, Forsyth, DR, Banks, GC and McDaniel, MA. A meta-analysis of the dark triad and work behavior: A social exchange perspective. *J. Appl. Psychol.* 2012;97(3):557–79, doi:10.1037/a0025679.

35. Smith, SF and Lilienfeld, SO. Psychopathy in the workplace: The knowns and unknowns. *Aggress. Violent Behav.* 2013;18(2):204– 18, doi:10.1016/j.avb.2012.11.007.

36. Babiak, P, Neumann, CS and Hare, RD. Corporate psychology: Talking the walk. *Behav. Sci. Law* 2010;28:174–93, doi:10.1002/ bsl.925.

37. Smith, SF and Lilienfeld, SO. Psychopathy in the workplace: The knowns and unknowns. *Aggress. Violent Behav.* 2013;18(2):204– 18, doi:10.1016/j.avb.2012.11.007.

38. Mathieu, C, Hare, RD, Jones, DN, Babiak, P and Neumann, CS. Factor structure of the B-Scan 360: A measure of corporate

psychopathy. *Psychol. Assess.* 2012;25(1):288–93, doi:10.1037/a0029262.

39. Caponecchia, C, Sun, AYZ and Wyatt, A. 'Psychopaths' at work? Implications of lay persons' use of labels and behavioural criteria for psychopathy. *J. Bus. Ethics* 2012;107(4):399–408, doi:10.1007/s10551-011-1049-9.

40. Scherer, KT, Baysinger, M, Zolynsky, D and LeBreton, JM. Predicting counterproductive work behaviors with sub-clinical psychopathy: Beyond the five factor model of personality. *Pers. Individ. Dif.* 2013;55(3):300–305, doi:10.1016/j.paid.2013.03.007.

41. Babiak, P, Neumann, CS and Hare, RD. Corporate psychopathy: Talking the walk. *Behav. Sci. Law* 2010;28(2):174–93, doi:10.1002/bsl.925.

42. Akhtar, R, Ahmetoglu, G and Chamorro-Premuzic, T. Greed is good? Assessing the relationship between entrepreneurship and subclinical psychopathy. *Pers. Individ. Dif.* 2013;54(3):420–25, doi:10.1016/j.paid.2012.10.013.

43. Ali, F, Amorim, IS and Chamorro-Premuzic, T. Empathy deficits and trait emotional intelligence in psychopathy and Machiavellianism. *Pers. Individ. Dif.* 2009;47(7):758–62, doi:10.1016/j.paid.2009.06.016.

44. Osumi, T and Ohira, H. The positive side of psychopathy: Emotional detachment in psychopathy and rational decision-making in the ultimatum game. *Pers. Individ. Dif.* 2010;49(5):451–6, doi:10.1016/j.paid.2010.04.016.

45. Chiaburu DS, Muñoz, GJ and Gardner, RG. How to spot a careerist early on: Psychopathy and exchange ideology as predictors of careerism. *J. Bus. Ethics* 2013;118(3):473–86, doi:10.1007/s10551-012-1599-5.

46. Mathieu, C, Neumann, C, Babiak, P and Hare, RD. Corporate psychopathy and the full-range leadership model. *Assessment* 2015;22(3):267–78, doi:10.1177/1073191114545490.

47. Mathieu, C, Neumann, CS, Hare, RD and Babiak, P. A dark side of leadership: Corporate psychopathy and its influence on employee well-being and job satisfaction. *Pers. Individ. Dif.* 2014;59:83–8, doi:10.1016/j.paid.2013.11.010.

48. Viding, E, McCrory, E and Seara-Cardoso, A. Psychopathy. *Curr. Biol.* 2014;24(18):R871–4, doi:10.1016/j.cub.2014.06.055.

49. Machiavelli, N. *The Prince*. Oxford: Oxford UP (2005; orig. pub. 1532).

50. Ali, F, Amorim, IS and Chamorro-Premuzic, T. Empathy deficits and trait emotional intelligence in psychopathy and Machiavellianism. *Pers. Individ. Dif.* 2009;47(7):758–62, doi:10.1016/j.paid.2009.06.016.

51. Witt, LA and Ferris, GR. Social skill as moderator of the conscientiousness-performance relationship: Convergent results across four studies. *J. Appl. Psychol.* 2003;88(5):809–21, doi:10.1037/0021-9010.88.5.809.

52. O'Boyle, EH, Forsyth, DR, Banks, GC and McDaniel, MA. A meta-analysis of the dark triad and work behavior: A social exchange perspective. *J. Appl. Psychol.* 2012;97(3):557–79, doi:10.1037/a0025679.

53. Kish-Gephart, JJ, Harrison, DA and Treviño, LK. Bad apples, bad cases, and bad barrels: Meta-analytic evidence about sources of unethical decisions at work. *J. Appl. Psychol.* 2010;95(1):1–31, doi:10.1037/a0017103.

54. Furnham, A, Trickey, G and Hyde, G. Bright aspects to dark side traits: Dark side traits associated with work success. *Pers. Individ. Dif.* 2012;52(8):908–13, doi:10.1016/j.paid.2012.01.025.

55. Khoo, HS and Burch, GSJ. The 'dark side' of leadership personality and transformational leadership: An exploratory study. *Pers. Individ. Dif.* 2008;44(1):86–97, doi:10.1016/j.paid.2007.07.018.

56. Horney, K. Neurosis and human growth. *Am. Scholar* 1950;19(4):409–21.

57. Nelson, E and Hogan, R. Coaching on the dark side. *Int. Coach. Psychol. Rev.* 2009;4(1):7–19.

58. Harms, PD, Spain, SM and Hannah, ST. Leader development and the dark side of personality. *Leadersh. Q.* 2011;22(3):495–509, doi:10.1016/j.leaqua.2011.04.007.

59. Robins, RW and John, OP. Effects of visual perspective and narcissism on self-perception: Is seeing believing? *Psychol. Sci.* 1997;8(1):37–42, doi:10.1111/j.1467-9280.1997.tb00541.x.

60. Chatterjee, A and Hambrick, DC. Executive officers and their effects on company strategy and performance. *Adm. Sci. Q.* 2007;52:351–86.

61. Padilla, A, Hogan, R and Kaiser, RB. The toxic triangle: Destructive leaders, susceptible followers, and conducive

environments. *Leadersh. Q.* 2007;18(3):176–94, doi:10.1016/j. leaqua. 2007.03.001.

62. Blair, CA, Hoffman, BJ and Helland, KR. Narcissism in organizations: A multisource appraisal reflects different perspectives. *Hum. Perform.* 2008;21(3):254–76, doi:10.1080/08959280802137705.

63. Judge, TA, LePine, JA and Rich, BL. Loving yourself abundantly: Relationship of the narcissistic personality to self- and other perceptions of workplace deviance, leadership, and task and contextual performance. *J. Appl. Psychol.* 2006;91(4):762–76, doi:10.1037/0021-9010.91.4.762.

64. Baumeister, RF, Campbell, JD, Krueger, JI and Vohs, KD. Does high self-esteem cause better performance, interpersonal success, happiness, or healthier lifestyles? *Psychol. Sci. Public Interes.* 2003;4(1):1–44, doi:10.1111/1529-1006.01431.

65. Hayward, M and Hambrick, D. Explaining the premiums paid for large acquisitions: Evidence of CEO hubris. *Adm. Sci. Q.* 1997;42(1):103–27, doi:10.2307/2393810.

66. Almlund, M, Duckworth, AL, Heckman, J and Kautz, T. *Personality Psychology and Economics.* 2011. NBER Working Paper No. 16822, doi:10.1016/B978-0-444-53444-6.00001-8.

67. Judge, TA, Bono, JE, Ilies, R and Gerhardt, MW. Personality and leadership: A qualitative and quantitative review. *J. Appl. Psychol.* 2002;87(4):765–80, doi:10.1037//0021-9010.87.4.765.

68. Hogan, R, Curphy, GJ and Hogan, J. What we know about leadership: Effectiveness and personality. *Am. Psychol.* 1994;49(6):493–504, doi:10.1037/0003-066X.49.6.493.

69. Van Velsor, E and Leslie, JB. Why executives derail: Perspectives across time and cultures. *Acad. Manag. Perspect.* 1995;9(4):62–72, doi:10.5465/AME.1995.9512032194.

70. Khoo, HS and Burch, GSJ. The 'dark side' of leadership personality and transformational leadership: An exploratory study. *Pers. Individ. Dif.* 2008;44(1):86–97, doi:10.1016/j.paid.2007.07.018.

71. Judge, TA, Piccolo, RF and Kosalka, T. The bright and dark sides of leader traits: A review and theoretical extension of the leader trait paradigm. *Leadersh. Q.* 2009;20(6):855–75, doi:10.1016/j. leaqua.2009.09.004.

72. Furnham, A, Trickey, G and Hyde, G. Bright aspects to dark side traits: Dark side traits associated with work success. *Pers. Individ. Dif.* 2012;52(8):908–13, doi:10.1016/j.paid.2012.01.025.

73. Raskin, R, Novacek, J and Hogan, R. Narcissism, self-esteem, and defensive self-enhancement. *J. Pers.* 1991;59:19–38, doi:10.1111/j.1467-6494.1991.tb00766.x.
74. Paulhus, DL, Westlake, BG, Calvez, SS and Harms, PD. Self-presentation style in job interviews: The role of personality and culture. *J. Appl. Soc. Psychol.* 2013;43(10):2042–59, doi:10.1111/jasp.12157.
75. Goncalo, JA, Flynn, FJ and Kim, SH. Are two narcissists better than one? The link between narcissism, perceived creativity, and creative performance. *Pers. Soc. Psychol. Bull.* 2010;36(11):1484–95, doi:10.1177/0146167210385109.
76. Grijalva, E and Harms, P. Narcissism: An integrative synthesis and dominance complementarity model. *Acad. Manag. Perspect.* 2013;28(2):1–56, doi:10.5465/amp.2012.0048.
77. Hurley, S. Social heuristics that make us smarter. *Philos. Psychol.* 2005;18(5):585–612, doi:10.1080/09515080500264214.
78. Gunnthorsdottir, A, McCabe, K and Smith, V. Using the Machiavellianism instrument to predict trustworthiness in a bargaining game. *J. Econ. Psychol.* 2002;23(1):49–66, doi:10.1016/S0167-4870(01)00067-8.
79. Binning, JF, LeBreton, JM and Adorno, AJ. Subclinical psychopaths. In: *Comprehensive Handbook of Personality and Psychopathology, Vol. 1: Personality and Everyday Functioning,* eds. JC Thomas and DL Segal. San Francisco, CA: Wiley & Sons (2006), pp.345–63.
80. O'Boyle, EH, Forsyth, DR, Banks, GC and McDaniel, MA. A meta-analysis of the dark triad and work behavior: A social exchange perspective. *J. Appl. Psychol.* 2012;97(3):557–79, doi:10.1037/a0025679.
81. De Fruyt, F, Wille, B and Furnham, A. Assessing aberrant personality in managerial coaching: Measurement issues and prevalence rates across employment sectors. *Eur. J. Pers.* 2013;27(6):555–64, doi:10.1002/per.1911.
82. Judge, TA, Piccolo, RF and Kosalka, T. The bright and dark sides of leader traits: A review and theoretical extension of the leader trait paradigm. *Leadersh. Q.* 2009;20(6):855–75, doi:10.1016/j.leaqua.2009.09.004.

CHAPTER 7

1. Kurzweil, R. *The Singularity Is Near: When Humans Transcend Biology.* New York: Viking Penguin (2005), doi:10.1016/j.techfore.2005.12.002.

2. https://www.psychologytoday.com/blog/the-narcissism-epidemic/201308/how-dare-you-say-narcissism-is-increasing.

3. Waugaman, RM. *The Narcissism Epidemic,* by JW Twenge and WK Campbell (review). *Psychiatry Interpers. Biol. Process.* 2011;74(2):166–9, doi:10.1521/psyc.2011.74.2.166.

4. Reynolds, EK and Lejuez, CW. Narcissism in the DSM. In: *The Handbook of Narcissism and Narcissistic Personality Disorder: Theoretical Approaches, Empirical Findings, and Treatments,* eds. WK Campbell and JD Miller. Hoboken, NJ. John Wiley & Sons (2011), pp.14–21, doi:10.1002/9781118093108.ch2.

5. Foster, JD, Campbell, WK and Twenge JM. Individual differences in narcissism: Inflated self-views across the lifespan and around the world. *J. Res. Pers.* 2003;37(6):469–86, doi:10.1016/S0092-6566(03)00026-6.

6. Stewart, KD and Bernhardt, PC. Comparing millennials to pre-1987 students and with one another. *N. Am. J. Psychol.* 2010;12(3):579–602.

7. Twenge, JM and Foster, JD. Birth cohort increases in narcissistic personality traits among American college students, 1982–2009. *Soc. Psychol. Personal. Sci.* 2010;1(1):99–106, doi:10.1177/1948550609355719.

8. Freud, S. Group psychology and the analysis of the ego. *Psychoanal. Q.* 1921;47(1):1–23, doi:10.1097/00005053-192410000-00117.

9. Church, AH, Rotolo, CT, Margulies, A et al. The role of personality in organization development: A multi-level framework for applying personality to individual, team, and organizational change. *Res. Org. Change Develop.* 2015;23:91–166, doi:10.1108/S0897-301620150000023003.

10. Kluger, AN and DeNisi, A. The effects of feedback interventions on performance: A historical review, a meta-analysis, and a preliminary feedback intervention theory. *Psychol. Bull.* 1996;119(2):254–84, doi:10.1037/0033-2909.119.2.254.

11. Grijalva, E and Zhang, L. Narcissism and self-insight: A review and meta-analysis of narcissists' self-enhancement

tendencies. *Personal. Soc. Psychol. Bull.* 2016;42(1):3–24, doi:10.1177/0146167215611636.

12. Atwater, LE and Yammarino, FJ. Does self–other agreement on leadership perceptions moderate the validity of leadership and performance predictions? *Pers. Psychol.* 1992;45(1):141–64, doi:10.1111/j.1744-6570.1992.tb00848.x.

13. Van Velsor, E, Taylor, S and Leslie, JB. An examination of the relationships among self-perception accuracy, self-awareness, gender, and leader effectiveness. *Hum. Resour. Manage.* 1993;32(1992):249–63, doi:10.1002/hrm.3930320205.

14. Harms, PD, Spain, SM and Hannah, ST. Leader development and the dark side of personality. *Leadersh. Q.* 2011;22(3):495–509, doi:10.1016/j.leaqua.2011.04.007.

15. Heidemeier, H and Moser, K. Self–other agreement in job performance ratings: A meta-analytic test of a process model. *J. Appl. Psychol.* 2009;94(2):353–70, doi:10.1037/0021-9010.94.2.353.

16. http://qz.com/670841/the-no-1-thing-ceos-want-from-executive-coaching-self-awareness/.

17. Mussel, P. Epistemic curiosity and related constructs: Lacking evidence of discriminant validity. *Pers. Individ. Dif.* 2010;49(5):506–10.

18. Kashdan, TB, Gallagher, MW, Silvia, PJ et al. The curiosity and exploration inventory-II: Development, factor structure, and psychometrics. *J. Res. Pers.* 2009;43(6):987–98.

19. http://fortune.com/2016/03/03/
best-companies-to-work-for-job-openings/

20. Jepma, M, Verdonschot, RG, van Steenbergen, H, Rombouts, SARB and Nieuwenhuis, S. Neural mechanisms underlying the induction and relief of perceptual curiosity. *Front. Behav. Neurosci.* 2012:6.

21. Bacon, ES. Curiosity in the American black bear. *Ursus.* 1980;4:153–7.

22. Berlyne, DE. A theory of human curiosity. *Br. J. Psychol.* 1954;45(3):180–91.

23. Collins, RP, Litman, JA and Spielberger, CD. The measurement of perceptual curiosity. *Pers. Individ. Dif.* 2004;36(5):1127–41.

24. Kang, MJ, Hsu, M, Krajbich, IM et al. The wick in the candle of learning: Epistemic curiosity activates reward circuitry and enhances memory. *Psychol. Sci.* 2009;20(8):963–73.

25. Engel, S. Is curiosity vanishing? *J. Am. Acad. Child Adolesc. Psychiatry* 2009;48(8):777–9.

26. von Stumm, S, Hell, B and Chamorro-Premuzic, T. The hungry mind: Intellectual curiosity is the third pillar of academic performance. *Perspect. Psychol. Sci.* 2011;6(6):574–88.

27. Harrison, SH, Sluss, DM and Ashforth BE. Curiosity adapted the cat: The role of trait curiosity in newcomer adaptation. *J. Appl. Psychol.* 2011;96(1):211–20.

28. Mussel, P. Introducing the construct curiosity for predicting job performance. *J. Organ. Behav.* 2013;34(4):453–72.

29. Gallagher, MW and Lopez, SJ. Curiosity and well-being. *J. Posit. Psychol.* 2007;2(4):236–48.

30. Perlovsky, LI, Bonniot-Cabanac, MC and Cabanac, M. Curiosity and pleasure. Presented at the International Joint Conference on Neural Networks, July 2010, Barcelona, doi:10.1109/IJCNN.2010.5596867.

31. Berlyne, DE. Curiosity and exploration. *Science* 1966;153(731):25–33.

32. Shane, SA. *The Illusions of Entrepreneurship*. New Haven, CT: Yale UP (2008).

33. Parker, SC. Intrapreneurship or entrepreneurship? *J. Bus. Ventur.* 2011;26(1):19–34, doi:10.1016/j.jbusvent.2009.07.003.

34. Schmidt, GM and Druehl, CT. When is a disruptive innovation disruptive? *J. Prod. Innov. Manag.* 2008;25(4):347–69, doi:10.1111 /j.1540-5885.2008.00306.x.

35. Leunter, F, Ahmetoglu, G and Chamorro-Premuzic, T. Assessing individual differences in entrepreneurial potential and success. *Pers. Individ. Dif.* 2014;60(2014):S26–S27, doi:10.1016/j.paid.2013.07.035.

36. Simonton, DK. *Creativity in Science: Chance, Logic, Genius, and Zeitgeist*. Cambridge: Cambridge UP (2004).

37. Chamorro-Premuzic, T. *Personality and Individual Differences*, 3rd Edition. Chichester: John Wiley & Sons (2014).

38. Talke, K and Heidenreich, S. How to overcome pro-change bias: Incorporating passive and active innovation resistance in innovation decision models. *J. Prod. Innov. Manag.* 2014;31(5):894–907, doi:10.1111/jpim.12130.

39. Cukier, K, and Mayer-Schönberger V. *Big Data: A Revolution That Will Transform How We Live, Work, and Think*. London:

John Murray (2013).

40. http://www.economist.com/blogs/graphicdetail/2014/06/daily-chart-1.

41. Youyou, W, Kosinski, M and Stillwell, D. Computer-based personality judgments are more accurate than those made by humans. *Proc. Natl. Acad. Sci. USA* 2015;112(4):1036–40, doi:10.1073/pnas.1418680112.

42. Yarkoni, T. Personality in 100,000 words: A large-scale analysis of personality and word use among bloggers. *J. Res. Pers.* 2010;44(3):363–73, doi:10.1016/j.jrp.2010.04.001.

43. http://www.ibm.com/smarterplanet/us/en/ibmwatson/developer-cloud/personality-insights.html

44. Davenport, TH, Harris, J and Shapiro, J. Competing on talent analytics. *Harv. Bus. Rev.* 2010;88:52–8.

45. Campbell, JP and Wiernik, BM. The modeling and assessment of work performance. *Annu. Rev. Organ. Pyschol. Organ. Behav.* 2015;2:47–74, doi:10.1146/annurev-orgpsych-032414-111427.

46. Levashina, J, Hartwell, CJ, Morgeson, FP and Campion, MA. The structured employment interview: Narrative and quantitative review of the research literature. *Pers. Psychol.* 2014;67(1):241–93, doi:10.1111/peps.12052.

47. http://www.nytimes.com/2013/05/21/science/mit-scholars-1949-essay-on-machine-age-is-found.html.

48. https://hbr.org/2015/04/should-your-voice-determine-whether-you-get-hired.

49. Werbach, K. (Re)defining gamification: A process approach. *Proceedings of the 9th International Conference on Persuasive Technology* 2014;8462:266–72, doi:10.1007/978-3-319-07127-5_23.

50. http://www.marketsandmarkets.com.PressReleases/gamification.asp

51. http://insanelydriven.archive.lessrain.co.uk/

CHAPTER 8

1. Cappelli, P and Keller, J. Talent management: Conceptual approaches and practical challenges. *Annu. Rev. Organ. Psychol. Organ. Behav.* 2014;1(1):305–31, doi:10.1146/annurev-orgpsych-031413-091314.

2. Gallardo-Gallardo, E, Dries, N and González-Cruz, TF. What is the meaning of 'talent' in the world of work? *Hum. Resour. Manag. Rev.* 2013;23(4):290–300, doi:10.1016/j. hrmr.2013.05.002.

3. Silzer, ROB and Church, AH. The pearls and perils of identifying potential. *Ind. Organ. Psychol.* 2009;2:377–412, doi:10.1111/j.1754-9434.2009.01163.x.

4. Meyers, MC, van Woerkom, M and Dries, N. Talent: Innate or acquired? Theoretical considerations and their implications for talent management. *Hum. Resour. Manag. Rev.* 2013;23(4):305–21, doi:10.1016/j.hrmr.2013.05.003.

5. Schmidt, IW, Berg, IJ and Deelman, BG. Prospective memory training in older adults. *Educ. Gerontol.* 2001;27:455–78, doi:10.1080/036012701316894162.

6. Hoorens, V and Harris, PR. Distortions in reports of health behaviors: The time span effect and illusory supefuority. *Psychol. Health* 1998;13(3):451–66, doi:10.1080/08870449808407303.

7. Endo, Y, Heine, SJ and Lehman, DR. Culture and positive illusions in close relationships: How my relationships are better than yours. *Personal. Soc. Psychol. Bull.* 2000;26:1571–86, doi:10.1177/01461672002612011.

8. Larwood, L and Whittaker, W. Managerial myopia: Self-serving biases in organizational planning. *J. Appl. Psychol.* 1977;62(2):194–8, doi:10.1037/0021-9010.62.2.194.

9. Felson, RB. Ambiguity and bias in the self-concept. *Soc. Psychol. Q.* 1981;44(1):64, doi:10.2307/3033866.

10. Svenson, O. Are we all less risky and more skillful than our fellow drivers? *Acta Psychol. (Amst).* 1981;47(2):143–8, doi:10.1016/0001-6918(81)90005-6.

11. Cross, KP. Not can, but will college teaching be improved? *New Dir. High. Educ.* 1977;17:1–15, doi:10.1002/he.36919771703.

12. Chamorro-Premuzic, T and Furnham, A. *Personality and Intellectual Competence.* Mahwah, NJ: Lawrence Erlbaum (2005), doi:10.4324/9781410612649.

13. Heidemeier, H and Moser, K. Self–other agreement in job performance ratings: A meta-analytic test of a process model. *J. Appl. Psychol.* 2009;94(2):353–70, doi:10.1037/0021-9010.94.2.353.

14. Friedrich, J. On seeing oneself as less self-serving than others: The ultimate self-serving bias? *Teach. Psychol.* 1996;23(2):107–9,

doi:10.1207/s15328023top2302_9.

15. Judge, TA, Piccolo, RF, Podsakoff, NP, Shaw, JC and Rich, BL. The relationship between pay and job satisfaction: A meta-analysis of the literature. *J. Vocat. Behav.* 2010;77(2):157–67, doi:10.1016/j.jvb.2010.04.002.

16. http://www.wsj.com/articles/everything-is-awesome-why-you-cant-tell-employees-theyre-doing-a-bad-job-1423613936.

17. Bukowski, C. *Women.* New York: HarperCollins (2014), p.279.

18. Condrey, SE, Selden, SC, Tools, HC, Burke, RJ and Cooper, CL. The human capital phenomenon: Putting people first. *Public Adm. Rev.* 2010;70(2):319–21, doi:10.1111/j.1540-6210.2010.02140.X..

19. *The Economist. Managing Talent: Recruiting, Retaining and Getting the Most from Talented People,* eds. M Devine and M Syrett. London: Profile Books (2006), p.4.

20. Sonnenberg, M, van Zijderveld, V and Brinks, M. The role of talent-perception incongruence in effective talent management. *J. World Bus.* 2014;49(2):272–80, doi:10.1016/j.jwb.2013.11.011.

21. Ross, S. How definitions of talent suppress talent management. *Ind. Commer. Train.* 2013;45:166–70, doi:10.1108/00197851311320586.

22. Cappelli, P and Keller, J. Talent management: Conceptual approaches and practical challenges. *Annu. Rev. Organ. Psychol. Organ. Behav.* 2014;1(1):305–31, doi:10.1146/annurev-orgpsych-031413-091314.

23. Lewis, R and Heckman, R. Talent management: A critical review. *Hum. Resour. Manag. Rev.* 2006;16(2):139–54, doi:10.1016/j.hrmr.2006.03.001.

24. Cappelli, P and Keller, J. Talent management: Conceptual approaches and practical challenges. *Annu. Rev. Organ. Psychol. Organ. Behav.* 2014;1(1):305–31, doi:10.1146/annurev-orgpsych-031413-091314.

25. Terpstra, D and Rozell, E. Human resource executives' perceptions of academic research. *J. Bus. Psychol.* 1998;13(1):19–29.

INDEX

(page numbers in *italic type* refer to illustrations)